PRAISE FOR *BUSINESS AS UNUSUAL*

Business As UnUsual is a must-read for anyone looking to adapt and thrive in the new normal. Yvanovich's insights and frameworks provide a clear roadmap for personal and professional growth.

Prof. Mathews Z. Nkhoma | Associate Deputy Vice Chancellor, College of Business & Law RMIT University Melbourne, Australia

Business As UnUsual shows how businesses can adapt and excel in times of uncertainty and change, such as the one we are experiencing now due to the COVID-19 pandemic. It involves being agile, adaptable, and creative in finding solutions and opportunities. This book is about flourishing in a period of transformation and innovation driven by technological, economic, and social changes.

Rick Yvanovich helps us to understand how to embrace disruption, be innovative, and have a growth mindset to succeed. The book shows us the importance of values, flexibility, innovation, and resilience in today's ever-changing business landscape. To thrive in the new renaissance, businesses need to think and act differently, taking a human-centric approach, focusing on purpose and sustainability, and leveraging technology to enhance customer experience.

The book explains the new ERA of leadership and how to embrace "Business As UnUsual" and adopt a growth mindset to thrive in the new renaissance, both in terms of financial success and social impact.

Dr. Doru Dima, Ph.D. | CEO Romania, CPO International, Great People Inside

Business As UnUsual is an exceptional resource for those determined to adapt, innovate, and thrive in today's market. Rick Yvanovich's expert guidance is highly actionable and refreshingly authentic, making it a must-read. Trust me; this book is a game-changer that will help you stay ahead of the game and achieve unparalleled success in the new normal.

David Perry | Author of *Hiring Greatness: How to Recruit Your Dream Team and Crush the Competition, Executive Recruiting for Dummies*, and *Guerrilla Marketing for Job Hunters 3.0*

Yvanovich's expertise in coaching shines through in *Business As UnUsual*. The book provides unique insights and tools for breaking free from ruts and achieving success.

Ajit Nawalkha | CEO, Evercoach, Author of *Live Big* and *The Book of Coaching: For Extraordinary Coaches*

I had the privilege of meeting Rick Yvanovich at a CEO gathering in Dubai in 2022, and I was immediately struck by his inspiring nature. His book, *Business As UnUsual*, captures the essence of his wisdom and provides actionable strategies for success in this era of unprecedented opportunities. The book's reference to a new renaissance is a brilliant reflection of the potential for a fresh start in both business and personal life. It takes you on a journey to question and reflect on your purpose, life force, mind's potential, true self, and the perils of the mental dungeon. Ultimately, it guides you to discover your own treasures and find your way to your own Castle. A must-read for anyone seeking to navigate these transformative times with confidence.

Winston Rivero | Founder & CEO, NEWTOMS

I highly recommend *Business As UnUsual* for anyone who wants to stay ahead of the game in the new normal. Rick Yvanovich's approach is highly practical, and his insights are invaluable. This book is a game-changer for anyone who wants to succeed in the face of adversity.

Nicholas Kemp | Founder of Ikigai Tribe,
Author of *Ikigai-kan*

Yvanovich's *Business As UnUsual* is a refreshing and inspiring read in these challenging times. The book's frameworks and exercises provide a clear path to personal and professional growth.

David Fuess | CEO, Henson Group

As someone who's been through the ups and downs of entrepreneurship, Yvanovich knows what it takes to succeed. *Business As UnUsual* is a practical and actionable guide for anyone looking to thrive in the new normal.

Rick Orford | Co-Founder & Executive Producer at
Travel Addicts Life and Bestselling Author of *The*
Financially Independent Millennial

If you're feeling stuck in your business or personal life, *Business As UnUsual* is the book for you. Yvanovich's coaching expertise and unique tools and exercises will help you break free and achieve excellence.

Glenn Hopper | CFO, Sandline Discovery, Bestselling
Author of *Deep Finance*

Business As UnUsual is a comprehensive guide for anyone looking to thrive in the new normal. Yvanovich's insights and frameworks provide a clear personal and professional growth roadmap.

Shawn Johal | Business Growth Coach, Elevation Leaders,
Bestselling Author of *The Happy Leader*

Business As UnUsual is an outstanding guide for anyone looking to succeed in the new Renaissance. Rick Yvanovich's unique

Castle metaphor is both creative and effective, offering practical strategies and actionable steps for success. His emphasis on developing critical skills for the next decade has helped me upskill and prepare for the future, and I feel more motivated and focused than ever before.

Sanjay Jaybhay | Author of *Invest and Grow Rich*

Yvanovich's coaching expertise and unique tools and exercises make *Business As UnUsual* an invaluable resource for anyone looking to break free from ruts and achieve excellence.

Trissa Tismal-Capili | *USA Today* and *Wall Street Journal* Bestselling Author, Founder of the Institute of Conscious Business Leaders Board

As the CEO of a Nurse Empowerment Academy, Life/Business Coach Consultant, and NLP Practitioner, I know the importance of adapting and growing. That's why I wholeheartedly endorse Rick Yvanovich's *Business As UnUsual*.

Rick's genuine, warm approach offers innovative insights, practical strategies, and actionable steps for overcoming adversity in the new normal. This book is an essential guide for anyone seeking to thrive in our ever-changing world.

Delving into *Business As UnUsual*, I found Rick's relatable narratives enlightening and inspiring. This must-read reminds us that our actions today shape our success tomorrow.

Kimyette Saunders-Bouie | RN, CNLP, Life & Business Coach, and CEO of SauBou Nurse Empowerment Academy

Having invested thousands of hours into his personal development and acquired first-hand wisdom through multiple ventures, Rick Yvanovich delivers an ultimate guide with simple but powerful techniques, prompts, and tools to help you lead a life of purpose and feel great doing it while uplifting others on your path. Step by step, he leads you on the journey to strengthen the pillars of your inner self and arms you with insight and strategies to become an impactful leader in uncertain times.

Igor Lasun | Managing Director and Head of Products (Americas), UBS Asset Management

If you (really) want to succeed personally and professionally in the new Renaissance, Rick Yvanovich's *Business As UnUsual* is an unavoidable must-read! Providing deep insights and a true treasure chest of actionable tools and models, Rick inspires and empowers all of us to succeed while being the best we possibly can be for ourselves and others!

Jens Pheiffer | CEO, Capricorn Holdings ApS

This is a business book with a difference. Rick Yvanovich offers a unique approach to match his title: *Business As UnUsual*. In fact, the book is as much about developing values that will lead to success as it is any business advice. It encourages you to explore and reach some personal milestones. It's all about succeeding with the central metaphor offered here: building your own Castle. As the author says, grab your weapon of choice and begin!

Gary Genard, Ph.D. | President, The Genard Method, Author of *Speak for Leadership: An Executive Speech Coach's Secrets for Developing Leadership Presence in Public Speaking*

Business As UnUsual was balanced, informative, and full of insight. Yvanovich did an excellent job in weaving a myriad of engaging worksheets and thought-provoking "assignments" into the book's framework, while also driving home the keys to undoing self-inflicted damage many entrepreneurs find themselves habitually acting out. A great read for anyone seeking to understand further how to provide value as a business leader, while at the same time never giving up on the pursuit of new and exciting entrepreneurial ventures.

Gregory Enjalbert | ex-VP/MD Asia Pacific, Bombardier Transportation, and Founder of A Cup of CoFi

The only business books I want to read are ones that give me direct access to a 'how-to' based on the author's expertise.

Business As UnUsual is just such a book—it is an insightful and practical guide for anyone looking to navigate the current business landscape with agility and success.

Yvanovich's strategies and tools for breaking free from ruts and establishing critical skills are invaluable.

Deiric McCann | Director, Genos International EU

Business As UnUsual by Rick is a must-read for anyone looking to thrive in the current business climate. Rick's extensive experience as a successful entrepreneur shines through as he delivers invaluable insights, practical strategies, and actionable steps to adapt and overcome the challenges of the pandemic.

What sets this book apart is the focus on the mindset and daily habits required to succeed in the "new normal." It's not just about making changes to your business, but also about changing your own approach and habits to stay ahead of the curve.

As someone who not only has the professional experience but also a big heart to contribute and help others, Rick's approach is refreshing and inspirational. The passion and dedication for helping others succeed is evident in every chapter, making this book not only informative but also a pleasure to read.

I highly recommend *Business As UnUsual* to business owners, managers, and aspiring entrepreneurs looking to break free from any ruts and get back in the game. Your actions today determine your success tomorrow, and with Rick's guidance, you'll have the perfect guide to navigating the current upheaval and coming out on top.

Liene Uresina | Business & Mindset Strategist and Author of *Everything Is OK With You*

Business As UnUsual is an incredibly insightful and practical guide for anyone looking to break free from the status quo and achieve long-term success. Yvanovich's insights into habits, motivation, and leadership provide a powerful foundation for achieving your goals and building a fulfilling life. Reading this book has had a transformational impact on my personal life along with my business.

Daniel Reed | Founder, Top Prospect Careers, Author of *Mastering a Winning Resume*

Business As UnUsual is an incredible guide to help you thrive in the new normal. Rick Yvanovich shares practical strategies and actionable steps to help you adapt, overcome, and succeed in your career and business. I connected immediately with the (new) concept of Dungeon Coaching. But be warned, once you read the introduction, you won't be able to put this book down.

Ray Brehm | CEO/Founder, Pubfunnels™, **Author of** *Book Profit Secrets*

Rick uses his experience, insights about life, coaching, and culture building to write *Business As UnUsual*, which provides a practical roadmap for change makers.

Huynh Cong Thang | CEO/Co-Founder, InnoLab Asia

Drawing on other works like *The Five Levels of Mastery*, Yvanovich's *Business As UnUsual* incorporates an exciting blend of various business philosophies and approaches, offering a truly comprehensive guide for setting your own journey towards thriving in motion.

Dr. Peter Chee | President and CEO, ITD World, **Author of** *Coaching for Breakthrough Success* **and** *The Five Levels of Mastery*

Reading *Business As UnUsual*, I felt like having a very nice talk with a kind, old friend. The amazing thing is that a concept so technical and apparently complicated as "business" is dealt with such clarity and friendly terms. All of a sudden, all the fog around this matter disappears. Through a powerful metaphor of a castle, Rick Yvanovich is teaching us a very simple method to reduce the distance between our goals and our own possibilities to fulfill them. I warmly recommend this book that provides a holistic way of approaching business in all aspects, a very creative and constructive modality of self-actualization in order to permanently renew our own being, which is the true mechanism of developing a business.

Dr. Beatrice Constandache | Sports Medicine MD

I love *Business As UnUsual* for the great amount of practical examples and DIY instructions. Throughout the book, Yvanovich is guiding us through a step-by-step process of improving ourselves as leaders and entrepreneurs. This book offers invaluable insights, practical strategies, and actionable steps to adapt, overcome, and succeed in the new normal. Amidst the challenges of the pandemic, *Business As UnUsual* outlines the mindsets, daily habits, and skills required to break free from any ruts and get back in the game—your action today determines your success tomorrow.

Paweł Górski | Founder & CEO, Tribee.io

A great book to help the disrupted leader to become the agile leader the world needs now, setting new examples and getting more out of themselves and their teams.

Floris Verhagen | Vice President, ROSEN Asia Pacific

As a healthcare leader, *Business As UnUsual* is just as relevant to healthcare teams as it is to corporations. Healthcare systems globally are deeply challenged with talent shortages due to burnout. *Business As UnUsual* is a foundational body of work collating knowledge from self-mastery, neuroscience of change, biology of high-flow teams, and transformational leadership. Rick synergizes this wealth of practical tools for both personal and organizational shift with his depth of coaching experience on a global level. Rick is an authority on the kind of transformational leadership needed to elevate human capacity beyond work and into our homes and communities. I am excited for our future in healthcare as we have such model mentors to learn from.

Brenda Lau | MD, FRCPC, FFPMANZCA, MM, CGIMS, FRCPC Founder (pain medicine), CIPS Clinical Associate Professor, UBC Dept. of Anesthesiology, Pharmacology & Therapeutics, Interventional Pain Specialist, CHANGEpain, Founder and Medical Director, CHANGEpain Clinic

UNLOCK
YOUR POTENTIAL IN A BUSINESS AS UNUSUAL WORLD

Uncertainty overwhelms, reducing productivity and growth opportunities.

- Are you fed up with the pandemic wreaking havoc on your workplace?

- Tired of grappling with unprecedented challenges, struggling to stay afloat in today's topsy-turvy world?

- You're not alone! Countless professionals, just like you, are striving to adapt and reinvent themselves to thrive in this "new normal."

TURN ADVERSITY INTO OPPORTUNITY:
START YOUR TRANSFORMATION TODAY!

Unlock your FREE resources and exclusive offers designed to empower you and your team in a Business As UnUsual world.

rickyvanovich.com/bauu/offers/

BUSINESS AS UNUSUAL

HOW TO THRIVE
IN THE NEW RENAISSANCE

RICK YVANOVICH
FCMA GCMA FCPA MSC CCMP CCMC CBC

ISBN: **978-1-923431-96-6** (ebook)
ISBN: **978-1-923431-94-2** (Paperback)
ISBN: **978-1-923431-97-3** (Hardcover)

To Sirian, Safena, and Katharina.
From now to the moon and back.
I've repeatedly failed to embrace, prioritise,
and acknowledge your feelings.
Thank you for giving me my time and space,
not that I gave you any choice.
We can't change the past, and it's time for me to
rebuild and balance.

Wanna build some Castles?
Let's get on with it!

To those who are caught in the malaise:
Mistakes and life happens, I've learned the hard way.
This book is your guide to escape.
Go build your Castle!

CONTENTS

INTRODUCTION

*I've learned that people will forget what you said,
people will forget what you did, but people will never forget
how you made them feel.*

Maya Angelou

In the face of COVID-19, businesses wobbled, and entire industries collapsed whilst entirely new ones emerged. The travel industry, for example, and all its branches, were greatly affected by the global pandemic.

Initially, some people hoped the pandemic would end soon, and we could all go back to business as usual. As the months passed, even more unusual things happened—lockdowns, restrictions, regulations, and closed country borders, each fuelling greater disruption, uncertainty, and fear.

As the pandemic began to draw out, it became clear we'd not be returning to business as usual and thus the "new normal" was coined. However, I don't subscribe to that, as there's nothing normal about it and business remains very unusual. That triggered the name of this book, *Business As UnUsual* (BAUU) as we need to accept that business will continue to be unusual.

In our BAUU world, the way companies function and motivate their people is changing. It's a new renaissance understanding what needs to be done in today's BAUU world as people are also changing, evaluating, and re-evaluating their lives and work.

Holding purely transactional meetings, blaming people who are lacking skills and understanding, and motivating people by shouting at them and their work is an outdated style of doing business.

Businesses now require a different style, one that prioritises coaching over punishing and correction over discipline. Business now means more than providing a service; it means making people and the surrounding community better than they were before.

Businesses now need to prioritise their employees by helping them grow as people, (remember they *are* people as well as employees), especially in this disconnected, hyper-stressful, and rapidly changing unusual world. People need to feel a business and its leaders encourage their personal growth and professional development. By creating people who are satisfied, motivated, inspired, aligned, and engaged, a business will flourish and more importantly, the impact of those people will ripple out, creating a legacy that will forever change the world.

Who Am I?

Leaders aren't born, they are made. And they are made just like anything else, through hard work. And that's the price we'll have to pay to achieve that goal, or any goal.

Vince Lombardi

I've been told that my career looks random and unusual, and I'm grateful to Daniel Reed[i] for reframing it as eclectic leadership, I do so much like that! My name is Rick Yvanovich, and I'm a serial entrepreneur whose purpose in life is to inspire and transform professionals for consistently higher achievement.

I've worked in various industries since my first career as a Management Trainee at Sainsbury's, a large UK supermarket chain. From managing finances for an oil company to cloud accounting implementations for hotels and nearly everything in between, I have been able to compound my experiences

---

[i] Daniel Reed is a resume writer and career coach at Top Prospects Careers. https://www.linkedin.com/in/daniel--reed/.

along the way, to build myself and create a business (TRG International) along the way.

TRG started off as my accidental entrepreneurial dream to implement accounting systems. When the company first started, I was running the entire show. Implementation, upkeep, support, client presentations, marketing, and just about everything else you could think of. Eventually, the business started growing too fast for me to handle on my own. I hired one person, then another, and before I knew it, I was managing a large group of people, including multiple leaders and their staffs in various departments.

We began scaling outside of Singapore and Vietnam (my current home base). Soon, we were working with customers in eighteen different countries. I thought we would be done with eighteen countries, but we continued to grow, introducing hotel chains to our client list. Hotel chains by their nature have sites in many countries and so we added even more countries. The company then morphed from supporting financial ERP to manufacturing ERP, on premise, on cloud, and hybrid.

As the business continued to grow organically, I was hitting a wall. As an accountant I'm a numbers person rather than a people person. I know the number formulae; I didn't know the people formulae. Up until that point, as a start-up, I'd been working very hands-on alongside other people. This was no longer going to work as we grew, and it was up to me to learn how to lead and motivate many and varied teams, interns, and leaders and drive innovation across multiple countries and time zones. I was committed to making every employee in the company happier and better than when they started, if only I had the right formula.

The accountant in me sought a scientific formula for people. There had to be one, and I stumbled upon psychometrics, the science of measuring people. That opened my eyes and piqued my curiosity, and I dived into the science of success and started relentlessly studying the books and teachings of business giants. I've attended thousands of hours of seminars and live events, learning, unlearning, relearning, and discovering countless models and tools. I've spent decades working on myself, my business, and building up people to make their lives and the world a better place. In this book, I'll share some of my eclectic leadership knowledge and experience with you and show you how to thrive in the new renaissance, with a view of making you feel something worthwhile.

THE CASTLE

Figure 1. The Castle Metaphor[ii]

[ii] Castle Illustrations in this book are credited to Elena Richardson. © Richard Yvanovich 2023.

Every big castle was once started with a single block;
despise no small beginnings. A little step taken every day builds
up the hope of greater accomplishments. Do something every day!

Israelmore Ayivor

As a visual learner, I searched for a visualisation and a metaphor to use and came up with a Castle. Let me explain. In 1604, the English judge, Sir Edward Coke (1552–1634), declared that "the house of everyone is to him as his Castle and Fortress as well for defence against injury and violence, as for his repose."[1] Over the years, Coke's quote was simplified as "a man's home is his castle."

A Castle symbolises so many things including home, safety, sanctuary, refuge, sanctity, structure, strong foundations, nobility (of character and mind), worthiness, honour, respect, aspirations, community, impact, and legacy. It's a powerful metaphor and visualisation.

The Castle has several structures, and I'll name and explain what they represent briefly here and go into detail throughout the book. As it's a metaphor, I've taken the liberty to merge multiple historical castle building concepts.

The Castle's innermost structure is its strongest, and it's your stronghold. It's called the Inner Keep. It's innermost as it's internal, inside you. In our metaphor it has four Towers:

- The **Tower of Purpose** (Chapter 1) represents your values, life purpose, goals, and legacy.
- The **Tower of Life Force** (Chapter 2) represents how you manage your Health, Energy, Rest, Balance, and Stress.
- The **Tower of Mind** (Chapter 3) represents how you show up, your habits and kaizen (which I interpret as lifelong learning and growth).

- The **Tower of Self** (Chapter 4) represents the four "selfs": self-confidence, self-efficacy and self-worth/self-value, and self-motivation.

Are you curious why there are four Towers? A bit of cognitive bias on my part from my past helps to explain. See if you can connect my dots:

- The Latin phrase *unus pro-omnibus, omnes pro uno* is the unofficial motto of Switzerland where I lived for some years. My wife is also Swiss.
- The French version, *un pour tous, tous pour un,* (one for all, all for one) came from the 1844 novel *The Three Musketeers* by Alexandre Dumas which I read (in English as my French is *merde*) as a child.
- The many English language film adaptations of *The Three Musketeers* transformed the motto to the well-known *all for one and one for all.*
- *All for one and one for all* is an example of a chiasmus, an English literature device in which the second part of a sentence is the mirror image of the first, one of the many (or is it few?) bits of knowledge I recall from school.

Thus, *all for one and one for all* means solidarity: each Tower acts to support the Inner Keep, and the Inner Keep acts to support the Towers.

This book starts with the Inner Keep, the innermost section of the Castle, as a person cannot conquer the outside world without first mastering their inside world.

Infinitely curious, I researched the roots of the Inner Keep. The French word *donjon* means "an inner tower in a castle" and was originally used in English interchangeably with "keep." From the fourteenth century the English word *dungeon* appeared and referred to the underground prison in a Castle, usually below the Inner Keep.

This is the next building in our Castle metaphor and is underneath the Inner Keep.

- **The Dungeon** (Chapter 5) represents coaching.

Surrounding the Inner Keep is an area called the Bailey. The Bailey expands over time as we foray beyond our castle walls extending our reach/domain and Bailey buildings grow. The Bailey comprises three buildings:

- **The Great Hall** (Chapter 6) represents community, culture, and leadership.
- **The Stables** (Chapter 7) represent looking forward, transforming, and searching for satisfaction.
- **The Treasury** (also Chapter 7) represents your finances.

Building your Castle (Chapter 8) helps you see which areas of your life you need to focus on to maintain balance and fulfil your life purpose.

Why Should You Read This Book?

I think books are like people, in the sense that they'll turn up in your life when you most need them.

Emma Thompson

Building your Castle takes time, and you never stop expanding your domain. One premise of Business As UnUsual (BAUU) is sharing knowledge openly. In this book, I'll share the knowledge, including relevant tools and models, that made the most significant impact on me. You may also share and coach other people using the models and tools provided.

This book is a collection of the many learnings, knowledge, and wisdom I've garnered throughout my lifelong pursuit of growth and understanding about how people tick. It's a combination of those insights offered by thought leaders around the world as well as my own.

This book is a blueprint that will help you identify where your personal and professional goals are right now and where you want to go. Instead of attending thousands of hours of personal development and coaching seminars like I did, you can use the tools, teachings, and techniques I provide to bridge the gap between where you are and where you want to be.

Learning about the secrets of success, influence, and legacy are right here for the taking. The time to completely overhaul your systems and adopt new ways of motivating employees, driving results, and making the lives of people better is right now.

I share all this information because it's my passion to help people. Enhancing someone's life goes beyond bolstering their skill set alone; leaders need to enrich their people's overall well-being. So, whilst you are working to grow and inspire your company, don't forget that you, too, are worth an investment of your time and energy.

Too often, I see wildly successful people—even business owners—who feel like something is still missing. I'm not talking about a work life balance—that's too simplistic. They feel they're undercutting their own potential, as if they *could* be doing so much more. They have a gnawing sensation that something's a bit off. They want to make a change but don't know where to start or in which direction to go. BAUU will help you overcome that feeling. Be sure to let me know when it does and if it doesn't.

CHAPTER 1
THE TOWER OF PURPOSE

TOWER OF PURPOSE

He who has a why to live can bear with almost any how.

Friedrich Nietzsche

One cause for dissatisfaction in life is a lack of progress. When we aren't actively moving forward, we feel we are failing or merely drifting. When we feel stuck professionally, we aren't taking steps towards becoming the person we want to be. We aren't growing.

What underscores a lack of progress is universal: Purpose. Lack of progress in both life and business is generally due to a lack of personal purpose.

Without purpose, we stall on our projects, procrastinate, get hung up or consumed by minor details, get frustrated more easily, and further disconnect from our support systems. Lack of purpose (of an individual or of a business) and the lack of alignment of an individual's purpose with that of the company's purpose also results in stunted business growth and a lack of innovation. Without purpose, we've lost the plot; we've lost the point. What are we doing each day? Why are we doing it, *really*? Misaligned, unclear goals, coupled with a lack of true purpose and passion, lead to unsurprising unequivocal dissatisfaction.

Purpose brings clarity, direction, measurable goals, and growth. Arguably, the Tower of Purpose is the tallest Tower in the Inner Keep, as it acts as your guide, compass, and north star. It needs to be visible above the treetops to guide you on your journey. As you journey further, your Tower of Purpose also grows higher.

In other words, your life journey is your purpose, guided by your Tower of Purpose. Following a path relentlessly is what propels a person to achieve their desired results in life. The Tower of Purpose is here to remind us that life is not about making it to the final destination, but rather a journey on which we realise our purpose each step of the way.

Every person, whether they work for a business or not, has a unique purpose and diverse needs and will be motivated by different things.

- As a human, you are concerned about your own purpose. However, will you support the purpose of others too?
- As a leader, you are concerned about your business's purpose. However, will you support your own or your employees' purpose too?

Your Life Purpose should give way to larger Life Goals. Get specific about the larger goals you want to achieve in life.

- What are they?
- Are they based on money or life experiences?
- Are they in alignment with your purpose?
- Acting on these big life goals and taking inventory of where you are in relation to them can help you get meaningful results.
- What deadlines can you set for yourself?
- As humans, we must continuously evaluate the present environment and shift with the currents and tides to meet our changing and evolving needs.
- As decision-makers for our businesses, we must continuously evaluate the present environment and shift with the currents and tides to meet the evolving needs of our business and our people (employees).

The Tower of Purpose is made up of your Core Values, your Life Purpose, your Life Goals, and your Legacy. I'll touch all four in this chapter and provide a model to formulate Life Purpose at the end of the chapter. It may feel like a circuitous route as all the parts of the Tower of Purpose are linked together. Remember, this is your Castle and your Tower of Purpose. It's unique to you and its size and shape are up to you.

The Meaning of Life

Whatever we are, whatever we make of ourselves, is all we
will ever have—and that, in its profound
simplicity, is the meaning of life.

Philip Appleman

Forty-two. That's "the answer to the Ultimate Question of Life, the Universe and everything" as calculated by Deep Thought, the enormous supercomputer in *The Hitchhiker's Guide to the Galaxy* by Douglas Adams.[2] The only problem was that after 7.5 million years of working it out, no one knew what the exact question was.

Deep Thought aside, everyone will have a different view of the meaning of life, but I like to take a cue from Monty Python's "The Meaning of Life." In the movie, the meaning of life is simple: try to be nice to people, avoid eating fat, read a good book every now and then, get some walking in, and try to live together in peace and harmony with people of all creeds and nations. In other words, it's important to focus on improving ourselves, being kind to others, and taking care of the world. You'll sense these meanings throughout the book.

I encourage a basic/simple non-materialistic kind of life because happiness and fulfilment come from looking internally to see how you feel about the way you're living. Are you empowered to take care of yourself and meet your own emotional, physical, and mental needs? Are you encouraging continuing growth for your mind, body, spirit, and business? Remember that life is a journey on which we realise our purpose each step of the way.

Having a life purpose guides all our values, decisions, and motivations. It allows us to see the entire picture rather than a random assortment of puzzle pieces. Instead of focusing intensely on the smaller pieces and getting hung up on them, look at the big picture. What is your life's purpose? Is it to bake the best muffin or be an amazing parent? Is it to offer a creative and innovative idea to solve a complex problem? The thought of you just thinking about what your Life Purpose is gives me goose bumps. It's another example of the new renaissance in our BAUU world.

Life Purpose Examples

Where your talents and the needs of the world cross, there your calling can be found.

Aristotle

To help inspire you, here are some sample life purpose statements from real people just like you:[iii]

- Inspiring and transforming professionals for consistently higher achievement. (Rick Yvanovich)
- Inspiring and helping people to live with personal agency. (Gregory Engalbert)
- Inspiring People to Achieve Wholesome Success and in turn Pay It Forward to Make This World A Better Place. (Kian Leong Phang)
- Exponential Growth Innovation in Organizations. (Guy Rowse)
- To inspire people through coaching & mentoring for innovative results. (Angela Samson)
- Coaching and transforming leaders for a better world with love. (Dr. Peter Chee)

[iii] Life Purpose Examples and other resources can be found at RickYvanovich.com/BAUU/.

Values

In order to stand out, we have to know what we stand for.

Simon Sinek

Our values are beliefs about what is good or bad or desirable or undesirable. Many values define us, and since each of us is unique, we also have unique values. There will be similar values within groups of like-minded people, less so with disparate, unrelated groups of people.

Values help us grow, develop, and create the future we want. Decisions reflect our values and solid values keep us grounded. We use values to make ethical decisions, as they determine our moral compass of what is right or wrong. Values are motivational, while morals and ethics are constricting.

As an individual, are there some values you must have? No, I think not, as each of us is unique and different. Regarding leadership, are there some values a leader must have? That's a tricky question. The leader *first* needs their core values. Then they need to align them *and* be able to demonstrate such alignment, with those of their organisation.

Life Goals

Your plans may change, don't be attached to your plans, only be attached to your life purpose.

Wanda Bonet-Gascot

Some people I work with greatly underestimate the potential their reach and impact can truly have over the course of several years. I've found most people overestimate what they can do in the short term, in six months or a year, but greatly underestimate what they can achieve in five or ten years if they keep working towards their goals.

I have always set goals for myself. As I've aged, I've developed more life goals as opposed to just any old goals. I formed my life purpose only in the last five years; in my case, goals came first. When I found my life purpose, I needed to revisit my goals to ensure each of them drove my life purpose; if not, I dropped them. Keeping my life purpose in mind helped me prioritise which goals were most important, and thus, worthy of time and energy towards achieving them.

When we look at life goals, we are focusing on our life purpose. To achieve that, we need a vision and goals. When our goals align to our life purpose, we can achieve them faster.

Beyond SMARTEST Tool

Dreams are free. Goals have a cost. While you can daydream for free, goals don't come without a price. Time, Effort, Sacrifice and Sweat. How will you pay for your Goals?

Usain Bolt

SMART	SMARTER	SMARTEST	BEYOND SMARTEST
Specific **M**easurable **A**ttainable **R**elevant **T**ime-bound	**S**pecific **M**easurable **A**ttainable **R**elevant **T**ime-bound **E**ngaging **R**ewarding	**S**pecific **M**easurable **A**ttainable **R**elevant **T**ime-bound **E**ngaging **R**ewarding **S**atisfying **T**eam-Based	?

HOW CAN WE GO BEYOND SMARTEST?

Figure 2. What's beyond SMARTEST?

George T. Doran created the SMART acronym as an easy reminder for goal setting back in 1981.[3] Since then, the meaning of each of the letters has changed and multiple authors have added the additional letters ER and EST. *Figure 2* above depicts the evolution, and below I explain the SMARTEST acronym.

- **S**pecific. What outcome do you want to achieve, exactly?
- **M**easurable. How will you measure your progress and know whether you have attained this objective?
- **A**ttainable. Ensure the goal is possible and achievable. How much control do you have over the outcome? How can you increase your level of control?
- **R**elevant. Is it a worthwhile goal? Do you see a link to your company and/or life purpose?
- **T**ime-bound. By what date or time will you achieve this goal?
- **E**ngaging. On a scale of 1 to 10, how motivated are you to achieve this goal? How can you increase your motivation? If it's already at 10, how will you make it an 11?
- **S**atisfying. What satisfaction will you gain by achieving this goal?
- **T**eam-based. Who will you choose to be part of your team to achieve this goal?

I've always been curious: if goal setting can be SMART, SMARTER, and SMARTEST, what is *Beyond SMARTEST*? Is there even such a thing? In my mind, there is. We go beyond SMARTEST by adding another acronym, **B**-SMARTEST for BEYOND SMARTEST.[iv] *Figure 3* below depicts the evolution, and I explain the BEYOND acronym.

[iv] B-SMARTEST and other resources can be downloaded from RickYvanovich.com/BAUU/.

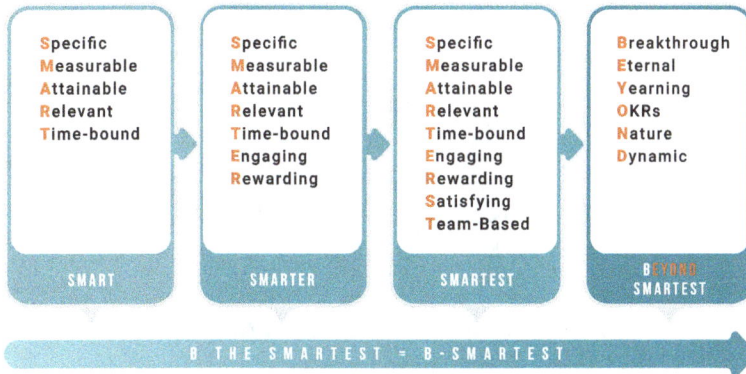

Figure 3. BEYOND SMARTEST

- **B**reakthrough means the goal is significant and makes a clear difference. These goals are way outside our comfort zone as we need to break through to something even greater. As there are multiple other acronyms used with big goals, let me put Breakthrough into more context. They're bigger than Covey's Wildly Important Goal (WIG)[4] or Collins' Big Hairy Audacious Goal (BHAG),[5] more like Tom Peters' Clear & Compelling Audacious Goal (CCAG).[6]

- **E**ternal means forever, endless, infinite. I was inspired by Simon Sinek's book *The Infinite Game* [see Infinite (growth) Mindset in the Tower of Mind in Chapter 3].[7] We're playing the infinite game; we're not just playing to win a finite game (where someone wins and someone loses).

- **Y**earning is a deep internal drive to achieve a goal; it's "engaging" on steroids. It feeds the deepest part of your soul.

- **O**KRs are Objectives and Key Results. We link your B-SMARTEST goals to OKRs and achieve them even faster! OKRs is a goal-setting methodology first introduced by Andy Grove at Intel in the 1970s and he wanted answers to two questions: "Where do we want to go?" (Objective) and "How will we pace ourselves to get there?" (Key Result).[8] OKR methodology was introduced to Google in 1999 by John Doerr. Larry Paige, co-founder at Google said, "OKRs have helped lead us to 10X growth, many times over," in the forward of Doerrs book about the OKR framework.[9]

- **Nature.** We're highly cognisant of the goal's impact on humans, humanity, and Mother Nature. We want to leave the planet and people better than we found them.
- **Dynamic** means we're constantly revising and fine tuning our goals as we progress.

If you are not making progress on your life goals, the question is *why not*? Are the actions too big? If so, the solution is to break them down into multiple smaller ones. Are you not feeling motivated enough? Say your purpose out aloud daily as a reminder to yourself (and others). Saying it brings it to life and turns it into a positive affirmation.

Ask an accountability buddy [see Self-motivation (Motivation) in the Tower of Self in Chapter 4] or coach to help keep you in integrity and committed to following through on your action steps. For companies, revisit your mission and vision and reword them to make it more vivid.

Good to Great Goals

On November 7, 2012, I attended a conference featuring Brian Tracy. During the conference, Brian said, "Raise your hand if you have goals." More than half of the three hundred people in the room put their hands up. Then Brian said, "Now raise your hand if you've written down your goals." More than half the room lowered their hands—I saw only a few scattered hands still raised in the crowd. Brian continued to say that not even 5 percent of people write their goals down. That was our homework after the conference, to immediately write down our goals and become part of the 5 percent.

I was one of the 95 percent who hadn't written my goals down. I'd been kidding myself that I had goals. As Brian made abundantly clear on that November day, you can't be successful until you've really committed to your goals. Commitment starts with writing them down. Are you kidding yourself, too? If you haven't committed your goals to paper yet, stop reading and write them down now!

The first step in goal setting and planning is realising where you are and, maybe, admitting to yourself you don't have all the answers. This is where it helps to learn from Marshall Goldsmith (see Chapter 5) and Simon Sinek. Both gurus have mastered the art of asking for help and clarity. Goldsmith encourages us to ask for help unabashedly, whilst Sinek likes to be the stupidest person in the room by asking people to explain things to him in the most rudimentary way possible.

Neither hesitates to admit he doesn't know or might be wrong. That is really, really important because most of us will not admit to *ourselves* that we don't know something, let alone ask for help. It can seem weird to say, "Hey, I don't see the point of life. Can you help me?" When the student is ready to receive help (by way of asking, of course), then and only then, will the teacher appear.

When the student is ready, the teacher will appear.
When the student is truly ready... The teacher will Disappear.

Tao Te Ching

After that conference with Brian Tracy in 2012, I felt elated, wanting to become one of the five percent. I sped home to write down my goals. If you're imagining me furiously writing goals whilst listening to the Rocky theme song, it didn't quite go like that. Like Rocky, yes, I struggled. I didn't like what I first wrote down because it was so *meh* and uninspiring. Was that it? Before Brian, I had read, met, and joined other self-development corporate trainers/coaches who had imposed their own goals on us—doubling sales, increasing hires, expansion, growth, and acquisition—but these aren't the sort of goals that necessarily excite you when you're sitting at home. In the end, were these the goals I *really* wanted?

My answer? No, not really. Is doubling sales what genuinely motivates me? No, not really. There is a real disconnect. I was dissatisfied and not fully committed with my personal goal setting, until I took a certified coaching and mentoring course (CCMP).[v] During one of the sessions, we were pairing up and as we had an odd number, I volunteered to pair with the instructor, Dr Peter Chee. During the forty-five-minute exercise, he helped me extract my life purpose and he triggered inspirational life goals all in alignment with my life purpose. Ever since then, I've taken a very different trajectory. My goals are much more tangible, meaningful, and fulfilling to me. I now see life more holistically and have created goals that supported my evolution in more than just a business or numbers sense. This book is one of those life goals.

I bumped into someone recently who no longer works for my company. They said they were now coaching as well as running their own technology company. During our conversation, I perceived they were moving their business in a circle. I told them it seemed like they were clear on their purpose, but I was curious about their personal life goals. Did their life goals align with their company purpose? Did their company purpose align with their life goals?

This person was not exactly lost, but I got the sense they did not have clarity of exactly where they were heading. They had the map, but they didn't know their destination, they weren't asking for help, and I could observe they were not happy as

---

[v] CCMP (Certified Coaching and Mentoring Professional) is an International Coach Federation (ICF) certification for advanced coaching and mentoring from ITD World.

they were not progressing, and I could feel their frustration and confusion.

Although a company appears to have it all from an outsider's perspective, they might not have it all together internally. This CEO had doubled (or more) the company revenue in a handful of years and had a list of notable achievements. However, they still struggled with their direction and goals. I offered to coach them and after working together, we helped establish their life purpose, clarity on their life and company goals and tied all the goals into alignment with their life purpose. They're now enthusiastic and bursting with energy, have a sparkle in their eye when they talk about what they're doing and yes, they're flourishing personally and professionally.

Goals inform your game plan. Without a destination to plug into your GPS, your movement, no matter the direction, is aimless. The BEYOND SMARTEST goal-setting technique can help you take your goals into the beyond.

Four Questions

You need to consider four questions when building your personal game plan. I have considered and reconsidered these questions when looking at my life purpose and each of my goals. These questions help you clarify your purpose and align your goals to your life purpose. The four questions are:

- What do you need to believe?
- Who do you need to become?
- How do you want to feel?
- What do you have to visualise?

What do you need to believe? To make the seemingly impossible possible, what do you need to believe to be true about yourself? Your business? What about the world? Get clear on what your beliefs are right now and see where you may be limiting yourself. Flip these beliefs on their heads and start investing in their more positive alternatives to see opportunities where there once were only roadblocks. Your values (see above) stem from your beliefs.

You can't make the possible impossible, but you can make the impossible possible. Believe (I'm)Possible.

Sirian Yvanovich

Who do you need to become? In the future, you will require upgraded personal beliefs, upgraded daily habits, upgraded organisation, sleep, boundaries, energy, and much more. Like upgrading the software on your phone, you accept the change and thus you take accountability for these changes in your life. This also means having a thick skin and not letting the little things add up to big things. The ability to handle these changes also helps build your resilience, your ability to cope with change. Take a moment to visualise the future you. Who is that person, and in what ways does that future you need you to evolve?

How do you want to feel? Take charge of your emotional state and understand that the outside world will always change. If you want to get to the next level of life, you need to take control of your emotions which will help you make clearer and quicker decisions with more confidence. One way I have learned to regulate my emotions is through breath work (see the Power of Breath in Chapter 2—The Tower of Life Force) and awareness. By awareness, I mean being deliberately conscious of what's going on, both internally and externally. As stuff happens, how does it make you feel? Be conscious of those feelings and be aware of what triggers them.

Mindfulness is a human ability to be fully present, an in-the-moment awareness of our thoughts, feelings, bodily sensations, where we are, what we're doing, and not being overly reactive or overwhelmed by what's going on inside and around us. As an example, as you read this section, how did it make you feel? Pausing and being deliberately aware is an application of mindfulness. This book does not cover mindfulness in detail; you'll need to wait for one of my future books.

What do you have to visualise? Visualisation is the next level of success. Olympians mentally rehearse their races, executives mentally rehearse their presentations, and you need to start visualising your goals. Your brain responds to visual rehearsal, and if you can see something in your mind, then you can experience it in real life. Continue to rehearse mentally the things you want to experience in your physical reality, and you will find they will magnetise themselves to you!

Whatever you vividly imagine, ardently desire, sincerely believe, and enthusiastically act upon must inevitably come to pass.

Jim Sirbasku, 1939–2010

I share with you a philosophy from Shawn Achor's book, *Happiness Advantage*. He describes *The Losada Ratio* (Chapter 6 Losada Ratio), which is the sum of the positivity in a system divided by the sum of its negativity.[10] This is the idea that we need 2.9013 positive interactions to each negative interaction—that's a mathematical number which is reinterpreted as being three. Additionally, high performance was linked to a score in the range of three to six. So, it takes at least three positives to counteract the effects of one negative comment, and we need to stay above this 3:1 ratio or line and aim for more.[11] For example when someone laughs and jokes at my new tie, it'll take three to six, likely a lot more (as I love ties!) more positive interactions for me to get over their negativity about my fabulous tie dress sense.

If the positive to negative ratio dips below 3, performance suffers. The opposite idea, then, is to ensure there are six positive experiences for every one negative experience to create a better sense of mental and social well-being. Being aware of this ratio means that we must be cognisant of the power of what we say and do, actively seek to praise, and lift others up rather than criticise, judge, and pull them down. By withholding judgement of others, we also reduce those negative interactions and thus improve the ratio.

With these four questions and a Losada mentality, you can start getting a game plan ready for yourself and your business that will make you excited about life and business over the long haul.

Legacy

If you're going to live, leave a legacy.
Make a mark on the world that can't be erased.

Maya Angelou

Your Legacy is what you leave behind when you reach the end of your life. It's what others will remember you for. The key is impact. How many people will remember the impact you had on them? You may impact one single person, or you may impact many people. The more impact you have on others, the more lasting your legacy.

Altruism is doing things for other people with no expectation of reward; it's a selfless concern for others. Altruistic emotions and behaviours are associated with greater well-being, health, and longevity.[12] Being better humans for a better humanity. I have to say I get enjoyment from helping others, so there's bias and a bit of selfishness there, too.

It's your Legacy, and it's your choice how altruistic and impactful it is; only you can decide how much is enough.

Life Purpose Formulation

Life isn't about finding yourself.
Life is about creating yourself.

George Bernard Shaw

This is a journey. It's up to you how fast you want to travel. There are a series of steps designed to explore, uncover, and gather your thoughts and stories. As you go through the steps and gather more and more thoughts, you may want to go back and revisit a previous step to add to or change it, as the steps are related to each other.

During this journey I'm acting as your guide and coach. You can journey by yourself or with your partner or coach. If you are a coach, you can use this with your coachees.

On this journey I need you to keep a record. So, arm yourself with your favourite weapons to record your thoughts and answers: pen/pencil, paper, journal, app, word cloud, sticky notes, spreadsheet, etc.

Each step consists of one or more of the following:

- **Record** your thoughts and answers using your weapons of choice. When recording your stories, imagine you are filming them, so describe the scene being played.
- **Explore and uncover** using the various prompts and questions (there is no need to answer every question), word lists, and templates.
- **Milestone**. The records you create may be long and we need to whittle them down to the Top 1–5, try these tips:
    - Do you notice any common themes? Group them together.

- Do you notice similar meanings? Consolidate them into fewer meanings, and discard the ones that resonate less.
  - Look at your list—give each one a 1–10 rank of importance and rank them in order.
  - Discard the bottom two. Then repeat until you only have five left.
  - Pick a pair, keep one and discard the other. Keep picking pairs until you have none left.
- **Identify** facts, feelings, patterns, and themes. Record the facts and your feelings, and search for patterns and themes.
- **Categorise** themes into contributions (use action verbs, typically your superpower/strength) and impacts (your belief/hope of what you (and/or others) deserve to feel).
- **Checkpoint**. We synergise multiple steps and milestones.
- **Formulate**. We put it all together and formulate our Life Purpose Statement.

The questions/milestones/templates/word lists, etc. are available for download.[vi]

Step 1: Explore and Uncover – Core Values

Your core values are the deeply held beliefs that authentically describe your soul.

John C. Maxwell

[vi] The Life Purpose Formulation prompt questions/milestones/templates/word lists etc. can be downloaded from RickYvanovich. com/BAUU/.

Values are our beliefs, the things that are important and matter to us. They motivate us. They influence our behaviour and are linked to our character and are what we want to be. Use the questions below as a guided prompt and record your answers using your weapons of choice.

1. What's important to you in your personal life?
2. What stories inspire you?
   - What about them inspires you?
3. What values do you admire in others?
4. What values do other people say you have?
5. Think of the most meaningful moments in your life.
   - What were you doing?
   - Who were you with?
6. Think of the moments you felt the **least** satisfied.
   - What were you doing?
   - Who were you with?
   - What caused the lack of satisfaction?
7. Think of the moments you felt the **most** satisfied.
   - What were you doing?
   - Who were you with?
   - What caused the feeling of satisfaction?
8. What were some of your **worst** life experiences?
   - What were you doing?
   - Who were you with?
   - What caused it?
9. What were some of your **best** life experiences.
   - What were you doing?
   - Who were you with?
   - What caused it?
10. Think of the moments that make you angry or frustrated or annoyed.
    - What were you doing?
    - Who were you with?
    - What caused it?

11. Think of the moments that make you happy or excited.
    - What were you doing?
    - Who were you with?
    - What caused it?
12. What value do you need to find in your work?
13. What do you believe in with respect to your values?
14. If you could get a tattoo to remind you of your life, what would it be?
    - Visualise its shape and colours.
    - Visualise where on your body you would tattoo it.
    - Who would you want to show it to?
    - Why would you want to show it to them?

Use the list of Value Words List in *Figure 4* below as a further prompt and capture your answers using your weapons of choice. *Acceptance* on the list below.

Accountability	Autonomy	Collaboration
Accuracy	Awareness	Commitment
Achievement	Balance	Community
Adaptability	Beauty	Compassion
Adjusting	Being true to	Competence
Adventure	yourself	Competency
Affection	Belonging	Competition
Agency	Blessing	Competitiveness
Agile	Boldness	Completion
Altruism	Calmness	Compromising
Ambition	Carefulness	Confidence
Appreciation	Caring	Connectedness
Arts	Challenge	Connection
Assertiveness	Change	Consistency
Attentiveness	Cheerfulness	Contentment
Authenticity	Citizenship	Continuous
Authority	Clear mindedness	Improvement

Contribution	Environmental	Generosity
Control	Awareness	Goodness
Cooperation	Equality	Grace
Correctness	Equanimity	Gratitude
Country	Esprit de corps	Growth
Courage	Ethics	Happiness
Courtesy	Excellence	Hard Work
Creativity	Excitement	Harmony
Curiosity	Exhilaration	Health
Decisiveness	Experiment	Helping Others
Democracy	Expertise	Helping Society
Democratic	Exploration	Honesty
Dependability	Expressiveness	Honour
Design	Fairness	Humility
Determination	Faith	Humour
Devoutness	Faithful	Imagination
Diligence	Fame	Improvement
Discipline	Family	Independence
Discovery	Family Happiness	Industrious
Discretion	Family-oriented	Influence
Diversity	Fast Pace	Influencing Others
Dynamism	Fidelity	Ingenuity
Economic Security	Fitness	Inner Harmony
Economy	Flexibility	Innovation
Education	Fluency	Inquisitiveness
Effectiveness	Focus	Insightfulness
Efficiency	Focus	Inspiration
Elegance	Forgiveness	Integrity
Empathy	Freedom	Intellect
Encouragement	Friendliness	Intelligence
Enjoyment	Friendship	Intimacy
Enlightenment	Friendships	Intuition
Entertainment	Frugality	Involvement
Enthusiasm	Fun	Joy

Just and Fair
Justice
Kaizen
Kindness
Knowledge
Leadership
Learning
Legacy
Love
Love for family
Loyalty
Magnificence
Making a
difference
Mastery
Meaningful Work
Merit
Mindfulness
Ministering
Modesty
Money
Morality
Mystery
Nature
Obedience
Open-mindedness
Openness
Optimism
Order
Originality
Passion
Patience
Patriotism
Peace
Perfection

Perseverance
Persistence
Personal
Development
Personal
Expression
Personal growth
Piety
Planning
Play
Pleasure
Poise
Politeness
Popularity
Positivity
Power
Practicality
Preparedness
Privacy
Professionalism
Prudence
Purity
Quality
Radiance
Recognition
Relationships
Reliability
Religion
Reputation
Resourcefulness
Respect
Respectful
Responsibility
Restraint
Results-oriented

Rigour
Risk
Safety
Security
Self-acceptance
Self-actualization
Self-care
Self-compassion
Self-control
Self-development
Self-forgiveness
Self-reliance
Self-respect
Selflessness
Sense of
Community
Sensibility
Sensitivity
Sensuality
Serenity
Service
Sexuality
Shrewdness
Simplicity
Skilfulness
Sophistication
Soundness
Spark
Speculation
Speed
Spirituality
Spontaneity
Stability
Status
Strategic

Strength	Thoroughness	Understanding
Structure	Thoughtfulness	Uniqueness
Success	Thrill	Unity
Support	Timeliness	Usefulness
Sustainability	Tolerance	Variety
Teaching	Toughness	Vitality
Team Spirit	Traditionalism	Wealth
Teamwork	Trust	Well-being
Temperance	Trustworthiness	Winning
Tenderness	Truth	Wisdom
Thankfulness	Truth-seeking	

Figure 4. Value Words List

Step 1: Milestone – Core Values

A highly developed values system is like a compass. It serves
as a guide to point you in the right direction when you are lost.

Idowu Koyenika

From your "Step 1: Explore and Uncover Core Values" records, whittle down your list to the top five. It's your choice to write them down or highlight them using your weapons of choice.

Step 2: Explore and Uncover – Passion

Nothing great in the world has ever been
accomplished without passion.

Georg Hegel

Think about what really gets you going. What do you care deeply about? What fuels you? Use the questions below as a guided prompt and record your answers using your weapons of choice.

1. What makes your heart sing?
2. What are the things you love to do?
3. What are your hobbies?
4. What are some things in life that you always have the energy to do?
5. What activities are you are most attracted to?
6. What do you do that would be hard for you to do without?
7. What do you do or experience that brings you the most joy?
8. What learning do you most look forward to?
9. When you're engaged, what are you doing?
10. When you're energized, what are you doing?
11. When you're enjoying life, what are you doing?
12. What is it that you do or experience that makes you feel most alive?
13. What is it that you do or experience that makes you feel most fulfilled?
14. What are the things you do for yourself that bring you feelings of enjoyment or fulfilment?
15. What are the things you do for others that bring you feelings of enjoyment or fulfilment?
16. What activities are you doing that feel meaningful to you?
17. What activities are you doing that feel worthwhile to you?
18. If money was no object, what would you be doing?
19. What lights you up when you talk about it?
20. You realise that you've forgotten to eat/drink. What were you doing that made you lose track of time?
21. Do you prefer to help people you know, or people you don't know?
22. Do you prefer to help people you know, or people close to you?
23. What do you never get bored with?

24. What would you do more of to feel more fulfilled?
25. What would you do more of to feel more engaged?
26. What would you do more of to feel more energised?
27. What would your parents say are your greatest passions?
28. What would your partner say are your greatest passions?
29. What would your friends say are your greatest passions?
30. What would your work colleagues say are your greatest passions?
31. What would most other people say are your greatest passions?
32. What are you passionate about?
33. What do you feel are your greatest passions?

Step 2: Milestone – Passion

People with great passion can make the impossible happen.

Jeremiah Say

Reflect on your "Step 2: Explore and Uncover Passion" records. Identify any facts, feelings, patterns, and themes. Whittle your Step 2 record list down to your top five. It's your choice to write them down or highlight them using your weapons of choice.

Step 3: Explore and Uncover – Achievements

The value of achievement lies in the achieving.

Albert Einstein

Reflect on your past and your life story to date. Using the prompts below as a guide, make a list of all the achievements you're proud of, using your weapons of choice.

- In sports
- In hobbies
- With friends
- In the community
- Your certifications
- Awards and prizes
- In primary school
- In secondary school
- In college
- As a young child

- As a teenager
- In your 20s
- In your 30s
- In your 40s
- In your 50s
- In your 60s
- In your 70s
- In your 80s
- In your 90s

Step 3: Milestone – Achievements

Who you are is not what you became through your achievements, but by the price you paid to get them.

Manuel Corazzari

From your "Step 3: Explore and Uncover Achievements" records, whittle down your list to your top five. It's your choice to write them down or highlight them using your weapons of choice.

Step 4: Explore and Uncover – Talents

The person born with a talent they are meant to use will find their greatest happiness in using it.

Johann Wolfgang von Goethe

What are you good at? Use the questions below as a guided prompt and record your answers using your weapons of choice.

1. What are your greatest strengths?
2. What are you most effective at doing?

3. Where do you have the most impact?
4. What would your parents say are your greatest talents?
5. What would your partner say are your greatest talents?
6. What would your friends say are your greatest talents?
7. What would your work colleagues say are your greatest talents?
8. What would most other people say are your greatest talents?
9. What do you feel are your greatest talents?

Step 4: Milestone – Talents

Use what talents you possess; the woods would be very silent if no birds sang there except those that sang best.

Henry Van Dyke

Reflect on your "Step 4: Explore and Uncover Talents" records. Identify any facts, feelings, patterns, and themes. Whittle your Step 4 record list down to your top five. It's your choice to write them down or highlight them using your weapons of choice.

Step 5: Checkpoint 1 – Synergise Steps 1–4

Discover the intersection of your unique passion, talent, and value to leave this world a better place than you found it.

Rick Yvanovich

Reflect on your Milestones from Steps 1–4 and identify any facts, feelings, patterns, and themes. Based on your reflection, what are the most important things you can do that synergise your top passions and talents and align with your values?

Whittle it down to no more than five (less is better) using your weapons of choice. I suggest you reflect on what you've written and make iterative improvements. It's encouraging to have a partner or coach help as you iterate.

> **The most important things I can do that leverage my top passions and talents and aligns with my values are the following:**
>
> 1. _____
>
> 2. _____
>
> 3. _____
>
> 4. _____
>
> 5. _____

Step 6: Explore and Uncover – Best Roles

To be beautiful means to be yourself. You don't need to be accepted by others. You need to accept yourself.

Thich Nhat Hanh

Think about your previous roles including any jobs, and the type of work you'd like to do in the future. Use the questions below as a guided prompt and record your answers using your weapons of choice.

1. Which of your previous roles or jobs fit you well?
   - What did you love about those roles? What would you like to do more of?
2. Which of your previous roles or jobs do you feel were a poor fit?

3. What about those roles or jobs would you like to avoid in the future?
4. If you were in the flow, what would you be doing, exactly?
5. If you could choose any job or project, what would you choose to do?
    - What do you love about this job/project?
6. What unpaid volunteer work would make you lose track of time?
7. What is the one type of work you would like to fill your days with?
8. Describe your best day. It can be one you already had, or it can be one that you imagine.
    - What does it look and feel like?
9. Describe your best week. It can be one you already had, or it can be one that you imagine.
    - What does it look and feel like?

Step 6: Milestone – Best Roles

There are many roles you can play in life, but you know there's one role you must play: to be yourself and live it to the fullest.

Wilson Kanadi

Reflect on your "Step 6: Explore and Uncover Roles" records. Identify any facts, feelings, patterns, and themes. Whittle it down to no more than five (less is better) using your weapons of choice. I suggest you reflect on whatever you've written and make iterative improvements. It's encouraging to have a partner or coach help as you iterate.

The Best Roles I can do that leverage my top passions and talents and aligns with my values are the following:

1. _____

2. _____

3. _____

4. _____

5. _____

Step 7: Explore and Uncover – Stories

*The stories we tell literally make the world. If you want
to change the world, you need to change your story. This truth
applies both to individuals and institutions.*

Michael Margolis

Think about your meaningful and vivid stories (past, present, future), both highs and lows, involving you by yourself or with other people. Identify any people, facts, feelings, patterns, and themes in each story.

Use the questions below as a guided prompt and record your stories and answers using your weapons of choice.

1. What's a recent experience (does not have to be at work) that you absolutely loved being part of?
2. Who is a person that significantly influenced you, resulting in the unique person you are today?
   - Vividly record the story and their impact on you.
3. Who is another person that significantly influenced you, resulting in the unique person you are today?
   - Vividly record the story and their impact on you.

- Repeat for each person who has had a significant impact on you.
4. Who are your heroes and role models?
   - What's the story behind this?
5. As a young child, who did you aspire to be when you grew up?
   - What's the story behind this?
6. Today, who would you want to be (who do you want to become), if you could be any of your heroes or role models?
   - What's the story behind this?
   - What do you want to feel if you become this?
7. As a young child, what type of work did you aspire to do when you grew up?
   - What's the story behind this?
8. As you grew older, how and when did your aspirations change?
   - What's the story behind this?
9. Record a specific, vivid, happy, joyful childhood memory.
   - What's the story behind this?
10. Record another specific, vivid, happy, joyful childhood memory.
    - What's the story behind this?
    - Repeat if you have more stories from your childhood.
11. Record a specific, vivid, happy, joyful memory.
    - What's the story behind this?
12. Record another specific, vivid, happy, joyful memory.
    - What's the story behind this?
    - Repeat if you have more stories that pop into your mind.
13. At your funeral, what stories would you want your partner to be telling about you?
    - What's the story behind this?

14. At your funeral, what stories would you want your family to be telling about you?
    - What's the story behind this?
15. At your funeral, what stories would you want your friends to be telling about you?
    - What's the story behind this?
16. At your funeral, what stories would you want your colleagues to be telling about you?
    - What's the story behind this?
17. At your funeral, what stories would you want other people to be telling about you?
    - What's the story behind this?
18. What do you want to be remembered for?
    - What's the story behind this?

Step 7: Milestone – Stories

The ability of humans to read meaning into patterns is the most defining characteristic we have.

Eleanor Catton

Reflect on your "Step 7: Explore and Uncover Stories" records. Identify recurring feelings, patterns, and themes. Record up to twelve recurring/repeating patterns and themes, and for each, categorise them as either a contribution (use action verbs) or an impact. I suggest you reflect on whatever you've written and make iterative improvements. It's encouraging to have a partner or coach help as you iterate.

Step 8: Checkpoint 2 – Synergise Steps 5–7

Finding patterns is the essence of wisdom.

Dennis Prager

Reflect on Steps 5–7. Identify recurring feelings, patterns, and themes. Record up to twelve recurring/repeating patterns and themes, and for each, categorise them as either a contribution (use action verbs) or an impact. Split into two lists, one for contribution (use action verbs) and one for impact. I suggest you reflect on whatever you've written and make iterative improvements. It's encouraging to have a partner or coach help as you iterate.

Feel free to backtrack and review/update each of the previous steps.

Step 9: Formulation – Life Purpose Statement

As the struggle for survival has subsided, the question has emerged: Survival for what? Ever more people have the means to live, but no meaning to live for.

Viktor Frankl

Now we get to put it all together. Remember it's a journey and will need many drafts and iterations. The format of the Life Purpose Statement is this:

Action Verb	Target Audience	Added Value
Understandable Simple Clear Service-driven Contribution	Who	Added value to audience Impact on audience Infinite (not finite) Growth-oriented Desirable/aspirational Feels good/right to you Gives you goose bumps

The Action Verb is from the Contribution in Step 7 and 8. The Added Value is from the Impact in Step 7 and 8.

Earlier in this chapter I gave some Life Purpose Examples. See how some of them fit:

	Action Verb	Target Audience	Added Value
1	Inspiring and transforming	professionals	for consistently higher achievement
2	Inspiring and helping	people	to live with personal agency
3	Coaching and transforming	leaders	for a better world with love
4	To inspire	people	through coaching and mentoring for innovative results
5	Inspiring	people	to Achieve Wholesome Success and in turn Pay It Forward to Make This World A Better Place
6	Innovation	in organisations	Exponential growth

The first draft is going to be very rough. Don't expect it to be perfect, and it likely makes limited sense. That's OK, the idea here is to capture the gist of it and give it a go.

As an example, look at number 6 in the table, it makes more sense if we change the order to Added Value + Action Verb + Target Audience. So yes, you can do that if it grammatically lands better for you.

Helping others is the way we help ourselves.

Oprah Winfrey

Now it's your turn!

Draft	Action Verb	Target Audience	Added Value
1			
2			
3			

Keep iterating until it inspires you and feels right, and if it gives you goose bumps then you've likely nailed it.

CHAPTER 1 KEY TAKEAWAYS

- Lack of progress is a cause of dissatisfaction.
- Lack of progress in both life and business is generally due to a lack of personal purpose.
- Our life journey is our purpose and is guided by the Tower of Purpose.
- Our life purpose gives our life meaning.
- Our values are beliefs about what is good or bad or desirable or undesirable.
- Our goals need to align with our life purpose.
- SMART, SMARTER, SMARTEST, BEYOND SMARTEST
- Write down your life goals and become one of the top 5 percent.
- Your Legacy is what you leave behind when you reach the end of your life. It's what others will remember you for.
- Life Purpose Statement formulation follows 9 Steps.
- Download Chapter 1 resources from RickYvanovich. com/BAUU/.

CHAPTER 1
REFLECTION PROMPTS

What's your **one** key takeaway from this chapter?

```
_____
_____
_____
```

And what else?

```
_____
_____
_____
```

What action will you take right away because of something you read in this chapter?

```
_____
_____
_____
```

And what else?

```
_____
_____
_____
```

CHAPTER 2
THE TOWER OF LIFE FORCE

TOWER OF LIFE FORCE

If an egg is broken by outside force, life ends. If broken by inside force, life begins. Great things always begin from inside.

Jim Kwik

Humans need life force energy to exist, and we don't have an endless supply of it. You cannot operate at your best if your body and mind are not both being taken care of. It's important to keep your mind sharp and your skills intact; it's equally important to ensure you are investing in your physical self as well. Thus, the purpose of the Tower of Life Force is to manage and take care of this life force energy.

Have you ever felt tired or exhausted or run-down? These and other symptoms are some of the physical and emotional flags that may inhibit our life force energy and signal the need to maintain your Tower of Life Force. When our Tower of Life Force isn't being maintained and cared for, we'll lack the life force energy to build up our Castle.

For those people who have had one or more challenging bouts with COVID and may be suffering from long COVID (that's me!), it's unsurprising the renaissance around health in our BAUU world.

Some (not all) of the symptoms are listed below:

- Body fatigue
- Exhaustion
- Feeling sleepy
- Brain fog
- Aching muscles
- Stiff back
- Feeling slow
- Lack of motivation
- Trouble sleeping/insomnia
- Moodiness
- Irritability/grumpiness
- Feelings of hopelessness
- Anxiety
- Absentmindedness

HERBS

The parts of the Tower of Life Force can be remembered by using the acronym HERBS: Health, Energy, Rest, Balance, and Stress, and we'll cover each of them below.

H = Health

*I believe that the greatest gift you can give your
family and the world is a healthy you.*

Joyce Meyer

One thing this pandemic has taught many people, is that without your health, you truly have nothing. Some people—and more so leaders—tend to be highly cerebral and dedicate plenty of time to working and growing their mind or social network; health isn't always their number one priority or even on their priority list. Yet, without your health, there is no you, and that would be a terrible loss to the world. Therefore, it's important to take care of you!

I manage my health, not as a one-off activity, but as a lifestyle. I make intentional choices to prioritise my health in my daily habits and routines. Instead of hyper-focusing on weight loss, a special diet, or purely aesthetic goals, I aspire to make small healthy choices every day. Living a generally healthy lifestyle reduces the risk of most diseases, keeps the body healthy, and promotes mental well-being. Thus, the Tower of Life Force also supports the Tower of Self and the Tower of Mind.

My daily habits for health are surprisingly simple. I keep a water bottle handy and hydrate with two to three litres of plain water a day. (Sometimes I add lemon or lime and a few grains of Himalayan salt, though my cardiologist says cut out the salt and long COVID resulted in lemon/lime tasting yuck—not as

I remember lemons/limes should taste). In a study published by the Georgia Institute of Technology, the researchers found that dehydration can lead to a decline in cognitive function.[13] If you're not staying hydrated, it could lead to more errors during attention-related tasks.

I have also cut out all alcohol and sugar. These substances did nothing but make me feel lethargic and cloudy. Sure, people enjoy them socially, but those substances don't hold any of the nutritional value your body desperately needs to operate at its peak. Ditch the chemicals, trashy snacks, and microwavable TV dinners to see a drastic change in your vitality.

Instead of eating processed stuff, I focus on fuelling my physical body with real food. It helps to buy fresh fruits and vegetables in season and eat them daily. Even frozen fruit and spinach work for smoothies (sounds strange together but trust me on this one!). I also eat plenty of fish and white meat for protein or skip the meat entirely and opt for any of the numerous plant-based protein options. These foods are packed full of the macro and micronutrients your body needs to stay in tip-top shape.

My final health habit is daily exercise. This may sound daunting, but it's because most people needlessly overcomplicate exercise. The human body is meant to be in motion, and all that "exercise" means to me is moving my body. This can be a lunchtime stroll or evening walk. There's certainly nothing wrong with doing some press-ups and planks in the morning. I've recently taken up skipping rope. It's nurturing for my heart, and it makes my wife and kids laugh—especially if I'm still wearing my suit. Laughter is, of course, uplifting for your health too (as is hugging, though the pandemic put a temporary curb on that).

Reflect on your eating and exercise habits, are they helping or hindering your health?

E = Energy

*Recharging your batteries is giving life and love to
yourself and consequently to others.*

Rick Yvanovich

When it comes to managing yourself, many people immediately
jump to time management as a priority when they really should
be focused on prioritising managing their energy. The amount
of time and energy an activity takes should dictate where it falls
on your to-do list and schedule, depending on your natural
energy levels.

Your energy is like a personal battery pack. We all take a
different amount of time to charge, we drain steadily between
charges, and we need to manage our energy so we can keep going.
We also recharge differently. Unlike the battery in my phone that
can be replaced with a new one, humans don't have that option,
so let's be careful we don't kill our own battery!

To implement good energy management, start by understanding your natural energy levels. Notice at what time of
day you feel the most energised and at what time of day your
energy starts to dip. Make the time between these times your
normal operating hours, and then start time-blocking your
day ruthlessly. The activities and projects that require the
most energy should be done when your energy is at its peak.
The less energy-demanding tasks can be scheduled around
those peak times.

Doing things at the right time helps optimise the energy
required to do them and avoids wasting that energy. People can
block out time in a variety of ways. Sitting in a chair all day is
bound to have a negative effect on energy, so taking breaks to
stand up and stretch, hydrate, and get a bit of fresh air is of the
utmost importance to sustaining your daily energy.

One time-blocking strategy is the Pomodoro® Technique created by Francesco Cirillo in the late 1980s.[vii] The idea is to break up a 90-minute work block into three 25-minute chunks, each followed by a 5-minute break. One 25-minute work block plus one 5-minute break is called a Pomodoro. Your entire day is broken out into Pomodoros, and you string more or fewer Pomodoros together for the task you are working on. Instead of working all day with back-to-back Pomodoros without rest, when you complete four Pomodoros take a longer twenty- or thirty-minute break, then repeat.

Another time-blocking strategy is scheduling your time and only doing what is scheduled in that time block. This means starting and ending per the schedule and saying no to anything that's not scheduled. Simple to say but can be challenging to do. Time management is beyond the scope of this book (you'll have to wait for the next one).[viii]

R = Rest

Rest is not idle, not wasteful. Sometimes rest is the most productive thing you can do for your body and soul.

Erica Layne

Rest is how we recharge our batteries. It's also how we get new ideas, synthesise complicated information, and reflect on our choices and processes. As we constantly expend energy, we must constantly replenish it. And with long COVID, I prioritise my

---

[vii] The Pomodoro® Technique is a time management technique designed to help individuals and teams manage time effectively. "Pomodoro®" is a registered trademark by Francesco Cirillo.
[viii] Time Management resources can be found at RickYvanovich. com/BAUU/.

rest as I feel my batteries seem to take longer to charge, hold less charge, and deplete faster than pre-COVID. Rest needs to be scheduled into your day just like any other priority to make sure that you are taking it without guilt. Rest is an investment in your sustainability and longevity and one of the foundational bricks in the Tower of Life Force.

Different activities consume different types of energy, resulting in the need to recharge with different types of rest. I learnt from the TEDx talk by Saundra Daulton-Smith and from her book *Sacred Rest: Recover Your Life, Renew Your Energy, Restore Your Sanity*, that there are seven types of rest.[14,15] Each different type of rest recharges different batteries and this is likely why sometimes one might have had one type of rest and then still feel not rested.

1. **Physical rest**. Passive rest is sleeping (and napping). Active rest is restorative, such as massage, stretching, and yoga.
2. **Mental rest**. Brain fog alert! Take regular breaks (give the Pomodoro a go), grab a snack, hydrate, immerse yourself in nature, walk in the woods, or smell some flowers.
3. **Sensory rest**. Turn down or turn off those sensory stimuli. There are major cultural sensory overload problems, for example, there are no noise laws in some places (like Vietnam), and I find other people's noise noisy even though I'm partly deaf! Or am I partly deaf because it's so noisy? Make a point to turn off lights, screens, all notifications that involve pinging/buzzing/beeping/ringing. Giving your senses a break can help you recharge and feel rejuvenated.
4. **Creative rest**. Lack of innovation, writer's block (that's happened far too many times during the creation of this book), frustration, inability to finish a project, and more are all a sign you need creative rest. Do something

that needs no creativity: Take a walk, read a book, watch Netflix... No, don't surf social media!

5. **Emotional rest**. Take a "yes" vacation and start setting some boundaries! Try saying "no" more often. If that's too bold, say, "I'll think about it." Give yourself time out to pause and tend to your own emotional needs through silence, journaling, or simply *being* without expectations from others or emotional output.

6. **Social rest**. As a generalisation, social settings drain introverts and recharge extroverts. Make a two-column list. On one side, list the people around whom you feel energised, supported, and uplifted. On the other side, list the people who you find draining, demanding, or exhausting. Spend more time with the first group and reduce time spent with the latter.

7. **Spiritual rest**. If you've been focusing on personal goals (losing weight, getting that promotion, passing that exam), it's time to engage in an activity that gives you a feeling of belonging and love.

B = Balance

Perfect is the enemy of the good.

Voltaire

Balance is important because one person simply cannot do everything and thus choices need to be made. Some people strive for the *perfect* balance, but remember perfection gets in the way of achieving good or good enough. By balance I'm not talking about work-life balance. I mean keeping the elements of your Castle in balance.

I know at this stage of the book I have not covered the whole Castle. However, when building your Castle, we need to balance the Inner Keep (Chapters 1–4) and the Bailey (Chapters 6–7) and look to see which parts need attention (which are stronger, which are weaker and need further development) to help balance. Taking inventory is the first step to know *where* to start making improvements to balance. Focus on implementing the habits needed to strengthen and improve the Tower of Life Force first, to ensure you have the life force to build and maintain and balance the rest of your Castle.

Managing my balance was so important for me because I had to accept that I couldn't do everything and needed to be wise about my commitments. Saying yes to one thing typically means saying no to another.

S = Stress

Stress should be a powerful driving force, not an obstacle.

Bill Phillips

Stress is our body's reaction to a threat and anxiety is the body's reaction to that stress. Stress and anxiety impact our mindset and ability to see things in an infinite and growth-oriented way (see Infinite Mindset, Chapter 3). Whilst having some stress and anxiety can be a sign you really care about what you're doing, we may tend to hold onto unhealthy levels of these draining emotions. Even when these emotions threaten to overrun us, stress and anxiety are states that we can control with a strong mindset. Whoa! I can hear you saying, "I want one, how do I get it?" I feel your curiosity and enthusiasm, and we'll be diving into that in the Tower of Mind (Chapter 3).

Without a strong mindset, the impact of stress and anxiety will begin to weigh mentally and emotionally. These emotions undoubtedly trickle over into work. For most adults, stress and anxiety are unavoidable at times. What is important isn't that you feel these emotions, it's whether you have the skills, tools, and support needed to process these emotional states without a profound negative impact on your life. During human evolution, we've been wired to protect ourselves from threats and now the tendency is to react to negative stimuli more intensely than positive, thus we overestimate threats, underestimate opportunities and resources. This is known as the negativity bias.[16]

Your mindset affects your level of satisfaction at work because our emotional state will always colour how we perceive reality.

People ask questions like, "Is the glass half full or half empty?" If people know you're talking about a glass, then they're making a conscious choice. I tend to make an unconscious choice. I always see the glass as half full. Always, always, always.

If I had to make a choice and think about it deeper, I'd say that trying to classify the glass as half full or half empty isn't even helpful. Why are you restricted to only a glass half full of water when the other half is full of air? Why do we only see the glass as being 100 percent? Air is everywhere, as it is infinite. Sometimes, being so focused on the glass means we miss the bigger picture and lose sight that an entire universe of possibility exists outside that glass!

We always have an option to view our glass differently. This happens when people may not like the options they have. One option, we might say, doesn't seem like much of an option, yet it is still an option. We always have a choice, even when choosing between bad options.

Why? Because the ability to choose is critical to being motivated or being satisfied. If you choose, you have a sense of autonomy, agency, and control. Not liking your choices isn't the point. The point is that nothing is ever being forced upon you. You are choosing one direction over another time and time again. Open yourself to all the choices and a wider lens of the world to allow yourself room to expand.

*The greatest weapon against stress is our ability to
choose one thought over another.*

William James

When I get stressed, I need to let off steam. My initial stress
response (and bad habit) is to internalise my stress and anxiety. I
bury it deep inside me, and I need to provide it with an outlet, or
else it'll unexpectedly explode, usually at the most inconvenient
time, which causes more stress. One outlet is running. It took
me years to enjoy running, at least five years, and at times I feel
I can't live without it. Truth be told, I don't run fast (I'm slow)
but it helps me clear my mind and refocus. I call it my Running
University Meditation.

I also don't listen to music on my runs, but I do listen to
Audible audiobooks. I run the same route repeatedly. It's
mindless; sometimes I run farther than planned when I lose
myself in books. I find myself adding extra laps. If it's a good
book or a good chapter, I'll get into a state of flow, run 5k, 10k,
and keep going.

For me, running quiets my mind. My mind is so full of
thoughts and ideas all the time, it's hard to shut it up. I need
to concentrate on something and lose myself in it. When I'm
running, my mind quiets, empties itself, and wanders. I can get
new, clearer, and more innovative thoughts whilst consuming
knowledge from my Audible book and getting healthier
with exercise. It's a boost to my DOSE (dopamine, oxytocin,
serotonin endorphins), the happy neurochemicals.

- **Dopamine** is released when you reach your goals. It's
  that feel-good satisfaction of achieving something.
  That's why it's also called the feel good or victory
  chemical.
- **Oxytocin** is released when we feel compassion and care
  between people we love and/or are important in our

lives. It's that warm and fuzzy feeling. It's also called the love chemical.

- **Serotonin** is released when you feel a sense of pride, appreciation and/or significance from others. So, when others acknowledge your achievements and sing your praises, you'll get a feel-good feeling as a result. It's also known as the leadership chemical as it motivates leaders to excel more to receive more feel-good praise. Additionally, followers also do well as they don't want to let their leader down, so it's an upward spiral for all.
- **Endorphins** are released as a response to pain. After a physical workout you can feel that runners high. That's where the saying "no pain, no gain" came from (Jane Fonda's exercise videos from 1982), or even from a deep belly laugh (you laugh so hard it hurts).

During the pandemic, I wasn't able to run like I used to. We've had intermittent lockdowns, some with a strict curfew, such as each household was allowed to have one person go out three times a week (twice to go shopping and once to the pharmacy). This means running for pleasure was not an option. Instead, I'm pacing the terrace and clocking up to one kilometer of movement during my lunchtime walk whilst listening to Audible and eating my sandwich. It's not the same as running, it's BAUU, and it's all about making things work for you.

This book has taken longer than planned, and whilst I was in the UK editing it, I caught COVID, and as of writing this, I haven't run for months. Even walking tires me, so my running university meditation may no longer work, and I've morphed back into reading without the running.

I've learnt that irrelevant of whatever acts as your go-to de-stressor today, it would be better if you are aware of what else helps to de-stress you. In BAUU, we need to be able to change, as things will change.

Anxiety and Your Nervous System

It's normal that people experience anxiety. It's our
body and brain's way of keeping us alert and it can
actually improve performance.

❧

Hayley Vaughan-Smith

I often marvel at the power of the human brain. Our brain is
our best asset in achieving satisfaction, which also means it can
be our greatest threat to the same state. A state of anxiety can
threaten to dampen a moment of happiness that we could have
achieved. Knowing how important the human brain is to our
ability to achieve a happy life, we must understand a little more
about the brain's inner workings, and specifically our nervous
system, which is how our body sends signals and coordinates
actions.

There are two sides to the autonomic nervous system—the
parasympathetic and the sympathetic. The *parasympathetic* side
tends to the "business as usual" functions of the body and makes
sure they happen. This includes things like regulating the glands
that produce tears and saliva. The *sympathetic* side speeds up the
heart, dilates the pupils, and inhibits digestion in response to a
threat.[17]

The amygdala is part of the limbic system and is the
emotional and behavioural part of the brain. It's also known as
the lizard or reptilian brain. The amygdala is constantly scanning
our environment for threats to our emotional and physical well-
being. If a threat is detected, the sympathetic nervous system
is activated, putting our body into a state of fight (prepare to
defend against the threat), flight (run away), freeze (get stuck
or dissociate), or fawn (people-pleasing and pacifying).[18, 19] This
state slows down our other bodily responses and creates the
build-up of stress hormones.

When our sympathetic nervous system is activated, we can become trapped by our body's instant automatic response (fight, flight, freeze, fawn), which can result in stress and anxiety, and thus can trigger a feeling that we're stuck. We can't clearly see our options or a path to safety because we are caught up in one thing: survival, and our bodies are in overdrive dealing with it. This overactive reaction can lead to chronic stress. If the sympathetic nervous system is like the gas pedal in a car, pumping fuel/energy throughout the body, then to slow down we need to apply the brakes of the parasympathetic nervous system, which gets the body to relax and be chill and calms the body down. This is the fastest way to regain clarity and control when you feel your nervous system activate. There are a few ways to apply the brakes:

- **Relaxation**. Breathing techniques (see the Power of Breath below), yoga, decluttering (see Declutter below), and images of relaxing scenes all have a relaxing effect. The impact differs from person to person so be sure to try them all and find out what works better for you.
- **Physical activity**. Exercise has a calming effect as it encourages deep breathing and can relieve muscle tension through movement.
- **Change your attitude towards stress**. If stress is seen as undesirable and thus a threat, then changing our attitude towards it as non-threatening and desirable hacks our brain and perceives it as our friend.[20]

The Power of Breath

Breathing is the greatest pleasure in life.

Giovanni Papini

I consider running to be a kind of meditation. Books or videos about meditation always start with a conversation about breathing. I misunderstood the link between meditation and breath until I started reading about proper breathing. Once I learned more about it, I realised I was breathing incorrectly during my runs and in general.

Instead of correctly breathing deep into my belly (diaphragmatic breathing), fully filling my lungs with each breath, I would breathe vertically, shallow, and ragged. Running, I would start panting, unable to breathe through my nose because my mouth was open.

To practice diaphragmatic breathing, place one hand on your chest and the other on your belly. Breath in through your nose and push your belly out, breath out slowly and steadily through your mouth keeping your lips pursed. The hand on your upper chest should hardly be moving at all.

Reading *Breath: A New Science of a Lost Art* by journalist James Nestor helped open my eyes to a different breathing technique.[21] Nestor teaches us that you shouldn't open your mouth whilst breathing. Breathing through your nose is better because the nose is a complex organ, and nose-breathing requires conscious awareness. You concentrate more on your breath when it comes in and out through your nose.

Further, your nose has a massive filtration system, as compared to your mouth, which offers zero filtration. Thanks to Nestor's book, I changed the way I breathe, which changed the way I run. I no longer open my mouth, and I can adjust my pace as needed. If I feel I need a bit more air, I'll slow down. Generally, I breathe easier now, and the act of breathing has become more relaxed.

In a study conducted in 2017, researchers asked people who suffered from generalized anxiety disorder to try either alternate nostril breathing (also a yogic breath control known in Sanskrit as *nadi shodhana pranayama*) or mindful breath awareness for ten minutes, two days in a row. They found that practising alternate nostril breathing was about three times more effective at reducing people's feelings of anxiety than simply being aware of your breath with no specific breathing pattern attached.[22]

To breathe properly is to live properly.

Robin Sharma

Here's a quick exercise to raise awareness of physical stress and how its linked to breathing. Try it by following the four steps before reading and further.

1. Clench your fist as tight as you can and start counting to at least 10. Notice your breath—are you holding it?
2. Now unclench your fist and take a deep breath.
3. Make another fist and start counting to at least 10. Take slow relaxed breaths.
4. Notice how your fist starts to relax as you exhale.

This exercise was a demonstration of the Relaxation Response (from Dr. Herbert Benson), "a physical state of deep relaxation in which your body releases chemicals that slow down your breathing and heart rate...and the opposite to the fight-or-flight response."[23,24] Dr. Benson also shares that deep belly breathing (diaphragmatic breathing) helps the mind and body relax.

Whilst I'm not saying that breathing will help treat an anxiety disorder, practising deep belly and alternate nostril breathing are tools that help curb feelings of stress and anxiety and promote relation. Try them and discover which one you prefer.

Five Finger Breathing

Any time you are feeling stressed, you can do a little exercise called Five Finger Breathing.[25] Here's how it works:

1. Place your index finger on the outside of your pinkie finger of your other hand. As you breathe in, run your

finger up to the tip of your pinkie finger. Breathe out and trace down the inside of the pinkie finger.

2. Inhale again and trace up your ring finger. As you exhale, trace down the other side of your ring finger.
3. Move to the middle finger. Inhale, tracing up one side. Exhale, tracing trace down the other side.
4. Continue tracing each finger until you have traced your entire hand.
5. Reverse the process.

As stress and worry threaten to overtake our mind and push our peace further away, use this breathing technique. Five-finger breathing helps you cut through the stress to find the calmer, more at peace you.

Stress and Gaming

When we play games, our brains respond differently to stress and obstacles. We're better able to control our attention and ignore distractions.

Jane McGonigal

Whilst unchecked stress can have you ready to blow a gasket in response to the wrong look, there is such a thing as a healthy level of stress. To a certain extent, stress comes from investing in a specific outcome. Any time you desire a particular outcome in a situation, there will naturally be accompanying stress. This is the type of stress that makes you wake up early and prepare for your big presentation. It's the kind of stress that makes you iron your tie the night before and double-check that you packed your laptop charger. These types of stress levels help us be our best. But if we're ready to have a meltdown because someone didn't clean out the coffee pot the right way, we need a stress intervention.

The type of stress we experience, whether positive or negative, is largely determined by our own perceptions. When we anticipate a threatening situation, our body releases stress hormones that help prepare us to face our fear in the presence of a threat or challenge. Our brains can't differentiate between the possibility of a lion attack and an approaching deadline. It merely detects a threat.

On the other hand, if we believe we have control over the outcome of a situation or threatening stimuli, our body doesn't need to prepare us for the threat in the same way. We can anticipate the challenge, but our bodies aren't experiencing stress in the same way, and we are better able to control our emotional reactions and stay more open to innovative solutions for our problems.

Instead of seeing challenges as something to overcome, engaging with something like a game forces us to change our perception. When we approach a challenge like a game, we tackle tough problems more creatively, with more determination and optimism, and we are more likely to reach out for help.

Also, when it comes to games, we often try and fail repeatedly. When you try at something and fail, you internalise that failure, you learn, and you are less likely to engage in that behaviour or action again. You try new approaches. This means we can start getting better a lot faster. This is much like when your character is killed in a video game. You can always come back and try again.

Some people believe that video games are not good for us. I believe that they can be good for us and yes there is science to back up this claim and some people are investing into it. *SuperBetter* is a book by Jane McGonigal, a game designer who designed a game to build resilience to aid her recovery after a severe concussion, including a decade's worth of scientific research, resulting in a proven game plan (for a better life) and a game (called SuperBetter).[26]

I have not failed. I've just found
ten thousand ways that won't work.

Thomas Edison

The willingness to fail often means we can find all the solutions that don't work more quickly, increasing our chances of finding something that does work even sooner and thus success.

Declutter

The best way to find out what we really
need is to get rid of what we don't.

Marie Kondo

The *Cambridge Dictionary* definition of declutter is "to remove things you do not need from a place, in order to make it more pleasant and more useful."[27]

One perspective of "things" are the physical things. Having too many physical things can cause stress. I wear neckties; I like them. Some were gifts, some hold special memories, some are from iconic brands, but do I really need a hundred (I kid you not) of them? Choosing which one to wear can be stressful. What about you, are you cluttering up your cupboards and getting stressed about what to wear? Netflix brought Marie Kondo and her Kon Mari method into many homes, raising awareness of what it means to get rid of the physical things that aren't serving us and those that don't bring us joy.[28, 29]

Another perspective of "things" are the non-physical things—information overload, too many choices, too many decisions to make. Decision fatigue is the result of having to make too many decisions and the more decisions we make the lower the quality of our decisions.[30] In the "Paradox of Choice," psychologist Barry Schwartz explains that the success of your next innovation will depend on whether you are marketing to "Satisficers" or "Maximisers."[31] When shopping, people need to make decisions. Satisficers take the first product that meets their requirements and maximisers take the best product and best deal available. He points to the famous Jam Experiment, where shoppers were presented with twenty-four jams on one day and only six on another. The result was ten times more jam sold when there was a smaller choice. Less choice, more sales, less stress; more choice, more stress and poorer decisions. Similarly, Steve Jobs, Mark Zuckerberg, and Jeff Bezos all wear pretty much the same clothes each day so they don't have to spend any thought on what to wear and reduce decision fatigue.

You will not find WiFi in the forest, but
you will find a better connection.

Anthon St. Maarten

With all this talk of clutter and decisions, it's time to take a walk outside in nature and breathe some fresh air. Step away from the commercial nature and hustle and bustle of life to be present with Mother Nature. Realise that the past is gone and will never return, so let it go. All you have is this moment in nature and only this moment. Ask yourself what is most important to you right now? This is the Japanese concept of shinrin-yoku (forest bathing or taking in the forest atmosphere), which encourages practitioners to leave the constraints of the hustle of the now and simply be one with the world of nature.[32] Get out of doors and into a forest or field and in nature, be quiet and listen, be in and with nature, and just be yourself.

Though I live in a bustling city, after the pandemic lockdowns I couldn't wait to get out into nature and breathe. With the lockdowns hopefully over, let's make a regular date with nature.

CHAPTER 2
KEY TAKEAWAYS

- Remember that the meaning of life must be rooted in feeling well, thinking well, and doing well. Focus on doing more of those things, and the rest of life will take care of itself.
- The purpose of the Tower of Life Force is to manage and take care of our life force energy as we don't have an endless supply of it.
- HERBS = Health, Energy, Rest, Balance, and Stress.
- Certain levels of stress can be healthy, and it's important to manage our stress so that we aren't put in a state of fight, flight, freeze, or fawn.
- Your energy is like a personal battery pack. It needs recharging. We each drain differently and recharge differently. Rest is how we recharge our batteries.
- There are seven types of rest, each one recharges different batteries: Physical, Mental, Sensory, Creative, Emotional, Social, and Spiritual.
- Relaxation, physical exercise, and changing our attitude to stress are ways to reduce stress.
- Utilising breathwork (deep belly, single nostril, five-finger) can help regulate our emotions and control our nervous system.
- SuperBetter is a video game/tool to build resilience.
- Decluttering reduces stress.
- Shinrin-yoku (forest bathing) is a natural destressor.
- Approaching life's problems with a gaming mindset helps our minds create innovative solutions and makes us more open to receiving feedback and help.
- Download Chapter 2 resources from RickYvanovich. com/BAUU/.

CHAPTER 2
REFLECTION PROMPTS

What's your **one** key takeaway from this chapter?

```
_____
_____
_____
```

And what else?

```
_____
_____
_____
```

What action will you take right away because of something you read in this chapter?

```
_____
_____
_____
```

And what else?

```
_____
_____
_____
```

CHAPTER 3
THE TOWER OF MIND

TOWER OF MIND

The empires of the future will be empires of the mind.

Winston Churchill

The Tower of the Mind, whilst not necessarily the tallest tower, must be one of the most robust, resilient, and agile. I picture this tower as a sturdy, squat structure that helps hold this group of Towers in the Inner Keep together. Without a strong Tower of the Mind, it's incredibly hard to persevere through challenges, see opportunities in what appear to be dead ends, and continuously pursue growth.

Leaders who are looking to create a legacy will experience plenty of failure and rejection. The key to success is being able to push forward despite these obstacles. Building a resilient mindset comes when you align yourself with kaizen and build the mental habits needed for lasting success.

Kaizen

Nothing is perfect, we can always make it better.

Rick Yvanovich

LIFELONG LEARNING

LEARN SOMETHING EVERY DAY

改 + 善
KAI + ZEN
CHANGE FOR GOOD

DAILY GROWTH

CONTINUOUS IMPROVEMENT

Figure 5. Kaizen

Kaizen is a Japanese word that means continuous improvement. It comes from two Japanese words: *kai* (change) and *zen* (good). I have come to embrace kaizen as a core value. I interpret the original term as meaning that nothing is perfect, thus, we embrace and commit to never-ending, lifelong improvement of ourselves and all we do. A 1 percent improvement compounded every day becomes a 3,778 percent improvement over a year. Daily, small-scale improvements over a long time make a significant difference. Conversely, a 1 percent worsening each day compounded for a year would result in a 97 percent loss. So, aim to be just 1 percent better each day.

Every day, part of our job is to work on ourselves. We don't always have to aim to do our best, but we can aim to do the best that can be done under the circumstances, and then seek to make it even better.

Kaizen comprises three key components: lifelong improvement, reflection, and an infinite mindset. I describe each of these below.

Lifelong Improvement

Learn, grow and make things better today than they were yesterday.

Rick Yvanovich

The greatest athletes in the world, even the world-record holders, have coaches who help them improve. People at the top of their field or industry always have more to learn, maybe from their peers in the same industry or from a mentor in an entirely different industry. Before we can improve, we must first be willing to admit that we don't know it all, that we all have more to learn, and areas in which we need to improve.

We often hear *learning* and *growth* being used together and, sometimes, they're even used interchangeably. But when we consider the definitions of these words, they are quite different. Whilst learning is the act of acquiring knowledge or a skill, growth is the germination of that knowledge and the increased capacity that occurs as a result. Lifelong improvement requires both learning *and* growth.

Reflection

Without reflection, we go blindly on our way, creating more unintended consequences, and failing to achieve anything useful.

Margaret J. Wheatley

As humans, we ruminate as a way of reliving the past in our minds again and again. We hyper focus on negative things, situations, or people from the past to avoid encountering them again, and this habit tends to become intrusive. Letting the past control and consume our present thoughts and emotions causes us to lose sight of the value and opportunity in the present moment.

Reflection is vastly different from living in the past. The biggest difference between reflecting and ruminating is that reflection is brief, purposeful, and devoid of emotional attachments. When done in an active and deliberate way, reflection is a proactive part of learning.

Regularly reflecting on our improvement, learning, and growth helps us see how far we have come (or not) in relation to our major life goals. When we reflect, we feel empowered to adjust our actions and habits according to the progress we have made towards our goals.

I used to assume everyone knew how to reflect, but then I wondered whether I knew how to do it "properly" as I can't ever remember anyone teaching me any method apart from being told to reflect on stuff and thus, I realised people in general probably don't know how to do it. Those who do reflect don't all do it the same way, either. It seemed to me that without a common way of doing it, the results could only be random.

Unsurprisingly, pondering this dilemma piqued my interest and drove me to come up with a solution and, voilà, I developed my own reflection model which I call the Reflection 4 Reaction Reward and Repeat Model:

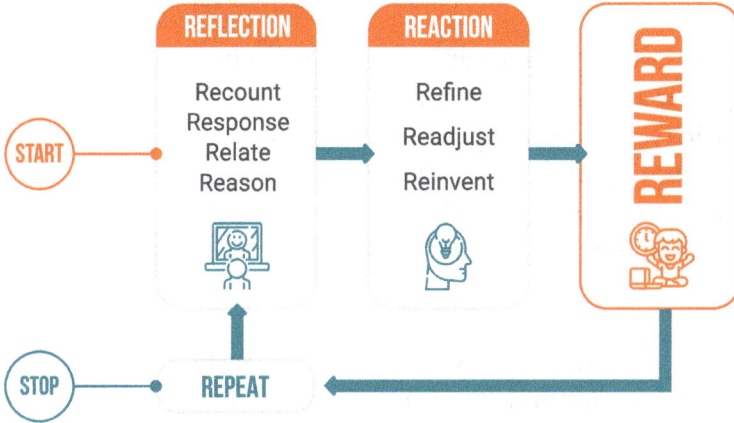

Figure 6. Reflection 4 Reaction Reward and Repeat Model[ix]

To be helpful, reflection needs to be deliberate. Thus, the Reflection 4 Reaction Reward and Repeat Model comprises the following four steps, which are described below:

1. Reflection
2. Reaction
3. Reward
4. Repeat

Typically, the Reflection is recorded. Some people love to journal this daily or weekly or periodically. In a work context, this can be more formalised with a report.

[ix] Reflection 4 Reaction Reward & Repeat resources can be downloaded from RickYvanovich.com/BAUU/.

Step #1: Reflection

Every time your mind shifts, your world shifts.

Byron Katie

This is where you actively look back on the past week, month, or quarter and describe what's happened. Ask yourself where you are in relation to your goals and the balance of your Towers. Are you moving in the right direction or veering off course? Using a framework when you visit the past will help you avoid getting hung up or stuck on it. Follow the sequence of prompts below, to help guide your reflection:

1. **Recount.** – Describe what's happened in the past week/month/quarter. What is the status, and what are the key aspects of whatever's happened?
2. **Response.** – Explore your emotional response(s) to these issue(s). How do you feel about the Recounting? Be honest about what emotions may be coming up and ask yourself what might have caused you to feel this way.
3. **Relate.** – What was good or bad about the Recount and Response? What connections do you sense between these things or issues you've recounted and your KASH, your existing Knowledge, Attitudes, Skills, and Habits? (More detail on KASH in Chapter 7.)
4. **Reason.** – Analyse the underlying facts. Go deep and try to make sense of it all. What have you learnt? What conclusions can you deduce?

Step #2: React to the Reflection

Everything in your life is a reflection of a choice you have made. If you want a different result, make a different choice.

Anonymous

Your reaction can be fine-tuning details (refining), making a bigger change (readjusting), or making a very significant change (reinventing). Don't be afraid to change the things that aren't working. Be creative, apply design thinking (creative problem-solving), and come up with multiple options from which to choose. Reach out to peers or professionals for accountability and support and put a plan in place that will support you in moving forward.

Step #3: Reward Yourself

Remember: Rewards come in action, not in discussion.

Tony Robbins

Yup, even after completing only two steps of the process, it's time for a reward. Make yourself a hot cocoa, blast your favourite song, write yourself an encouraging note, or do something else that will give you a little pleasure. Humans, by nature, are less inclined to do things unless we will be rewarded for them. Reward yourself for progress, no matter how small, and do it often.

Step #4: Repeat the Process

Success is the sum of small efforts, repeated day in and day out.

Robert Collier

Reflection isn't a onetime activity. This method works best when it's done habitually. Reflect periodically. Weekly is good, and daily (journaling) is even better. Sometimes there is no need for further reflection on a matter (for example, when a project is over), so you can stop.

These steps are captured in the following model:

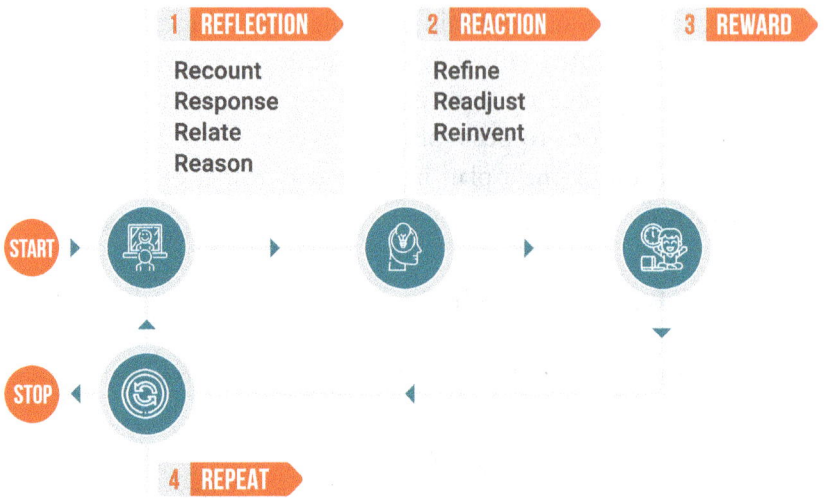

Figure 7. Reflection 4 Reaction Reward and Repeat Flowchart

Infinite Mindset

To infinity and beyond!

Buzz Lightyear (Toy Story)

As the pandemic disrupted lives, it also exposed gaping holes in many mindsets. We could clearly see the negative patterns of our minds and how they manifested every day. We noticed how easily and quickly we can fall into a rut and lose our sense of direction. With all the changes we're dealing with currently, including the emotional ups and downs each new day brings, we need to assess how are we coping—that is, if we're coping at all.

Instead of seeing disruption as a roadblock, view it as a call forward, a chance to innovate and grow into a new role, market, or industry. This belief that we can adapt and continue to thrive directly results from the growth mindset within. Instead of putting ourselves or our business into a limiting box and insisting that *we can't*, the pandemic has challenged us to ask ourselves *how can we?* This is a small but distinctive shift we're seeing in successful people and businesses across the board, and why I'm sure you're reading this book now.

Many long-lasting companies like Apple, Nike, Google, Coca-Cola, and Amazon have begun to shift their language and expectations. These companies all started at the same place, as businesses looking to serve a niche. Through their growth mindset and forward-thinking attitude, they have been able to innovate beyond their original scope to become global powerhouses in their industries.

Promoting a growth mindset in yourself and others may seem like it is out of your control, but I assure you it's not. Just like these other million-dollar corporations, a growth mindset is something that each person can instil in themselves, and then let it ripple out to others.

Fixed Mindset vs. Growth Mindset

> *Once your mindset changes, everything on the*
> *outside will change along with it.*
>
> *Steve Maraboli*

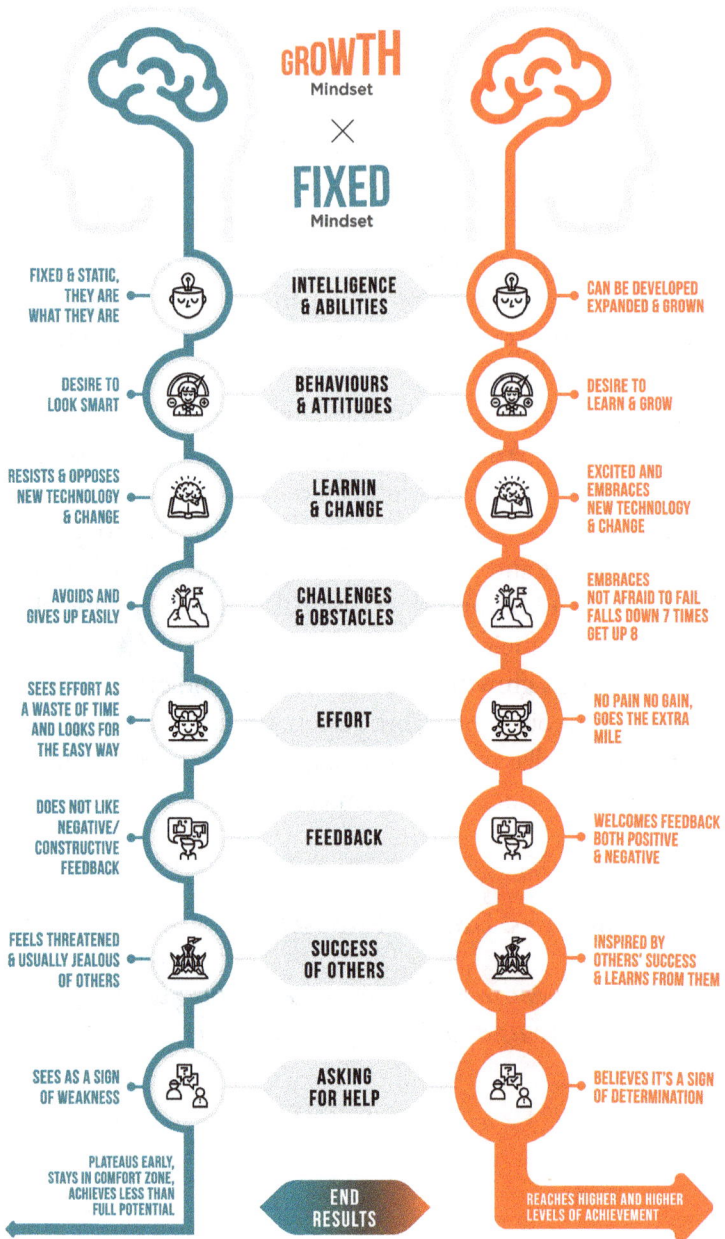

Figure 8. Fixed vs. Growth Mindset

The idea of having a fixed mindset or a growth mindset stems from a belief (or lack thereof) in our ability to learn and grow. Many people have a growth mindset in one area of life and a fixed mindset in another. No matter what mindset you currently have, a growth mindset is always available. All we must do is become aware of our fixed mindset and look beyond it to see the limitless possibilities that are available for growth. Let's take a moment to understand these two very different mindsets as depicted in *Figure 8* above.

A **fixed mindset** is the belief that we cannot change or improve something, no matter how hard we try. It's the idea that I was born with a set capacity for knitting or cooking when, in fact, I can improve these skills simply by putting time and effort into learning them. People having a fixed mindset believe their intelligence, skills, and abilities are fixed at birth. Their capacity for playing chess or skateboarding is fixed, and they are what they are. This mindset doesn't allow room for growth and ultimately holds us back from achieving our fullest potential both in business and in life. People with a fixed mindset focus on the challenges associated with a problem and don't believe they can improve through hard work and focused energy. A fixed mindset glues us to the spot, leaving us stuck.

Business As UnUsual requires us to be more agile to get through times of immense challenge and change. An open-minded attitude reflects a growth mindset, as it sees opportunity in challenges. In this current business model, we need the ability and awareness to break ourselves down and rebuild ourselves (and our businesses) from the ground up, if necessary. Without the right mindset to support transformation, we will not get very far. Having a growth mindset allows people to look past failures and challenges to see room for improvement and innovation.

A **growth mindset** believes you can go beyond the limitations to build your intelligence, skills, and abilities, even when success seems unlikely. People with a growth mindset don't see the success of others as a threat to their own abilities; instead, they use opportunity as a calling for personal development.

Whilst a fixed mindset is finite, meaning it has a limit and a maximum capacity, a growth mindset means you can change things. A growth mindset shows how limitless and infinite the human mind truly is and demonstrates the power it is capable of harnessing.

Neuroscience has proven that we can make ourselves smarter. The brain is elastic and can endlessly grow, change, and adapt based on new information, experiences, and skills. The more we practice using a growth mindset, the more effective we become at applying it in all areas of life. To truly take the next step as leaders, we must embrace the flexibility of the human brain. Go out into the world to try and fail, learn, and grow. You will become even more resilient.

Infinite (Growth) Mindset

An infinite mindset embraces abundance whereas a
finite mindset operates with a scarcity mentality. In the
Infinite Game we accept that "being the best" is a fool's errand
and that multiple players can do well at the same time.

Simon Sinek

An infinite mindset is having a growth mindset and then some. Simon Sinek popularised this thinking in his book, *The Infinite Game*.[33] When you have an infinite mindset, you don't play win or lose games. Those having an infinite mindset aim for an infinite future and a lasting legacy for the betterment of all.

Kaizen is inherently infinite because it embraces continuous small improvements. Improving means we grow, and growing means acquiring new knowledge and better skills. Kaizen isn't a destination to be reached; it is an attitude and a mindset that needs to be adopted.

In kaizen, there is no reward for arriving at the destination. These teachings are simply support beams to help prop you up and push you forward on your lifelong journey. Arguably, it is a journey that ends at death unless you've created a legacy that will enable your mission, vision, values, and impact to live on.

Using Sinek's framework, we can reframe the idea of a fixed mindset as a finite mindset. Likewise, a growth mindset is an infinite mindset. In *The Infinite Game*, Sinek wrote that "[b]usiness is an infinite game in which players develop their strategies without a fixed set of rules."[34] New players can join at any time; there is no beginning and no end.

A lot of games are finite. Football, for example, is a finite game. The game has rules and limits within which the players operate. You're allowed to play only for a certain amount of time. The point is to score more goals than the other team. It's finite. One team wins, the other loses, or you could have a draw. Chess is another finite game. Someone wins, someone loses. We know who the players are. There are fixed rules, and there is a clear end. The finite mindset of sports is evident. A beginning and an end. Winners and losers. You don't play Premier League Football to lose. You play to be victorious.

The infinite mindset is different. It's not about winning or losing any single game; it's more about focusing on the future and building sustainability. To keep going, keep going strong, and keep going healthy. When applied to businesses, the infinite mindset means we're not trying to beat the competition or achieve an end result. Instead, we're trying to build a healthy and robust infinitely self-sustaining organisation.

The most essential principles in Sinek's infinite mindset include purpose, trust, and courage. Businesses exist for a cause known as a *purpose*. Just as you need a defining purpose for your life, your business needs one as well. It's different from the usual strategy pyramid that asks the questions: "What's your mission? What's your vision? What are your values?" Those questions don't bring innovative answers.

The strategy pyramid is a planning tool typically used to help tell the story of the relationship of the steps from goal to action, from top to bottom. I've created and used an overly detailed one shown in Figure 9 below, and it reflects purpose (goal) at the pinnacle, which is why the pyramid is sometimes called the purpose pyramid. As you go down the levels, you may recognise some familiar concepts (I give some brief explanations below the figure). As you can see, purpose is the driving force that propels your business (by helping society or the environment) and allows you to connect with your ideal clients on a deeper level.

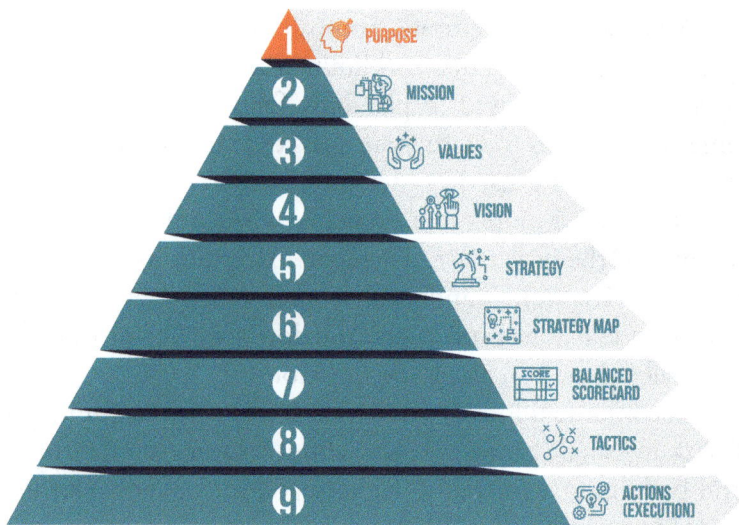

Figure 9. Strategy Pyramid

I'll quickly whiz through the nine levels, and if you already know them, you can skip this.

1. **Purpose**. Why do we do what we do?
2. **Mission**. What do we do?
3. **Values**. What's important to us?
4. **Vision**. Where do we want to be in the future?

5. **Strategy**. The game plan. How are we going to get from where we are to where we want and/or need to be?
6. **Strategy Map**. A visualisation of the company's primary strategic goals.
7. **Balanced Scorecard**. A performance measurement tool to track the Execution of the strategy through the use of multiple measurements (metrics/KPIs) focused on strategic objectives.
8. **Tactics**. What we need to do to achieve the strategy. There can be multiple tactics to achieve each strategic goal.
9. **Actions (Execution)**. The actions we need to take to achieve each of the tactics.

We need to build trust in teams. The word *trust* keeps coming up because it's super important. Trust needs to exist between people if they're going to work well together, and it is critical in teams. Without trust, you can't have a high-performing team, as without trust you have lower levels of productivity, retention, engagement, innovation, communications, transparency, agility, accountability, responsibility... I could go on and on, but I think you get the gist.

We need to have worthy rivals, not to beat, but to make us better. Having someone alongside us pushes us to innovate continually and encourages us to improve our performance, product, and service. We don't know what we don't know, but our rivals may know what we don't know. And we may know what they don't know. If we are competing, it makes us even better.

Let's return to our sports analogy. If you want to improve your personal best and the other athletes around you are better, they will spur you on because you will have something to aim for. Your rivals in business need to be businesses like your own that have the sort of success you would like to have. We don't want rivals who are out there to kill or beat us. We want contenders who make us better, just as we can help them be better too. All of us are constantly raising the bar.

We want every team to perform well and lift the others up. For the sake of sustainability, we need to figure out how to adjust quickly and effectively to changes such as the pandemic. We need the ability to pivot our business at a moment's notice, so we can continue to push forward. Regardless of what changes await you in the business world, you need to be prepared to cope with them; else, your business is not sustainable.

Finally, we must have *courage*. As a leader, you need courage to lead the rest of the team in this infinite mindset. It's not about crushing goals or driving towards results. That old mindset won't work. You need to look beyond this quarter to the next quarter, and the one after that, and the one after that, and the one after that. Your thoughts need to be on long-term sustainability.

Sinek's work is about thinking our way into the future we want and then taking the steps necessary to create it. It's the edge you need to build an infinitely sustainable business. It's a helpful approach to the challenges we now face. Let's think infinitely, let's be perpetual, and let's help others do the same.

Let It Go

"Let it go."

Marshall Goldsmith

Marshall Goldsmith is a world-renowned business educator and coach who helps CEOs and their management teams address change in the workplace.[x] Goldsmith notes that we often say,

---

[x] Dr. Marshall Goldsmith has been recognized as one of the Top Ten Business Thinkers in the World and the top-rated executive coach at the Thinkers50 ceremony in London since 2011. He helps successful people achieve positive, lasting change and behaviour; for themselves, their people, and their teams.

"I'll be happy when..." instead of finding things to be happy for right now.

We commonly hear people say, "I'll be happy when I get that job/promotion/car," but this is not how we are meant to think. Goldsmith calls this type of future thinking "the Great Western disease." The "I'll be happy when" symptoms are tying your goals to material things and expecting them to make you happy when, really, deep down inside, you are unhappy.

The Great Western Disease is that we fixate on the future at the expense of enjoying the life we're living now.

Marshall Goldsmith

You could argue that this feeling of "I'll be happy when..." is like Sinek's finite thinking, where we will be happy when we win the match, or when we reach the sales goal, or when we lose weight or get a promotion. Instead of enjoying the process of learning and growing, we become wrapped up in the specific outcome we're working towards and basing our emotional state on whether we achieve it. This can lead to disappointment, frustration, or (worst of all) giving up!

Marshall's discovery is based on his thirty-five-plus years' experience as a Buddhist practitioner. He writes that if we can't accept a situation for what it is, and we refuse to forgive the people causing it, ultimately, we will hurt ourselves. Being stuck and accepting defeat is a tell-tale sign of a finite mindset: getting stuck and staying stuck. This way of thinking limits our opportunity to find meaning or happiness because it depends on a future that may not materialise.

Marshall instructs us to *let it go*. Once we can accept that we failed, have understood the challenge, and accepted our role in the situation, we must let it go. We should look to these moments to learn and better ourselves, but we cannot hold on to them. Once you let things go and accept the reality of your situation, it is liberating. You will clearly see other options that will allow you to move forward.

Nobody is perfect. Whilst we are learning, trying, failing, and living, life gets messy. It's complex and layered. Not everything goes our way all the time, and when our plans fail or more problems pop up, rather than beat ourselves up for things that have already occurred and/or are not under our control we should *let it go.* We can choose to change our view of the world and of ourselves. Marshall writes that this is critical for self-evolution.

Marshall himself exemplifies this idea. People often ask him, "Why are you not on the list of top ten coaches when you're so well-known and so successful?" There are top ten lists and top twenty lists, and he's not included. They removed him from the list because he was always number one! He's already on the pedestal, and when you ask him how he's been so successful, he attributes all of it to the ability to *let it go.*

Goldsmith isn't playing the game and trying to win. He's playing the game, and he's enjoying learning the rules as he plays. He's coaching and driving success and helping individuals get a bit better than they were the day before. If the coachee doesn't care to change, then Marshall doesn't care to change them either, and he won't take them on as a client.

The belief that you can help others and make a difference is vital to success. You don't have to win everything; you need to pick and choose well. That means you can help those who want to change. If someone doesn't want to change, don't waste your time. Be big enough to let it go and move on to the next thing.

My Mindset and Results

Whatever your mind can conceive and believe, it can achieve.

Napoleon Hill

"Whatever your mind can conceive and believe, it can achieve." Those words were written by Napoleon Hill, the American self-help author, in his 1937 book, *Think and Grow Rich*.[35] It's a powerful statement that rings true for those who have experienced the power of the human mind. Perception is equally powerful. Many studies over the years have indicated that we have barely scratched the surface in understanding the capability of the human mind.

Given enough time and mental practice (visualising and rehearsing a task in your head), we can think our way out of most situations. We've fought and innovated our way out of this pandemic situation, that's for sure. We have harnessed the power of brilliant minds across the entire planet to help. Without that collaboration, we wouldn't have the vaccines that are available today. Early in the pandemic, no one would have believed a working vaccine could be ready so quickly. People were panicking, and they could see no light at the end of the tunnel. However, when the world was at its darkest, a light emerged (as it always will).

My Personal Mindset

> *Start by doing what's necessary; then do what's possible,*
> *and suddenly you are doing the impossible.*
>
> *Francis of Assisi*

My personal mindset is to believe anything is possible. This might sound overly simplistic, but we are limitless beings whose only limits are the limits we impose on ourselves. Sure, you must get out of your own way sometimes. There's that moment when you say, "I can't do this," and once you've said that, you've already decided. Once you've put forth a self-limiting belief, it becomes your limitation.

Whether you think you can, or you think you can't, you're right.

❦

Henry Ford

Rather than believing in limitations, I always focus my thoughts on the positive. I approach everything with the belief that I can do it and do it well. Whether I know how to do it, have done it before, or have no idea where to start, I can do it. I believe in myself and my resourcefulness to know I can work it out. I have confidence that I will always find a solution to the problem.

Anything is possible if you put your mind to it. If the goal you're chasing is in alignment with your life, purpose, and satisfaction, that's even better. It's like being supercharged, giving yourself internal drive and motivation every day. Can you make yourself do things you don't *want* to do by sheer force of will? Yes, it's possible, but it's tiring. There's a word for this: *drive.*

If you force yourself or others to rely on drive, you're using extra energy. It's like a firehose springing a leak. Somewhere, energy is being drained out and weakening the forward motion. Using drive or force means we don't really want to do something, but we feel it's something we *should* do. If we find ourselves saying we *should* do something, it's probably out of alignment with what we truly want to do. It creates internal resistance, like driving a car with the handbrake on. In this case, it's critical to find that alignment with purpose/objective/goal so we can clearly see what the point is and once we've done that, there is less internal resistance.

A lot of our mindset is developed by parents and coaches when we're kids. For a moment, recall that sports coach at school who was always trying to extract a little more out of you and encouraging you to believe you could accomplish anything by trying just a little harder. We learn that by trying harder, we can go further. I'm not exactly the athletic type, but when I was in school, I participated in crew (which is a fancy word for rowing). I was the coxswain, and it was my job to encourage, coach, and push the crew team harder during our races. With all the encouragement I was doling out, I started believing it along with my crew.

There will always be people who are smarter, faster, or fitter than you are. But if you try hard enough, you can narrow the gap. If you can outwork your competition and put in more effort, then you can often catch up, match, and exceed their mark. The ability to motivate and encourage both yourself and others helps you make things happen with less resistance and in a shorter timeframe.

More than anything, my mindset comes from an upbringing that regarded hard work as a part of life. You didn't question it. It just was. You put in the hours and achieved the goals your coach and the other adults set out for you. I made it happen then and continue to make it happen to this day. Thus, it's part of my mindset and not something I can turn off easily or at all. It works for me, and it might work for you. Is it tiring sometimes having to push and push myself? Yes, it is; however, as long as it is aligned with my purpose, and I feel its continuing my journey in the right direction, it's fine.

Happiness

*Folks are usually about as happy as they
make their minds up to be.*

Abraham Lincoln

Happiness needs to come from within. Most people pursue happiness in achievements, material possessions, social status, and relationships. Our hustle-and-grind culture only grinds us into the ground. The more we chase happiness, the more it eludes us. Instead of turning our attention outward, we must look inward.

The ability to remain optimistic in the face of adversity and challenge is a true test that requires a strong mindset. When you choose to look for happiness and fulfilment internally, you have more control over your state of mind than when you let your happiness be dictated by the outside world.

The Danish happiness concept of *hygge* was introduced to an international audience in *The Little Book of Hygge* (Meik Weiking, 2017), and this happiness craze began sweeping nations.[36] Hygge is not universally translatable; however, in general, it refers to the Danish concept of well-being, comfort, and cosiness.[37] This phenomenon became well-known because its premise is so simple and accessible. It reflects the Danish belief that happiness comes from feeling well taken care of, having an internal sense of comfort, and being at ease. These are aspects anyone can use anywhere in the world to create instant happiness.

Another refreshing take on happiness comes from the Swedish concept of *lagom*. Lagom sounds like *hygge's* more serious brother, but the concept isn't so uptight. Roughly translated, *lagom* means "just the right amount." *Lagom* represents the idea that happiness comes from harmony and balance in life.[38]

The two philosophies both provide a context for happiness beyond the commercial, external world. *Hygge* is centred on taking time out to feel cosy and safe, whilst *lagom's* emphasis on balance in all things can be more of a motivating philosophy. Applying these mindsets can help you reassess your priorities and take a cathartic step back from constant consumption.

Habits

If you pick the right small behaviour and sequence it right, then you won't have to motivate yourself to have it grow. It will just happen naturally, like a good seed planted in a good spot.

BJ Fogg

Habits make up most of our thoughts, emotions, and actions. We all need to overcome bad habits and encourage better habits. However, new habits don't always last.

New habits are built by doing something and learning that it creates a good feeling. Want that good feeling to continue? Then make what you are doing a habit. Soon you will motivate yourself to build even more new habits and routines, building them into existing habits. Eventually, your new habits will become automatic, like waking up or brushing your teeth, you'll no longer have to consciously think about them.

I'm sure you've made a New Year's resolution that fizzled out in January or committed to a new routine on a Monday only to abandon it by Wednesday. The way to make a new habit last is to focus on upgrading a current habit instead trying to eliminate it.

Implementing better personal (or business) habits will help achieve new personal (or business) goals. One can't achieve something new by repeating old habits. Old habits need to be upgraded if you want to keep moving forward and growing. We need to be agile enough to learn and try new methods. We need to abandon old ideas that no longer help us in this BAUU world and replace them with more innovative and creative ones.

Steven Covey's 7 Habits

Sow a thought, reap an action; sow an action, reap a habit; sow a habit, reap a character; sow a character, reap a destiny.

Steven R. Covey

Steven R. Covey's 1989 book, *The 7 Habits of Highly Effective People,* is perhaps the best-known among all business management and leadership books.[39] In it, Covey unlocks the secret to his success by identifying the seven habits that will skyrocket your growth and help you unleash your true potential. The seven habits are powerful and totally transformative. Here they are:

1. **Be proactive**. You must be responsible and accountable for yourself. Don't engage in blame. It's all on you. You're in charge of yourself. Remember you always have a choice and being proactive is a choice. As Covey writes, "I am not a product of my circumstances. I am a product of my decisions."
2. **Begin with the end in mind**. Focus and act on what you can control and influence. Let go of anything you can't control or influence because those things are time wasters. This is about having a vision of what you want to achieve. Covey says, "Your most important work is always ahead of you, never behind you." Focus on the forward motion and work backwards from your goals.
3. **Put first things first**. Take care of the most important tasks first. Prioritise and learn to say no to things that aren't priorities. This step is about balance and finding a holistic way to decide what matters and what does not. Covey urges you to live by the principles you value most, not by the agendas the world forces on you.
4. **Think win-win**. Collaborate with others so everyone can celebrate the wins. Don't let losing be an option for anyone. This gets to the core of what it means to build trust and connection. Find a common ground that excites and energises everyone.
5. **Seek first to understand, then to be understood**. This habit is about effective communication. We need to listen actively to understand. Weak and confusing communication is becoming far too common because of our current WFA (Work From Anywhere) model. Now more than ever, we must ensure that communication is

clear and understood by all parties. As Covey cautions, most people do not listen with the intent to understand; they listen with the intent to respond.

6. **Synergize**. When people come together and collaborate, that which they co-create is invariably better than anything they would come up with individually. Remember, we do not know what we do not know. That's why we strive to put diverse teams of people together. Synergy is better than "my way or no way;" it's *our* way. Synergy is not the same as compromise. In a compromise, one plus one equals one and a half at best. Something always gets lost in a compromise.

7. **Sharpen the saw**. Covey emphasises the importance of continuously improving yourself. You should always be improving, refining, and renewing. Renewal empowers us to move onwards and upwards in a spiral of growth.

Each of Covey's seven habits has played an important role in my own life. The first habit (being proactive) can be seen in our kaizen mindset of lifelong learning. This is also Step 4 of The Slight Edge (see The Slight Edge below). Every day I am learning, whether it's from a book or an article. I enrol in courses to learn from the best. When I feel I have come up short at being proactive, it triggers me to jump into action to fill the gap.

Habit six (synergize) is especially important today. Connection and collaboration have become increasingly important to Business As UnUsual. We have seen that, for example, in the handling of the pandemic. People and organisations came together to innovate new solutions to these novel problems. We put our minds together in unprecedented times and created something amazing.

There is a lot of knowledge and meaning in Stephen Covey's seven steps. His book hit bestselling status the year it was released and has since become a contemporary classic, as the lessons are timeless and universal. Although this book is over thirty years old now, it still packs a punch.

How I Show Up

CEOs are hired for their intellect and business expertise—and fired for a lack of emotional intelligence.

Daniel Goleman

Other people's perceptions of us depend upon how they see us, although an individual's perception may differ from reality. For example, your loving partner may think you walk on water, and that becomes their reality: they believe you can walk on water. Whether you can actually walk on water or not is irrelevant. Similarly, some people may think you're a jerk. To them, you'll always be a jerk, regardless.

Therefore, how you show up becomes important, and that's exactly what Emotional Intelligence is all about. Emotional Intelligence relates to the skills that help you perceive, understand, express, reason with, and manage emotions, both within yourself and others.

We can apply these skills to help us become more aware of our own and others' feelings. Having higher levels of emotional intelligence makes us more conscious of the influence emotions have on our decisions, behaviour, and performance. This, in turn, helps us minimise the unproductive influence emotions can have and maximise its productive qualities.

The way you show up determines the way people feel, and the way they feel determines the extent to which they can engage, and that impacts pretty much everything about the outcome of the relationship.

꧁꧂

Deiric McCann (GENOS International)

In short, Emotional Intelligence helps you show up the way you want to be perceived and thus enhance your effectiveness, influence, and mental resilience.

Reinvent Yourself

When I let go of what I am, I become what I might be.

꧁꧂

Lao Tzu

Have you ever seen a friend act one way in front of you and differently in front of their colleagues, and differently again when they're with friends they've known since high school, or in front of a new partner? This is because we are limitless human beings with the potential to reinvent ourselves repeatedly. We can be whoever we choose to be in this life, and most of the time, to make it to the next level, a better life requires a better version of who we are today.

Boost yourself and your own success by understanding and getting clarity on who the version of you is that needs to make these goals happen, and work on becoming that future you (remember the Four questions in Chapter 1) every day.

Does the person who has everything you want to have in the future wait to act on their goals, or do they go out there and make things happen? Are you acting in integrity with what you want to be? Are you taking steps daily to become the biggest, brightest version of yourself, or do you consistently sell yourself short?

Make the decision to go for it and really go for it!

The Slight Edge

For things to change, you've got to change. For things to get better, you've got to get better. It's easy to do. But it's easy not to do, too.

Jeff Olson

Direct sales guru Jeff Olson wrote *The Slight Edge* to give people a seven-step tool for making small, daily changes that lead to success and happiness in life, as depicted in *Figure 10* below.[40]

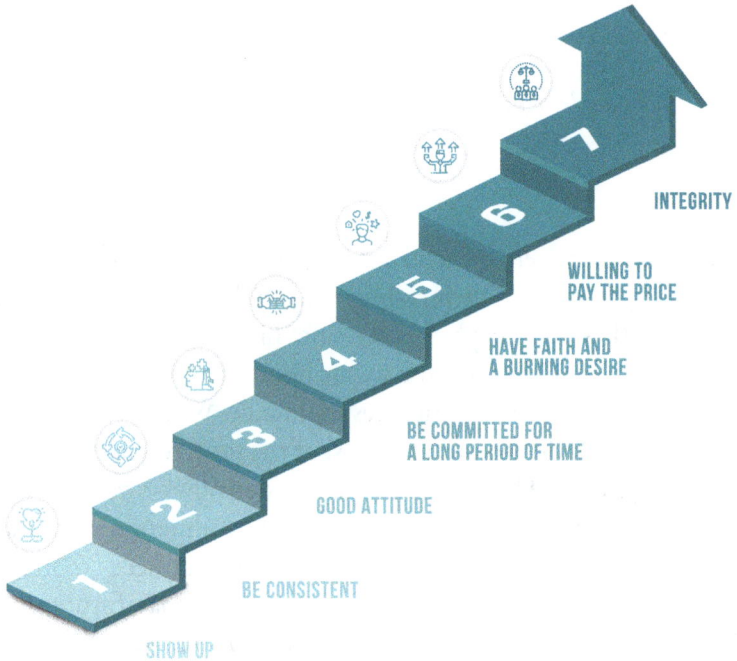

INTEGRITY

WILLING TO
PAY THE PRICE

HAVE FAITH AND
A BURNING DESIRE

BE COMMITTED FOR
A LONG PERIOD OF TIME

GOOD ATTITUDE

BE CONSISTENT

SHOW UP

Figure 10. The Slight Edge

1. **Show up!** Woody Allen is credited with saying that 80 percent of success is showing up. You must show up, come rain or shine. Don't let anything stand in your way. Be present and positive. Decisions are made by the people who are *in* the room. You must be there to have an impact.
2. **Be consistent**. Consistency serves to build trust with your people and community. It is also a way to build

positive habits. Just as you need to brush your teeth every day to prevent cavities, you need to be consistent with your other habits and attitudes.

3. **Good attitude**. Winston Churchill is credited with saying that attitude is a little thing that makes a big difference, and it's true. Leave your bad attitude at home and come to work with a good outlook. Intentionally starting your day in a positive way makes a big difference in your whole outlook.

4. **Be committed for a long period of time**. John Leonard is credited with saying it takes a long time to grow an old friend. In his 2008 book, *Outliers*, Malcolm Gladwell wrote that to develop expertise in any skill, you must practice the correct way to do something for a total of ten thousand hours. There are a million different ways to tell you that becoming an overnight success is a myth. Work hard and commit yourself to the long game.

5. **Have faith and a burning desire**. These are two qualities you must possess if you want to achieve success. You must have faith in yourself and a burning desire to win or achieve. As Napoleon Hill put it, desire gets you up early and keeps you up late. It keeps you pushing forward when everything seems bleak. It's an important ingredient for sustainable success.

6. **Be willing to pay the price**. Leaders are not born; they are made through hard work. There's always a price that must be paid to reach a goal. Vince Lombardi said it best, "Hard work is the price we must pay for success. I think you can accomplish anything if you're willing to pay the price." Whether this means investing in yourself, investing in a coach, or scraping up the money you need by any means possible, there's always a price.

*Hard work is the price we must pay for success. I think you can
accomplish anything if you're willing to pay the price.*

⁓

Vince Lombardi

7. **Integrity**. This trait is very important for your success.
    As American politician Alan Simpson put it, "If you
    have integrity, nothing else matters. If you don't have
    integrity, nothing else matters." Integrity gets to the
    centre of a person's being and marks them as authentic
    in everything they do and say.

The Slight Edge also teaches a powerful lesson about the
power of choice because, as the author points out so succinctly,
if something is easy to do (like brushing your teeth every day),
it's also easy not to do it (and forego brushing your teeth on
some days). You have a choice.

We are confronted with these simple choices every day. Will
I brush my teeth? Will I shower? Will I go to the gym? Will I
arrive for the meeting on time? Everything you do every day is
a choice. You need to make sure you're making the choices that
will get you where you want to go.

Figure 11 below shows a visualisation of the above concepts—
the impact of what's easy to do and what's easy not to do.

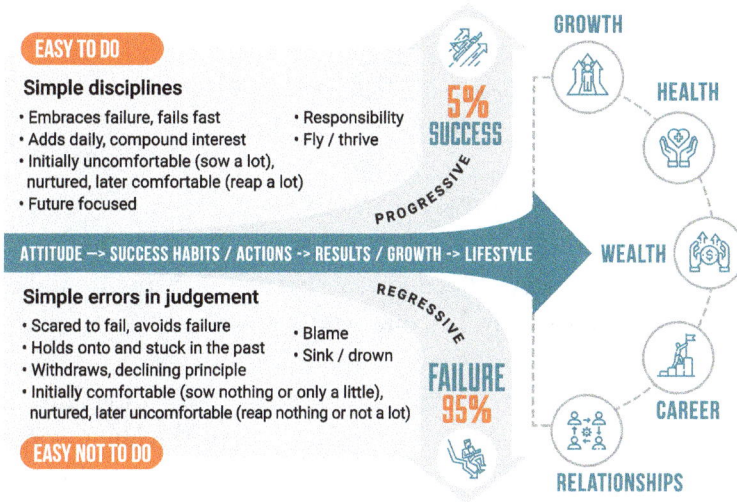

EASY TO DO

Simple disciplines
- Embraces failure, fails fast
- Adds daily, compound interest
- Initially uncomfortable (sow a lot), nurtured, later comfortable (reap a lot)
- Future focused
- Responsibility
- Fly / thrive

5% SUCCESS

PROGRESSIVE

ATTITUDE --> SUCCESS HABITS / ACTIONS -> RESULTS / GROWTH -> LIFESTYLE

REGRESSIVE

Simple errors in judgement
- Scared to fail, avoids failure
- Holds onto and stuck in the past
- Withdraws, declining principle
- Initially comfortable (sow nothing or only a little), nurtured, later uncomfortable (reap nothing or not a lot)
- Blame
- Sink / drown

FAILURE 95%

EASY NOT TO DO

GROWTH
HEALTH
WEALTH
CAREER
RELATIONSHIPS

Figure 11. Visualisation of the Impact of What's Easy to Do and What's Easy Not to Do

Living The Slight Edge

Simple, productive actions, repeated consistently over time.
That, in a nutshell, is the slight edge.

Jeff Olson

I live the principles outlined in *The Slight Edge* every day, and as it resonates so strongly, I recommend it to anyone.

Reading business books is one thing that, for me, didn't come easily right away. I loved reading science fiction and fantasy, but business books less so, even though I knew this habit would greatly improve my life. I knew there was underlying resistance, and I wasn't sure why. Sure, it would have been easy to continue to put off reading business books even though I knew it would be beneficial.

However, *The Slight Edge* triggered me to commit to reading ten pages every single day, and I have reaped significant rewards as a result. Since starting on this path in 2012, I've set annual reading challenges in Goodreads, though I failed two of the challenges and have read more than 900 books. It's staggering what a little target of only ten pages a day has resulted in.

I am so convinced that it's important to read at least ten pages a day that I instituted this habit as part of the founding philosophy at TRG International. People who work for the company are expected to read ten pages every day. I've found that it is an excellent way for continuous growth and learning. Watching a YouTube (or other) video can also be educational (I may be showing my age here as that was never an option in the past), but there is a lot of value in the written word of a book, so don't write it off as old fashioned or out of date.

To support our employees in reaching these goals, we've built a business library that contains over a thousand books. Some of them are the best business books on the market, and new books (that we take suggestions on) are added to the library each year. Fewer barriers mean less internal resistance. People are motivated by a thirst for knowledge and have sustained enthusiasm when there is an easy way to improve themselves.

We may feel we are all time starved and have no time to read. One can find time each day to consume part of a book, whether reading or listening to it. If you are driving, on public transport or walking, listen to an audiobook. When exercising, listen to an audiobook instead of music. I call this Running University. There are so many small opportunities for reading during our days.

A little bit more of pretty much anything (not just reading) compounded over time is more than you'd think. Every single time you commit to your goals, even a little more today than you did yesterday, makes a difference. Don't discount baby steps; they are still steps. Stay committed to the important things, even when they're not glamorous.

We always have a choice. We can choose to give in to our resistance, or we can choose to overcome it. Giving into resistance and fear by standing immobilised is much easier than moving forward despite our fear. We need to understand that resistance will always be there, but the greatest rewards don't come from being committed to something short term. Rather, they come over the long haul. So, take a step no matter how small.

When working on improving yourself, consider these questions that lead to deep reflection, awareness, and growth. What do I know, and what don't I know yet? Where do I need to improve, and how can I do something about it?

Look around for signs of *The Slight Edge* in people's performance, and you can tell who has embraced it because they are the ones who are thriving. I can tell just as easily when someone is merely paying lip service to the seven steps. It's easy to tell because those people struggle. They are missing that special slight edge.

CHAPTER 3 KEY TAKEAWAYS

- *Kaizen* is a Japanese word that means continuous improvement. *Kai* (change) and *zen* (good).
- Reflection 4 Reaction Reward and Repeat is a model to create a habit out of reflection.
- Looking at challenges as opportunities that can help you grow instead of as roadblocks will propel you forward.
- An infinite mindset is one of limitless opportunities and the desire/drive to improve oneself. It's not a matter of *can't;* it's a matter of *how can I?*
- Let go of your failures. Letting it go, allowing for forgiveness and mistakes in your life, will allow you to let go of the past so that you can clearly see the future and make decisions based on the present moment.
- Happiness is not about external things, but about your internal emotional state.
- Simplify your life and ensure every area is in balance. Create an internal sense of comfort and cosiness to feel deeply fulfilled.
- Habits determine the daily activities we do towards our goals. Aligning habits with our long-term plans leads to success.
- Our emotional intelligence determines how we show up. High emotional intelligence enables us to be aware of our emotional reactions, witness our patterns, and choose a more appropriate emotional state. Emotional intelligence also includes the ability to process your emotions in a healthy way.
- Reinvent yourself infinitely for continuous growth.
- Give yourself the advantage of *The Slight Edge,* follow the 7 steps, make them a habit and progress to success and happiness.
- Learn more about the slight edge in our Masterclass.[xi]
- Download Chapter 3 resources from RickYvanovich.com/BAUU/.

[xi] The Slight Edge Masterclass and other resources can be found at RickYvanovich.com/BAUU/.

CHAPTER 3
REFLECTION PROMPTS

What's your **one** key takeaway from this chapter?

```
_____
_____
_____
```

And what else?

```
_____
_____
_____
```

What action will you take right away because of something you read in this chapter?

```
_____
_____
_____
```

And what else?

```
_____
_____
_____
```

CHAPTER 4
THE TOWER OF SELF

TOWER OF SELF

Be yourself, but always your better self.

Karl G. Maeser

I created the concept of The Tower of Self many years ago. At the time, I was being continually asked, "How do people become successful?" I quickly realised that what these people really wanted to know was how do *they* become successful. I know and could talk all day about what I, personally, did to become successful, but that doesn't always translate to others. I wanted to be able to answer this question for others, so I did a load of research, spoke to a lot of successful people, and subsequently ran a bunch of events to help people with a solution.

The truth is that success is not an accident, nor is it a coincidence. Success is achieved on purpose. In the video "The Space Where Your Dreams Live," Mel Robbins says, "There is a massive gap, a massive gap between knowing what to do and actually doing it."[41] She couldn't have said it better. The Tower of Self is built by knowing what you need to do and how to go about doing it.

The Tower of Self comprises of four selves that bridge the *know* with the *go* (that is, forward action):

- The Know
  □ Self-Confidence
  □ Self-Efficacy
  □ Self-Worth/Self-value
- The Go
  □ Self-Motivation (Motivation)

Self-Confidence

> *Self-confidence can be learned, practiced, and mastered, just like any other skill. Once you master it, everything in your life will change for the better.*
>
> Barrie Davenport

Self-confidence is knowing and trusting in yourself and your abilities. Building confidence is instrumental in the Tower of Self. If you can't believe in yourself, why should anyone else believe in you? So, the first key to developing confidence is believing in yourself. It sounds simple, but "simple" is not a synonym for "easy," and developing confidence can be hard! As individuals, we may fail to stop and appreciate our accomplishments and instead focus on the next goal or accomplishment in our sights. Building confidence, like everything else in this book, needs to be done purposefully. It's a skill and attitude that needs to be honed through practice.

To start building your confidence, make a list of all the things you have accomplished in life. Here are some key things to think about:

- What have you accomplished so far?
- What do you think sets you apart from others who have been unable to reach those goals?
- For each accomplishment, what skills helped you reach that accomplishment?

What have you been able to learn, discover, and experience because of those accomplishments?

This exercise is about taking notice of, acknowledging, and appreciating your unique skills and talents and seeing how they've contributed to your success. Sustained success comes when you realise it's OK to be proud of yourself and confident in the skills you bring to the table.

One hack for building your self-confidence is the habit of journaling. Each day, write down what you achieved in a journal. This serves to acknowledge and appreciate your achievements in writing. Then, on those darker days when you need a little lift, open your journal, and read about all the amazing things you have already achieved!

Alternatively, each time you achieve something, write it down on a slip of paper, roll it up into a ball or fold it, and pop it into a jar. When you need a quick confidence boost, randomly pull out one of the pieces of paper from the jar and read about the amazing thing you achieved. When you finish, don't forget to roll it up and pop it back in the jar again. Pick a big jar and get creative by putting some decorations on it, too. Even better, get a new jar every year, so you'll have a roomful of jars as wonderful as you are.

Give your journal or jar a name to remind you what it really is: appreciation, acknowledgement, awesomeness, whatever you want to call it.

Never doubt your ability, you are awesome and don't you forget it.

Self-Efficacy

If I have the belief that I can do it, I shall surely acquire the capacity to do it even if I may not have it at the beginning.

Mahatma Gandhi

Self-efficacy is believing in your own ability to succeed. Looking at the list of your accomplishments and appreciating them will reinforce your self-efficacy because it serves as acknowledge that you have accomplished hard things in the past. Instead of focusing on how far you must go before you reach your next milestone, focus on appreciating the success you've already achieved and use that as proof you can accomplish anything you set your mind to.

One external way to build self-efficacy is to be an open source of information and encourage others to ask you for advice. When you give advice to someone else, you are more likely to believe in it yourself.[42] You can also try to approach your own problems as if you were giving someone else advice on the matter. Ask yourself, "If a friend or colleague were struggling with the same problem, what advice would I offer them?"

The answers we need are almost always held within ourselves. We need to learn to trust our senses and believe that success is possible for everyone who wants it.

Self-Worth/Self-Value

No one can make you feel inferior without your consent.

Eleanor Roosevelt

Self-worth/self-value is believing you are worthy of success and that you bring value to the world. Building a brand, a company, a mission, or a purpose can feel scary and lonely. Will people like me? Will people like my product? Does my service add value to the world? Is my service or time worth this much? It can be much easier to get sucked up into the tornado of *what-ifs* and self-doubt when you don't have the acknowledgements such as social proof or certifications to back it up.

One way to increase self-worth is to recognise, appreciate, and acknowledge your achievements. We can do this by journaling or the using the jar.

Life is too short to waste any amount of time on wondering what other people think about you. In the first place, if they had better things going on in their lives, they wouldn't have the time to sit around and talk about you. What's important to me is not others' opinions of me, but what's important to me is my opinion of myself.

C. JoyBell C.

Another way to increase self-worth is through positive thinking and positive future thinking. One simple tool for changing our negative thoughts and building positive ones is repeating a positive affirmation first thing in the morning and before bed at night. Daily positive affirmations help reinforce positive thoughts, and over time, this habit becomes automatic. Here are some examples of positive affirmations you can use:[xii]

- I'm awesome.
- I am worthy.
- I am capable.
- I grow with each challenge.
- I am growing every day.
- Waking up in the morning: Today I'm going to have another wonderful day
- Going to bed at night: Today I had another spectacular day.
- Before making a presentation: I'm so excited, my presentation will be magnificent.

Self-Motivation (Motivation)

Reasons have two functions. One is to justify ourselves and the other is to convince others.

Dan Sperber[43]

What exactly is motivation? Four dictionaries/encyclopaedias give similar but different definitions:

- "Motivation is the reason for which humans and other animals initiate, continue, or terminate a behavior at a given time" (Wikipedia).[44]

[xii] Positive affirmations and other resources can be found at RickYvanovich.com/BAUU/.

- "The need or reason for doing something" and the "willingness to do something, or something that causes such willingness" (*Cambridge Dictionary*).[45]
- "The mental processes that arouse, sustain, and direct human behaviour" (*Oxford Reference*).[46]
- "The act or process of giving someone a reason for doing something" and "a force or influence that causes someone to do something" (*Britannica Dictionary*).[47]

Which of these (or any others that you may know of) do you prefer and why?

Motivation is the reason humans do things.

Rick Yvanovich

I define **motivation** as "the reason humans do things." Let me explain my logic. Reasoning is an internal human thought process. We gather information/data, and as humans, we deduce one or more options from which we choose. Reasoning includes both need and process. And if motivation needs reasoning, then by its nature, it needs self-motivation, as it's the individual doing the reasoning. Thus, I define **self-motivation** as "the internal force that drives you to do something."

Self-motivation is the internal force that drives you to do something.

Rick Yvanovich

I know the motivation/self-motivation definitions are similar, and I recommend using the self-motivation one and calling it self-motivation. I am aware that we use the words motivation and self-motivation interchangeably. However, self-motivation is more precise and helps overcome the myth that one can motivate other people. It's a myth that we can motivate other people as individuals. "You can't motivate people"—but we can do something about it.[48]

I want you to pause and reflect about people you know today and in the past, whether at work or otherwise. In your opinion, how motivated were they? Statistically speaking (think of a normal distribution or bell curve), as you do this reflection, you'll see a spectrum from low to medium to high motivation. Clearly, different people have different degrees of self-motivation, and it's essential to take this into account when thinking about self-motivation.

> *Don't expect to be motivated every day to get out there and make things happen. You won't be. Don't count on motivation. Count on discipline.*
>
> *Jocko Willink*

The good news is that self-motivation is like a muscle, and we can build it up (into a taller Tower of Self). I believe we are all intrinsically motivated, and sometimes we need both intrinsic and extrinsic help finding our ON switch. So, instead of waiting for motivation to hit you, it's up to you to motivate yourself. Below are some questions and prompts to help you:

- What makes you jump out of bed in the morning? How can you do more of those things?
- What prevents you jumping out of bed in the morning? How can you do less or eliminate those things?
- What motivates you the most to achieve your goals and deadlines? How can you do more of those things?
- What de-motivates you the most to achieve your goals and deadlines? How can you do less or eliminate those things?
- Do you need external accountability? How can you get more of this?

- Do you need extrinsic rewards? How can you get more of these?
- Do you need verbal recognition and praise from others? How can you get more of these?

Figure out what makes you tick (turns your motivation ON), and lean into it when resistance pops up. Be aware that motivation comes and goes. Those who achieve lasting success commit themselves to the actions and habits (Chapter 3) that will keep them motivated long after the initial euphoria feeling from setting a goal fades. And for those of us who want/need a little (or a lot) of external motivation, I suggest a coach and/or an accountability buddy. An accountability buddy is someone you partner with to help you stick to your commitment. For example, to get this book written and get through the multiple edits (oh those red lines and critical [but true] comments stressed and de-motivated me), I used multiple accountability buddies to nudge me, remind me, and even cajole me to stick to my commitments. It worked—you're reading the book! So, thank you all my accountability buddies!

How do you find an accountability buddy? Here are a few ways:

- Ask a partner/friend/colleague
- Ask a coach
- Join *The Conspiracy* (I used this book as my Worthy Goal, so thank you Michael/MBS, Ainsley, the Ashes, and the Firs.)[49]

If you're in a team or leading people in one or more teams/ groups/organisations, you're maybe wondering how to best support other people with their motivation. Maybe your job or organisation has a requirement that you need to motivate your team/people. I can empathise, more so when the organisation is not aware of the myth that you can't motivate people. Read on!

Motivation—Theories, Models, and Tools

Motivation comes from working on things we care about.

~~~

Sheryl Sandberg

In the rest of this chapter, we'll look at multiple theories, models, and tools to help us better understand motivation.

Herzberg's Two-Factor Theory

The powerful motivator in our lives isn't money; it's the opportunity to learn, grow in responsibilities, contribute to others, and be recognized for achievements.

~~~

Frederick Herzberg

American psychologist Frederick Herzberg developed the *two-factor theory* (also known as the *dual-factor theory* or the *motivation-hygiene theory*) and co-authored *The Motivation to Work*.[50] Herzberg conducted his landmark study in 1959, and this work has helped define how businesses need to approach the administration and management of people.

Herzberg interviewed more than two hundred workers in the Pittsburgh area, focusing on engineers and accountants. He asked each person to describe moments when they had been very happy or very unhappy in their jobs. Through this work, Herzberg distinguished between two factors, which he called motivators and hygiene factors.

Motivators are the things that give a worker job satisfaction and arise from the work itself. They include acknowledgement for a job well done, the ability to take part in decision-making, and opportunities for career advancement. When these motivators exist in the work environment, all is well. When they do not exist, things start to break down. For example, if you receive praise for your work, you are energised and enjoy your work even more; however, when your work doesn't receive recognition and you expected it, you'll be unsatisfied.

Hygiene factors are the things that when they are going well, do not affect our happiness on the job, but when absent or flawed, contribute significantly to our dissatisfaction. Examples of hygiene factors include things like your salary, holiday time, or the work conditions themselves. These are affected by external forces such as company policies or management practices.

One takeaway concept is that employees have a fundamental set of expectations. It's part of their unwritten expectations when working for a company. When those basic expectations aren't being met, it can cause ripples of dissatisfaction.

There are motivational factors at play as well. These might not be an expected part of the job. Having motivational factors in place boosts morale, drives dedication to projects and connection to each other, and makes people feel like valued members of the team.

I observe that motivation is a word loosely used and relates to motivation and hygiene and satisfaction and dissatisfaction and happiness.[51] So, when leading others with this model in mind, we need to be cognisant that the word *hygiene* in the Herzberg (motivation-hygiene) context may not be understood by others. Don't assume others are as informed as you now are.

To better understand motivation, we need to also understand satisfaction and dissatisfaction, which we'll cover in Searching for Satisfaction in Chapter 7.

Maslow's Hierarchy of Needs

One can choose to go back toward safety or forward toward growth. Growth must be chosen again and again; fear must be overcome again and again.

Abraham Maslow

Also related to satisfaction, the psychologist Abraham Maslow introduced his hierarchy of needs theory in The Theory of Motivation.[52] Maslow believed you can grow and ascend the pyramid and reach what he referred to as *self-actualisation* (I like calling it *self-awesomeness*) by focusing on the positive things that are already in your life. Self-actualisation occurs when you have achieved true satisfaction in all areas of your life. *Figure 12* below depicts Maslow's hierarchy, modified to show how it applies in business today.

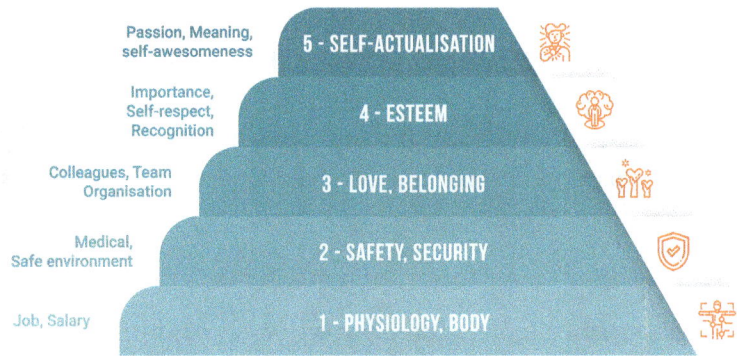

Figure 12. Maslow's Hierarchy of Needs in Business

In his hierarchy, there are five levels of human needs from physiological at the bottom of the pyramid to self-actualisation at the top. The order depicts the ascending importance. The need to grow, to ascend serves as a roadmap to individual's satisfaction in life and business.

Physiological needs are the basic things you need to survive. Examples of essential physiological needs include oxygen and water, which are provided by Mother Nature. However, other needs at the bottom of the pyramid need to be considered by employers for "survival." For instance, can your employees afford to pay their rent or mortgage on their current salaries? Are healthy food options available to your staff? Can they afford groceries, childcare, and other basic needs for survival? Having this dialogue with employees can be incredibly revealing. You may discover some employees are working second jobs just to make ends meet. Undoubtedly, some physiological needs are the responsibility of business leaders who can absolutely do better for their committed and loyal employees.

Safety gives you a level of comfort in life and includes personal health and financial security. As its one level up from the bottom, when we look at financial aspects it's beyond the "survival" level. Have you been able to foster an environment of safety in your place of business? Can your employees openly talk about what is happening in their life, both personally and professionally, without the fear of repercussions? Lack of psychological safety inhibits people from taking innovative risks, raising their voices when there is a problem, or sharing potential solutions.

Kim Scott in her book *Radical Candor: Be a Kick-Ass Boss Without Losing Your Humanity* introduced her radical candor model where "the whole point of Radical Candor is that it really is possible to care personally and challenge directly at the same time."[53] I mention the book here as this takes safety to a much higher level and one might want to consider that.

The whole point of Radical Candor is that it really is possible to care personally and challenge directly at the same time.

Kim Scott

Safety needs to be intelligently curated in every organisational environment, and employees should feel (ideally know) they always have the organisation's support. I believe it's important to inculcate safety into the organisational culture. Support and safety need to be nurtured and maintained. It's not surprising that safety is linked to emotional intelligence (see How I Show Up in Chapter 3). It's also one of the ten dimensions of high-performance teams (see Shaping Organisational Culture in Chapter 6).

The need for **love and belonging** relates to one's emotional well-being and support system, including relationships with family, friends, and colleagues. An intimate or close relationship is also crucial to survive throughout life. Does one feel valued, loved, and supported? Are individuals' ideas and voices heard and celebrated? Organisations need to take the time to let people know they add value to the organisation, and they are appreciated as people, not just as workers/employees/volunteers.

Should an organisation love their employees? Yes! If an organisation expects their employees to love their job and the organisation, then it's reasonable that the organisation loves their employees.

Esteem encompasses self-confidence, self-efficacy, and self-worth/self-value. Maslow classified esteem into two parts: firstly, self-esteem, and secondly, respect, recognition, status from others. Is feedback and feedforward (Chapter 5) taken seriously, or are they disregarded? Does one listen to others more than one speaks? Does one tend to delegate without actively listening? Remember, we have two ears and one mouth; they each need a turn and don't work well in tandem. Putting respectful policies into place helps people develop their self-esteem and allows them to carry these principles over to other people as well. People should take time to validate each other and provide space to lift each other up and spotlight each other's contributions so everyone gives and receives esteem.

Self-actualisation is the need to be the best you can be and achieve all your goals. Are people working on projects that light them up? If not, are they able to schedule their free time to do more of the things that are important to them, like meditation retreats or the ability to explore outside interests?

Looking at Maslow's theory through a lens of motivation requires looking beyond traditional forms of employee rewards and recognition. Organisations can easily make the mistake of believing that people are motived by and value only salary and bonuses. With this narrow idea in mind, organisations can easily miss the plethora of opportunities, including non-monetary, to grow people to higher levels of the Maslow pyramid. Motivating perks might be free lunches, extra paid time off, continuous training opportunities, creative idea incentives, memberships to business networks. Benefits such as these can serve as highly motivating rewards for people who seek fulfilment.[54]

The Hawthorne Effect

> *When leaders pay proper attention to people,*
> *motivation and productivity prevail.*
>
> *Rick Yvanovich*

The *Hawthorne effect* was developed by sociologist Henry Landsberger in the 1950s. He examined the results of a series of studies by Elton Mayo (psychologist), Roethlisberger and Whitehead (sociologists), and William Dickson (company representative) that measured how changing the lighting at The Hawthorne Works—an electrical plant in Cicero, Illinois— affected the workers' behaviours and output.

In the first of four studies, researchers had hypothesised that productivity would change with changes in the environment, in this case, the lighting. This study and one conducted in the late 1920s and early 1930 at the Elton Mayo factory showed that productivity did indeed improve when lighting levels were changed.

Landsberger discovered through his analysis (of the four studies) that some people work harder and perform better when they are being observed. This idea became the basis for his theory that workers' behaviour changed when they knew they were being observed as part of a research study, and not because of brighter lighting or better processes. Thus, the Hawthorne effect is the phenomenon that people behave differently when they know they are being observed or their activity is being recorded.

When people believe they are important in a project, anything works, and, conversely, when they don't believe they are important, nothing works.

Joanne Yatvin

There is controversy around the Hawthorne effect as the researchers did not give sufficient attention to the attitudes of the people. However, we can adjust for that and pay attention to people's attitudes. Thus, businesses should frequently ask employees to share their thoughts about making the workplace more harmonious. Treating everyone as people despite rank fosters feelings of community and camaraderie. These regular conversations and observations show a person that the organisation cares about them, their working conditions, and well-being.

Understanding the Types of Motivation

Intrinsic motivation comes from within you and is powered by your own dreams, aspirations, wants, and wishes.

Joanna Jast

Earlier I alluded to motivation as intrinsic or extrinsic. However, there are six types of intrinsic and extrinsic motivation according to Ryan and Deci.[55]

Intrinsic motivation is internal. This type comes from getting pleasure out of doing something for fun or for the challenge of doing it (which is fun). No external influence is needed. The drive comes from inside you, your grit, your drive. You are motivated to do what gives you satisfaction and a feeling of euphoria. For example, clearing your desk because you like it neat and tidy and devoid of distractions, or running a marathon. Intrinsic motivation also exists in the relation between individuals and activities. One is intrinsically motivated for some activities and not others. Not everyone is intrinsically motivated for a particular task. Other perspectives of intrinsic motivation are the following:

- *Sisu,* which is a Finnish word that is untranslatable. The closest is grit. It's an inner strength that allows you to push past and through significant hardships. It's courage in the face of adversity. It's never ever, ever giving up. I like the concept as it helps give greater meaning to that feeling.
- "Fall down seven times, get up eight" is a Japanese proverb.
- "Weebles wobble but they don't fall down" is a 1970s advertising slogan from Hasbro of a Weeble (a roly-poly toy) that could never fall down as they just roll back up again. It's one of those jingles that's stuck with me since I was a child and like a weeble, I imagine myself always getting up.

I want to make beautiful things, even if nobody cares.

Saul Bass

Amotivation is the lack of intention to act. It's the other end of the spectrum from intrinsic motivation. Amotivation is seeing an activity as not relevant, having no value, not feeling competent to do the activity, or not believing doing the activity will give the desired outcome. In short, if someone is amotivated, they're not going to do it as it's not relevant to them.

Extrinsic motivation contrasts to intrinsic motivation, where the activity brings a valued outcome that's separate from the simple enjoyment of the activity itself. According to Ryan and Deci, there are four types of extrinsic motivation with varying levels of nonautonomy: external regulation, introjected regulation, identification, and integration.

External regulation is a type of extrinsic motivation that is external, and it's the least autonomous. We do something only when we are being compelled to do it, usually by someone who has power over us. We might clear our desk daily only because the company has a clean desk policy and there's a penalty for failing to have a clean desk. Turn up on time, and you'll get full pay; turn up late, and you'll get a penalty. Too many corporate (and academic) motivation systems are based on such extrinsic rewards, where people are "bought" and then commanded. Carrot-and-stick rewards are typical of externally regulated, extrinsic motivation.

Introjected regulation is an external, extrinsic motivation. It's an internal self-regulation linked to anxiety, guilt-avoidance, or ego. When a task is not done, there's a feeling of pressure and tension. That's the self-regulation. You will work especially hard to avoid the shame of hearing your boss or teacher say your work isn't good enough and/or to boost your ego from their praise. Failure can be humiliating, made worse if it's done publicly.

Identification is a more autonomous and somewhat internal type of extrinsic motivation. Identification is when you self-value the activity, when you know it's important to you. As it is more autonomous, you decide whether and when to do it. An individual can choose not to act on a project for many reasons, and if this happens, revisiting how strongly they identify with the project may result in action. Typically, when one is struggling with identified motivation, there may be a lack of alignment and disconnect between their passion, purpose, and goals. Similarly, they may not be taking the daily actions needed to achieve their goals. Either way, it's an opportunity to re-evaluate the situation and create clarity and alignment.

Integration (or integrated regulation) is the most auton-omous and internal type of extrinsic motivation. We are aware of the identified regulations. We fully understood them and aligned them with our own values. As we internalise the rea-sons for doing it, the more self-deterministic and internal it becomes. It gets closer to being intrinsic motivation in that it is autonomous and unconflicted. However, it's still extrinsic motivation as its value is separate from the (intrinsic) joy of just doing it.

Intrinsic motivation trumps extrinsic motivation every time.

Perman

Intrinsic motivation is getting pleasure out of doing something for fun, or for the challenge. Individuals create goals as challenges for themselves. For example, athletes seek to improve on their personal best. It's a self-determined challenge.

What keeps us motivated to meet our goals? It takes two things: The first is to show progress, a sign we have achieved something. And the second is to celebrate! Whenever you show progress, you need to celebrate your achievement. You did one press-up? Celebrate! When we celebrate our success, we get a hit of dopamine that gives us a feeling of euphoria and makes us want to keep going so we can get a dopamine rush. Set small, achievable goals and celebrate each win along the way. Notice and acknowledge progress and build upon it. That drives internal motivation.

Money can extinguish intrinsic motivation, diminish performance, crush creativity, encourage unethical behavior, foster short-term thinking, and become addictive.

Daniel H. Pink

Organisations also set goals and goals may be imposed on individuals i.e., extrinsic motivation. Understanding which of the six types of intrinsic and extrinsic motivation is impacting an individual's motivation at any point will help determine how one should support that individual.

The Four Quadrants Theory (Punishments and Reinforcements)

The strengthening of behaviour which results from reinforcement is appropriately called 'conditioning.' In operant conditioning we 'strengthen' an operant in the sense of making a response more probable or, in actual fact, more frequent.

B. F. Skinner

The four quadrants of operant conditioning (punishments and reinforcements) involve adding or taking away aspects of a job as a reward or a punishment to result in the desired outcome. Since it's a bit of a mouthful and "operant conditioning" sounds so clinical, I'll be referring to this as "the Four Quadrants Theory." Before diving into it, first let's take you on a journey back in history, starting from the late nineteenth century, to understand where this all originated, then we'll see how we can apply it.

Ivan Pavlov was awarded the Nobel Prize for Physiology (medicine) in 1904. His studies on dogs accidentally resulted in what was originally called Pavlovian conditioning and later classic conditioning. In short: this is what the theory presented:

- Dogs would salivate when presented with food.
- Pavlov rang a bell, then fed the dogs. This paired the sound of a bell with food.
- This was repeatedly done which creates the conditioned response in the dog.

- Then when only the bell was rung (and there was no food), the dog still salivated.

Edward Thorndike is best known for his Law of Effect, where a behaviour that's followed by a pleasant consequence/reward is likely repeated, and conversely, if a behaviour is followed by an unpleasant consequence/punishment, it's likely not to be repeated. Thus, the reward encourages the behaviour, and the punishment discourages it.

John B. Watson followed a purely scientific approach to behaviour and believed all human (and animal) behavioural responses were the result of environmental stimuli. His famous (and controversial) Little Albert experiment conditioned a nine-month-old boy to fear a white rat, which extended to fear a rabbit, a dog, and a fur coat. This study showed how emotions can be conditioned (programmed) as a response.[56]

Give me a dozen healthy infants, well-formed, and my own specified world to bring them up in and I'll guarantee to take any one at random and train him to become any type of specialist I might select—doctor, lawyer, artist, merchant-chief and, yes, even beggarman and thief, regardless of his talents, penchants, tendencies, abilities, vocations, and race of his ancestors.

John B. Watson

Buurhus Frederic Skinner's studies were based around the idea that human behaviour is the consequent result of previous actions and human learning is a result of behaviour.

Pavlov, Thorndike, Watson, and Skinner's ideas have culminated in operant conditioning, whereby a stimulus leads to a behaviour and a behaviour leads to a consequence.[57]

Figure 13 below depicts each of the four quadrants of operant conditioning (positive punishment, positive reinforcement, negative punishment, negative reinforcement) to decide which motivating factors to add or remove when an individual performs a job well. Likewise, you can add or remove factors when an individual does not satisfy the job requirements or fails to make progress on their goals.

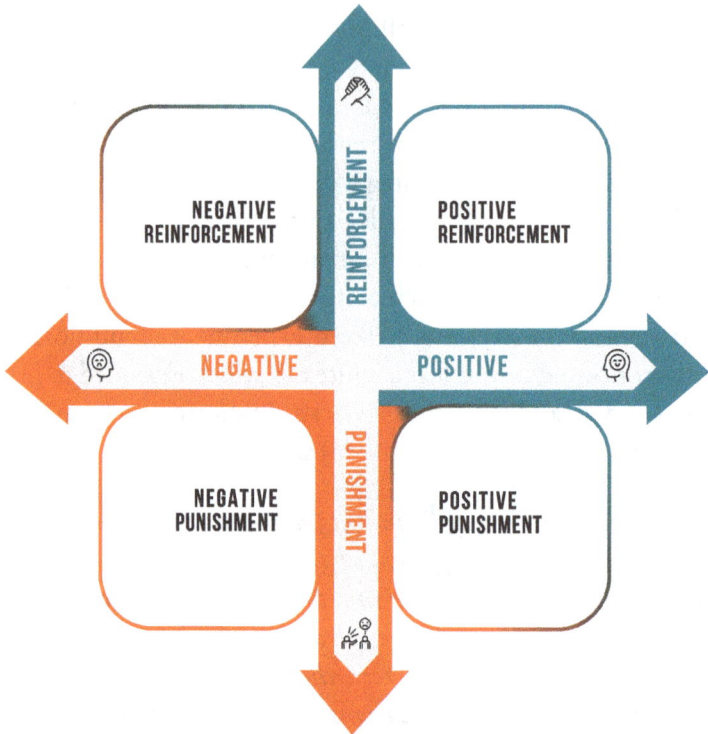

Figure 13. Four Quadrants of Operant Conditioning

A natural tendency would be to give individuals only positive reinforcement, right? Why would we ever take something pleasant away, or introduce something unpleasant? It's important to use all four quadrants and not favour one over the other. All four have advantages and disadvantages and different situations call for different tactics. The best practice is to base decisions on the behaviour of each individual either to encourage good behaviours or to discourage bad ones.

Positive punishment is when a responsibility or duty is added to decrease the chance an unwanted behaviour will reoccur. In an office setting, an individual who is significantly late to a meeting may be asked to stay and clean up the conference room. The goal is to ensure that individuals respect each other's time and to decrease the chance that the individual will be late for meetings in the future.

Positive reinforcement is when a reward is used to increase the frequency of the desired behaviour. For example, an individual who hits their sales quota might be rewarded with an Employee of the Month certificate and a small bonus. This extra perk motivates the individual to achieve their sales quota again the following month. The goal is to motivate other individuals to want the same reward.

Negative punishment is when something desirable is taken away as a penalty for undesirable behaviour. For example, if an individual badmouths the company or a peer, they might be removed from their role as a project leader. By removing something desirable, the chance the individual will engage in that behaviour again decreases.

Negative reinforcement is when something undesirable is taken away to increase a desired behaviour. For example, as an incentive for their hard work, the team with the highest sales quota for the month might be given permission to skip the weekly sales training on Friday afternoons. Making attendance optional serves as a reward and motivates all the sales teams to shoot for the highest quota the following month.

The use of the four quadrants needs to be balanced. No single quadrant is better than the other. They each do different things. It's also important to consider factors such as mental state, skill level, motivation style, leadership style, and the environment when applying the four quadrants theory. That way, the best decision is made for the business and the individuals. Understand that the success of the Four Quadrant Theory always depends on the person applying it—typically the manager—as it's up to them to apply more or less of each quadrant at any point in time. Pay attention to each individual and see how they respond (favourably or not) to each action taken.

Personally, I do not like the carrot-and-stick approach; however, I've included it in this book because it is a popular tool and part of the quadrant paradigm. You do not need to use it, but knowing it exists gives you more options, and you can choose to use it or not.

Think about how this information might be helpful in your organisation. How would you use the quadrants? What behaviours would you address? What would be encouraged? What would result in punishment? The more explicitly you define your expectations, the easier it will be to measure the success or failure of your intervention.

Love and Appreciation

There is more hunger for love and appreciation in this world than for bread.

Mother Teresa

The COVID pandemic created immense emotional tension on people. Some people have enjoyed spending more time together and relationships have flourished. Conversely, some people couldn't stand spending any more time together and relationships have withered and died.

When people speak completely different languages, then communication is challenging and potentially not feasible. When people speak the same language, there can still be misunderstanding, conflict, and arguments, which, if left unresolved, tend to fester, and may lead to an irretrievable breakdown of the relationship.

So, what's love got to do with BAUU? In *The 5 Love Languages*, author Gary Chapman shared how people give love and how they prefer to receive it.[58] The secret is to speak the right love language. There are five of them, and we each have a primary one. When individuals know their primary love language and that of their partner, then they can communicate using the right language, even though they are different. Another secret is to keep the emotional love tank full. Earlier in the Tower of Life Force, I said your batteries get drained and you need to recharge them. The emotional love tank is another type of battery (tank) we need to recharge (fill). We fill/recharge it by supplying the correct love language.

So, what's appreciation got to do with BAUU? In *The 5 Languages of Appreciation in the Workplace*, Chapman shares how to identify how people give appreciation and how they prefer to receive it.[59] Yes, this is the five love languages reframed and repurposed for the workplace. One way to build stronger connections, elicit positive emotions, and increase engagement is through appreciation. Appreciation is the foundation for motivation.

The five languages of appreciation look like this in the workplace:

- **Words of affirmation** (also known as verbal praise): positive verbal compliments. Congratulate people, express gratitude, give kudos (praise). Personalise compliments one-on-one or in front of others.
- **Acts of service**: expressing appreciation through physical action. Help someone with a task. Have others help you with a task you're working on.
- **Tangible gifts**: a meaningful gift that the recipient values. Their favourite coffee, drink, snack, book, tickets.
- **Quality time**: spending quality time with those you value. Give undivided attention, take time to actively listen. Schedule more time for one-on-one meetings. Create team building activities.
- **Physical touch**: at work with colleagues, this is a tricky appreciation language as in some countries physical touch can end in a lawsuit. So be culturally and legally sensitive. If allowed, a hug, a pat on the back, a high five.

CHAPTER 4 KEY TAKEAWAYS

- Success can only be achieved on purpose and is built by knowing what you need to do and how to go about doing it.
- The Tower of Self is one of four towers in the Inner Keep, and as such, it's internal. It comprises four selves that bridge the know (self-confidence, self-efficacy, and self-worth/value) with the go (self-motivation/ motivation).
  - Self-confidence is knowing and trusting in yourself and your abilities.
  - Self-efficacy is believing in your own ability to succeed.
  - Self-worth/self-value is believing you are worthy of success and that you bring value to the world.
  - Self-motivation (Motivation)
- Motivation is the reason humans do things.
- Self-motivation is the internal force that drives you to do something.
- You can't motive people, individuals motivate themselves.
- Herzberg's two-factor theory divides motivation into two factors: motivators, which encourage a person if present and hygiene factors, and which discourage a person if absent.
- Maslow's hierarchy of needs theory depicts five levels of motivation (physiological, safety, love/belonging, esteem, and self-actualisation). The order depicts ascending importance, the need to grow/ascend, and serves as a roadmap to individual's satisfaction in life and business.

- The Hawthorne Effect teaches that when you show your employees you care about them and their working conditions, you provide motivation that inspires them.
- There is a spectrum of motivation: Amotivation, Extrinsic Motivation (External Regulation, Introjected Regulation, Identification, Integrated Regulation) and Intrinsic Motivation.
- The four quadrants of operant conditioning (punishments and reinforcements) involve adding or taking away aspects of a job as a reward or a punishment to result in the desired outcome.
  - Positive punishment: Add penalty to reduce undesirable behaviour.
  - Positive reinforcement: Add reward to increase desired behaviour.
  - Negative punishment: Remove reward as penalty for undesirable behaviour.
  - Negative reinforcement: Remove penalty as reward for desired behaviour.
- An appreciation journal or jar helps build the selves.
- Setting small, achievable goals and celebrating each win along the way is how goals motivate.
- There are 5 love languages and 5 languages of appreciation in the workplace. Understanding your own and other peoples love/appreciation language fosters stronger connections, elicits positive emotions, and increases engagement.
- Want to know more about the five love languages? Go to: 5lovelanguages.com.
- Want to know more about the five languages of appreciation at work? Go to: appreciationatwork.com.
- Download Chapter 4 resources from RickYvanovich. com/BAUU/.

CHAPTER 4
REFLECTION PROMPTS

What's your **one** key takeaway from this chapter?

```
_____
_____
_____
_____
```

And what else?

```
_____
_____
_____
```

What action will you take right away because of something you read in this chapter?

```
_____
_____
_____
```

And what else?

```
_____
_____
_____
```

CHAPTER 5
THE DUNGEON

THE DUNGEON

*No one escapes pain, fear, and suffering. Yet from pain can
come wisdom, from fear can come courage, from
suffering can come strength.*

Eric Greitens

Dungeon Coaching is an evolution of my coaching philosophy. In this chapter, I'll take you on my evolutionary journey to explain Dungeon Coaching. As you progress through it, reflect on whether you want or need to be the Coach or the Coachee and as you choose to be one or the other, reflect more as to why you chose that.

Coaching and Mentoring Defined

Coaching is an empowering process of unleashing human potential by drawing out solutions from people through effective listening, asking great questions, using feedback, appreciating, and continuously supporting people to take ownership and be accountable for taking action to realise their goals.

Peter Chee & Jack Canfield

The International Coaching Federation (ICF) defines coaching as "partnering with clients in a thought-provoking and creative process that inspires them to maximize their personal and professional potential."[60] ICF also states that coaching is not mentoring or therapy.

So, a coach is someone who helps a coachee (client) unleash their greatness by using various coaching models, tools, techniques and, most importantly, by believing in the coachee. As a coach, it's deeply rewarding to guide coachees on their journey. A healthy coaching relationship is one where the coachee

- feels they are making progress;
- comes away from a coaching session feeling uplifted;
- looks forward to their coaching sessions; and
- is committed to the coaching objectives

Ideally, the coach feels the same way. As a coach, it's not your job to fix people; it's all about guiding them to make the best and most conscious decisions for themselves that also align with and support their goals. It's helping coachees navigate the emotional challenges that occur when they are learning and failing and growing. Most importantly, being a coach is about accountability and commitment (for both coach and coachee).

There are many reasons that stop people from receiving coaching, such as the following:

- They do not want to have someone look closely at their performance or behaviours.
- They do not want to be changed.
- They are unaware of their blind spots.
- Someone is forcing them (against their wishes) to be coached, typically a company trying to fix/change their performance/behaviour.

When this happens, it's important for the coach to focus on their coaching toolbox and meet coachees where they are. Some people need compassion instead of motivation, others need encouragement, and yet others need validation. Whilst a certain strategy might help you stay organised, it might not work for your coachee. As every person is unique, you may need to adjust your approach multiple times before you find a balance that works well for you and your coachee. You can't use a one-size-fits-all approach.

Mentoring is a relationship where a mentor becomes a role model to teach, advise and uplift the mentee through the sharing of knowledge, skills, experiences, and connections that inspires and develops the mentee.

Peter Chee & William Rothwell

The European Mentoring and Coaching Centre (EMCC) defines mentoring as "a learning relationship, involving the sharing of skills, knowledge, and expertise between a mentor and mentee through developmental conversations, experience sharing, and role modelling. The relationship may cover a wide variety of contexts and is an inclusive, two-way partnership for mutual learning that values differences."[61]

Reflecting on the definitions of coaching and mentoring, there are differences between them:

- When you're coaching, you are drawing out the solutions from the coachee and thus helping them move (take action) towards a goal. You are not giving them the answers. It tends to be shorter term (months) as its time bound by the goal(s) of the coaching.
- When you're mentoring, you are pouring into the mentee, sharing your knowledge, skills, experience and providing answers. It tends to be longer term (years) as it's an ongoing relationship and can last a lifetime.
- Subject matter expertise of the coach *is not* a requirement.
- Subject matter expertise of the mentor *is* a requirement.
- Coaching is more performance driven.
- Mentoring is more development driven.

People tend to delay action when they don't know what step to take or in which direction they should be moving. So, when you are *mentoring* someone, you are sharing your knowledge and experience and, in a lot of cases, you *can* provide the answers so the mentee can learn from your experience.

Coaching + Mentoring = Sports Coaching

I certified with CCMP and at first my mindset was to coach or to mentor. When coaching, I experienced that at times I knew the answer and/or had specific experience or knowledge to share. I found it frustrating and challenging to shut up, stay silent, and hold myself back and not give the answer. As a coach, I can ask permission (as should any coach) to give specific advice (à la mentoring) and thus step out of coaching and step into mentoring, then once the advice/mentoring has been given, step out of mentoring and back into coaching. This is necessary to ensure I don't damage the coaching relationship by offering *unsolicited* advice. You dear readers may or may not be aware (apologies if you are aware and know all this) that professional and certified coaches and mentors are bound by rules and guidelines from their certifying bodies, and this stepping into and out of coaching is normal for them.

Some coachees enjoy the coaching relationship specifically because it provides emotional support and accountability *without* being told exactly what to do.

However, for me, by following the rules, I was not in a good place, and the frustrations of flip-flopping (stepping in and out) were negatively impacting literally all aspects of my Inner Keep: How could I stay true? to my life purpose if the coaching was making me feel so stressed and out of balance? Additionally, how was this impacting my clients? Was I failing my clients and myself? I felt my Inner Keep cracking and crumbling.

> *Ask, and it shall be given you; seek, and ye shall find; knock, and it shall be opened unto you.*
>
> *Matthew 7:7*

During the pandemic in 2020, one *aha* moment materialised during CCMC as we were introduced to the concept of sports coaching for business, which blends coaching *and* mentoring. I immediately tried it and offered my clients coaching or mentoring or sports coaching, which I explained. I quickly realised I was more comfortable doing sports coaching, and I began to rebuild and reinforce my Inner Keep as I restored self-confidence and reduced stress.

I was immediately drawn to sports coaching over pure coaching or mentoring as I felt it's both performance and development driven and allows me to seamlessly switch between coaching and mentoring without asking for permission, as it's been agreed we'd not need do that. I felt that sports coaching gives us the option to use all our coaching tools to help drive coachees and mentees forward.

As I practiced, my perception was that sports coaching can leverage the principles of pleasure and pain. We need to make the habits associated with success more pleasurable and the habits associated with pain even more painful. In sports (the exercise kind), we reward the team and players for working hard during games and practice. We show the players what success will look and feel like when it's achieved. We also make it painful to give up, showing players what it would feel like if they were to fall short of their own potential.

Learning about the pleasure and pain principle in sports coaching was another *aha* moment. I realised that the threat of pain gets people to move.

It sounds cruel and nasty, but it's true. Two drivers motivate people to act: pain and pleasure. Some people run towards that shiny medal of victory and others simply run to avoid the pain of not winning a medal. As I reflected on this, it became clear that pain is more powerful than pleasure.

There is an old metaphor about pain. I've come across it many times in the past and it didn't fully register with me until I was asked by Peter Chee (see Dr. Peter Chee below) to help review a chapter of his upcoming *5 Levels of Mastery* book.[62] I've simplified the story below:

A man was sitting on his porch drinking coffee and he heard a dog whining next door. The man wasn't in the habit of getting into other people's business, but he was frustrated by the whining. He finished his coffee, went back inside, and carried on with the rest of his morning. In the afternoon, he returned to the porch to eat lunch, and he could still hear the dog whining.

As he wasn't a heartless man, he was concerned the dog might be suffering. He wondered if his neighbour was home and what might be causing the dog to whine. "I've got to do something about this," the man said to himself. So, he walked next door and saw his neighbour sitting on a porch swing whilst his dog whimpered and whined next to him on the ground.

"Um, excuse me, neighbour," he called over. "Is your dog okay? It's been whining all day. What's going on?" The neighbour waved his hand, "It's funny you should ask. I believe he's sitting on a nail." The man didn't understand. "But if he's sitting on a nail and he's in pain, why doesn't he just get up and move?" "That's the problem," the neighbour said. "He's obviously in pain, but not enough to make him want to move."

This metaphor illustrates how sometimes the pain isn't severe enough to stimulate us to change our situation. Like the dog, we can choose to endure the pain rather than putting in the effort to get relief. To end its suffering from the nail, the dog merely needed stop sitting on the nail. The dog only felt enough pain to whine about it. It was not painful enough to make him move and get off the nail.

I have come to realise that sometimes we must inflict pain. Not physical pain, of course, but make things painful enough to stop the whining and get away from the pain that's causing it. We need to show the coachee that staying on the nail will continue to cause them pain/whining. To get off it, they need to move (take action), and if they are not moving, we make it more painful.

Dungeon Coaching

> *One may live tranquilly in a dungeon;*
> *but does life consist in living quietly?*
>
> *Jean-Jacques Rousseau*

The importance of leveraging pain and pleasure inspired my idea for Dungeon Coaching. The Dungeon Coaching philosophy is based on the idea that growth means change and moving out of your comfort zone. Any resistance is discovered and sometimes painful. But the pain associated with growth is *minor* compared to the pain of remaining the same. I feel it's a coach's job to help illustrate the tremendous benefits that come with growth, and in dungeon coaching that may mean creating more pain.

There are no gains without pains.

Benjamin Franklin

In our Castle metaphor, we are investigating both intrinsically (the four Towers of the Inner Keep) and extrinsically (anything outside the Inner keep) to the individual. We need to work on the intrinsic; it's what keeps humans progressing and fulfilled.

With Dungeon Coaching, it's our job to address the Inner Keep. The more we try to treat or coach the problem (that is, the external conditions in the world), the more disconnected the coachee will feel. Instead, coaches need to help coachees gain awareness of the state of their Inner Keep so that they can discover where to focus and build it up.

As the towers of the Inner Keep build up, coachees take action towards their external goals, with less resistance and greater willingness. Because the Inner Keep can be the hardest area for coaches to access in their coachees, it's important to build that foundation of trust before the coaching even begins so that the environment is more comfortable for both of you.

If there is meaning in life at all, then there must be meaning in suffering.

Viktor Frankl

To make the best of every coaching relationship and feel confident and comfortable entering a coaching dynamic, it's important for coaches to pick coachees carefully. That's right, it's not just up to the coachee to decide if they want to work with the coach. The coach needs to be just as discerning about the coachee they choose to coach. A coach ought not to take on a coachee if it isn't a good match. A good match is not a 100 percent match, but you do need to have established a connection between coach and coachee, resulting in you both feeling it's a win-win situation, or else there is no point in moving forward with a coaching relationship. You won't be an effective coach, and they won't experience their desired transformation if the relationship isn't a win-win. There is power in saying no.

When in a coaching relationship, make each coaching session hyper-focused on what the individual coachee needs and how you as coach can best support them. Coaches should also focus on helping coachees achieve a holistic balance by being cognisant of the development of each of the parts of the castle. For example, it's poor balance if we have one massive tower when another tower has not even started developing yet. It's holistic balance as we balance the development of all the different elements of the castle.

This tends to happen naturally as the coach and coachees develop a more trusting relationship. Coaches need to know when to hold their coachees accountable and when to cut them some slack. Coaches also need to know when it's safe to push their coachees outside their comfort zone and when their coachees might not yet be ready. Balance for each person is as unique as people are unique and have different desires and needs.

And remember, it's all about the coachee. It's important to keep your energy focused on helping the coachee because coaching is all about them (the coachee) and not about you (the coach).

Tap Into the Inner Keep

This is where you can find your soul if you dare. Where you can touch that part of you that you've never dared look at before.

Laurie Halse Anderson

The challenge is to get into the Inner Keep, as individuals are fiercely protective about it, and it's in the Inner Keep that we need to uncover, discover, and challenge beliefs and needs and who the coachee is as opposed to focusing on the problem. The protective reflex is why we need to use pain and probing until we are allowed in to help. We need to remain conscious of the fact that this is the inner sanctuary; thus, we must tread lightly and gently to help nurture it instead of assailing it.

Coachees will get uncomfortable as they move out of their comfort zones. Venturing into uncharted territory means that we go into the situation with fear in our chests, wondering if each step is one step too far. For example, some people fear public speaking. I come across this fear frequently in interns and graduates entering the workforce. Sometimes, this fear manifests as the hesitancy to share ideas in meetings, whether the meeting has a hundred people or only a handful of people. Coaching such an individual, we must be careful not to push too far or too hard. We may need to return multiple times before they feel ready to proceed down a path because change cannot be forced.

Using Dungeon coaching, I typically discover how that fear or resistance might be linked to the Tower of Self (self-confidence, self-efficacy, self-worth/value, self-motivation, motivation). Here are some of the most common fears I hear:

- I don't feel I am worthy enough.
- People won't respect me.
- I'm not confident I can do it.
- I'm going to make a fool of myself.

To help in such scenarios, we need to build up these selves and uncover and document our abilities, successes, and achievements. We can also do this in a workshop scenario with complete strangers. The key is to have someone (ideally, a stranger) point out some of our positive traits. That strengthens the feeling of self-worth/value and self-confidence, and we start the upward spiral of building up all the selves as each self helps support the others:

- When we hear someone pointing out our positive traits, we get a boost to our self-worth/value as we feel we do have value as someone just pointed it out.
- When we get a boost to our self-worth/value we trust more in ourselves and get a boost to our self-confidence.
- As we get these boosts, we are more open to engage in more scenarios like this, boosting our self-motivation as we want to do it again to get a similar boost again.
- As we continue getting more and more input from others, we believe more in our ability to succeed (self-efficacy).

Our empowerment muscles are like a flywheel—once we get it going, it's relatively self-sustaining. Just like any big flywheel, there's some inertia at first, and effort is needed to get things moving.

Empathetic Listening and Laddering

In empathetic listening, you listen with your ears, but you also, and more importantly, listen with your eyes and with your heart. You listen for feeling, for meaning. You listen for behaviour. You use your right brain as well as your left. You sense, you intuit, you feel, 'you have to open yourself up to be influenced.'

Stephen Covey

For the coach to build trust with the coachee, to gain access to their Inner Keep, we can use the techniques of empathetic listening and empathetic laddering.

Empathetic listening is about listening to comprehend. The best empathetic listeners practice repeating what their coachee said in their own words or (re)framing what the coachee said in an empathetic context. An example would be: *My understanding is that you feel [name the feeling the coachee mentioned] because [name the feelings, thoughts, behaviours they mentioned].*

Empathetic listening goes with *empathetic laddering*. It's the "and what else" question reframed in an emotional context to dig a little deeper into the feelings/emotions of the answer. It's stepping into the shoes and understanding the perspective of the coachee. Empathetic laddering allows the coach to dig deep without placing a burden on the coachee to share anything specific. This technique allows the coachee to remain in control of the conversation, enabling them to share incrementally parts of their Inner Keep without you taking a wrecking ball to the tower walls.

When trying this technique, coaches might try asking questions such as the following:

- And what else? (Reframe it as an emotion to dig deeper.)
- How did you feel about that?
- When did you last feel that way?
- What triggered that feeling within you?
- What do we need more clarity about?

The coach needs to be curious which triggers them to ask questions. You are empowering your coachee to make more informed and empowered actions and make choices for themselves.

Coaching Gurus

If I have seen further, it is by standing on the
shoulders of giants.

Sir Isaac Newton

There are many great people who back up their teachings with proven tools and philosophies. We do not need to reinvent the wheel. A place to start is by learning from the greats, applying what you learn, and then improving upon it. We can facilitate growth and progress when we reach out to ask for help. My intense desire to learn more about myself, my ability to lead in business, and my use of coaching to help people grow triggered me to enrol in the Certified Chief Master Coach (CCMC) certification, where I have learnt from some of the best coaches in the world as well as become part of a community of master coaches.[xiii] Part of CCMC's philosophy is the idea that to see and go further, we (as people and coaches) "ride on the shoulders of giants." That quote always stayed with me because it's so inspiring. The idea that we can become good enough to stand on the shoulders of these giants is a powerful image. Standing on their shoulders evokes the feeling of flying higher and seeing further in every direction. It resonates with the tall towers of the Inner Keep.

I have been fortunate to learn from some of the top coaches in the world. From each of these experts, I have gleaned slivers of knowledge, universal laws, and scientific truths, all of which have

---

[xiii] The Certified Chief Master Coach (CCMC) certification is provided by ITD World. This International Coach Federation (ICF) approved program enables leaders for various coaching competencies including life coaching, executive coaching, disruptive team coaching, strategic business coaching, and coaching culture. For more information, visit RickYvanovich.com/BAUU/.

impacted my personal coaching philosophies and helped grow my Inner Keep.

There's a cliché that you've got to learn from the best to be the best. The people in this chapter have informed, influenced, and resonated with me and my coaching. I hope they resonate with you too and pique your curiosity further.

Dr. Marshall Goldsmith

Successful people become great leaders when they learn to shift the focus from themselves to others.

Marshall Goldsmith

Marshall is the number one executive coach in the world, and his mission is simple: to help successful leaders achieve positive, lasting changes in behaviour for themselves, their people, and their teams. With four decades of experience helping top CEOs and executives overcome limiting beliefs and disempowering behaviours to achieve greater success, Marshall doesn't need any more fame or accolades. He does this work because he genuinely loves helping people.

Marshall is a beacon of altruism, and it's not just hollow words. He demonstrates his commitment to giving every day in his business and personal life. If you visit his website, you'll see he gives away his materials for free. During the CCMC program, he coached me one-on-one, and that was an unforgettable, inspirational, and transformative experience.

Having learnt so much from Marshall, I believe two main components of his work, in particular, have shaped me and I trust you'll love them too: **Feedforward** and **I Need Your Help.**

Feedforward

*Feedforward represents other people's ideas that
you should be using in the future.*

Marshall Goldsmith

Marshall's Feedforward concept is an antidote to traditional feedback.[63,64] Feedback's major shortcoming is that it addresses only what took place in the past. However, Feedforward gives people multiple non-judgemental suggestions for the future and thus gives them the option to choose which suggestion(s) to use to help them achieve their goal. Feedforward is particularly helpful when you need to effect a change in behaviour in cases such as the following:

- A successful adult who has no interest in changing.
- A partner/husband/wife/friend who isn't making an effort to change.
- A parent who is stuck in their ways.

Just because you hash out a past problem with someone doesn't mean they will have the tools or the know-how to make a different choice the next time they are faced with a similar situation. Unless someone is willing to change their behaviour, traditional feedback won't have much effect on that person.

Feedforward helps shift the focus from the past to the future, and for that reason, it is my current favourite. It's a non-judgmental, future-focused, empowering, and autonomous tool that can be used with individuals and with teams to bring about behavioural change. It's one of many introductory building blocks for trust, team building, and high performance in teams. When applied well, Feedforward can shift entire cultures within a team or a company.

From a team perspective, Feedforward is about having the most high-performing group dynamic possible. Instead of pitting team members against one another by forcing them to compete for the same bonuses and promotions, it's much more beneficial to encourage each team member to leverage their own skills, so all members can encourage and support one another to reach the collective goals. When we have an aligned and well-supported team, then the individuals will also be high performers. When all our teams are high performing, we'll have a high-performing organisation.

I Need Your Help

To help others develop, start with yourself.

Marshall Goldsmith

Another of Marshall's concepts, *I Need Your Help*, is about having that courage and authenticity to say, "I don't know how to do that. Can somebody help me?" In a competitive business environment, people sometimes worry about admitting shortcomings or gaps in knowledge to their immediate leaders. Sometimes it's a matter of pride, but other times, it's imposter syndrome or fear.

I immediately thought of this principle whilst reading Jocko Willink's 2018 book *The Dichotomy of Leadership*.[65] One dichotomy is that you can't be a perfect leader unless and until you show authenticity. Contrary to popular belief, to be an authentic and trustworthy leader, you must demonstrate that you don't always have the answers or know how to do things. Executives make the mistake of thinking they must be the smartest person in each field and sector they oversee when really, they need to be the best at leading and managing the business.

For example, if you're running a business, you should be an expert on running your entire business from a leadership and management perspective. Running your business doesn't mean being a digital marketing or technology expert; it's about leading, motivating, and supporting the people you hire for those roles. In turn, the people you hire to run digital marketing should be digital marketing experts, and the people you hire to create your websites should be technology and design experts.

If you act is if you know all the answers, people won't trust you. And honestly, why should they?

Dr. Peter Chee

In my previous book, *Habits for Success*, I talked about Jim Sirbasku, who sparked something in me, and Deiric McCann who acted as a catalyst.[66] If you were to synthesise those two together, you'd get Peter.

Peter is both the fuel and the accelerant, and he's one of my coaches. Peter has been coached and mentored by Marshall. I'm privileged to call Peter not only my coach but also my mentor and friend. Peter coaches and mentors from a place of energy, love, happiness, and success. He regularly volunteers to coach leaders, using his signature Sunrise Eureka Beach Coaching which is legendary in the coaching community.[xiv] Peter has helped transform the lives of hundreds and thousands of people worldwide.

I first became aware of him at a distance in 2012 and then more personally in 2018 when I first attended the CCMP certification from ITD World, which Peter created and taught.

Peter is a force of nature, and his teachings are extremely relevant to our discussion of Business As UnUsual. My biggest takeaways from my time with Peter to date have been:

[xiv] For more information, see https://itdworld.com/gcce-love-the-world-initiative-by-itd-world/, or https://www.100coaches.com/coaches/peter-chee/.

- He's full of energy and curiosity, and shares ideas about how to make things better, how to improve models. He asks for and tests ideas. It's very uplifting for all involved.
- He continuously checks in with people he has coached (like me) to see how things are going and how he can help further growth.
- His models are situational, so they're flexible, and that inspires me and others to build models that are flexible and agile, too.

One of Peter's best innovations is his Situational Coaching Model (SCM), which comprises six patterns you can use to navigate a coaching conversation and was featured in the book, *Coaching for Breakthrough Success.*[67]

A genius coach knows how to shift seamlessly
from one conversational paradigm to another, to best meet
the needs of the situation for optimum results.

Jack Canfield and Peter Chee

Mastering conversational paradigms means knowing how to move a conversation forward to inspire immediate action in those around you by focusing on the solution instead of the problem. By moving away from blame and toward corrective action and support, Peter gets people excited about working on solutions.

Dr. Marcia Reynolds

People need to feel seen, heard, and valued
to have the desire to grow.

Marcia Reynolds

In her book, *Coach the Person, Not the Problem: A Guide to Using Reflective Inquiry*, Marcia teaches the art of reflective inquiry.[68]

"Reflective statements include recapping, labelling, using metaphors, identifying key or conflicting points, and recognising emotional shifts. *Reflective inquiry* combines questions with reflective statements."[69] When you reflect a person's words, you give them the opportunity to process information differently. When the coachee hears their own words repeated out loud, their brain can process the information more objectively and come up with their own solutions. In doing so, they will find deeper understanding. It's about creating transformation through conversation. Marcia is a supremely experienced coach who shows us that to change an outcome, we need to coach the person to create their own solutions instead of coaching on the problem. During one of her CCMC sessions on the topic of coaching leaders, enabling people to do things without you, she explained it's all about shifting from "I" to "we" to "they." That was a huge *aha* moment (the shift from we to they) for me and was the tipping point when I just got it.

Another great contribution is Marcia's *ripple effect* theory, which states that the full impact of an action reaches well beyond the spot where the stone falls into the pond. The impact you have on a coachee ripples beyond the individual and affects everyone with whom they connect and interact. When a coachee shares your knowledge with others, your impact ripples even further.

John Mattone

Nobody sees your "Inner core" except you... if you choose to see it.
If you do, this becomes the key to unleashing
your massive leadership potential.

John Mattone

John is the world's top executive coach. He was Executive Coach to Steve Jobs. When John speaks, it makes me want to sit up and listen. From John's sessions during CCMC, he shared his belief in four pillars that support authentic and intelligent leadership: Growing your leadership, growing your leadership, Securing your legacy, and securing your legacy. I reflected on what he said, read several of his books, articles and blogs and I share with you my takeaways and understanding of the four pillars.

- Igniting your inner core. The inner core refers to an individual's character, sense of self, values, thoughts, emotions, references, beliefs, and behavioural tendencies. These inner core strengths make each individual *"individual"* and thus unique. Igniting the inner core means *"everything that matters in life is determined entirely by the strength, maturity, and vibrancy of our inner-core."*[70] This resonates with the Inner Keep of the Castle and the concept of building strong and tall towers.

- Growing your leadership. John defines leadership as a set of inner qualities and competencies that allows a person to inspire and guide a team toward a common goal.[71] This resonates with my own life purpose (Chapter 1) and the Castle (via leadership in the Great Hall, Chapter 6), the Tower of Purpose (Chapter 1) and the Tower of Mind (Chapter 3).

- Living an abundant life. John says, "[t]he way to get ahead in life is to adopt the abundance mindset and create abundant value for others... It may seem counterintuitive at first, but giving people value is the only perfectly logical way to attain success in leadership and life in general."[72] With an abundance mindset, we believe in unlimited opportunities created through collaboration and providing value to others. This is also a win-win attitude which is another ingredient to lasting success.

- Securing your legacy. John says, "Every leader should be concerned with their legacy, not only for their own reputation, but for the well-being of the overall organization... Everyone knew that Steve Jobs couldn't possibly be replaced, and he knew it, too. But he also knew that his legacy could be carried on because of the way he infused the entire organization with passion for creativity and innovation."[73] Steve Jobs is a good example of a legacy. Legacy is part of the Tower of Life Purpose (Chapter 1).

John began embracing these four pillars in 2010 at the age of fifty-two, which he claims is better late than never, and so he urges people to act now rather than waiting later in life as he did. Here are two more sharings from John:

- The 50 Laws of Intelligent Leadership
- The Four A's

John Mattone's 50 Laws of Intelligent Leadership

Law #48: You will never achieve anything worthwhile in life unless you have also brought Abundant value to others—in your personal life and in business.

John Mattone

I'm inspired by John's 50 Laws of Intelligent leadership, which he encourages us to read, reflect, and share, which is why I mention them here so you can benefit from them too.[xv]

[xv] John Mattone's 50 Laws of Intelligent Leadership can be downloaded from his website https://johnmattone.com/wp-content/uploads/2020/01/JohnMattone_50LawsOfIntelligentLeadership.pdf.

The Four A's

*The 4 A's are the seeds to achieving sustained greatness in
leadership, life and creating a lasting legacy.*

John Mattone

The Four A's are altruism, affiliation, achievement, and
abundance. John believes these are the seeds for achieving
sustained greatness and creating a lasting legacy.

Altruism can be best understood as putting the well-
being of others before ourselves. Some understand altruism
as karma, whilst others interpret it as energy. Our hearts feel
good when we contribute to our community. Altruism is
about selflessness and the commitment to doing as much good
as possible in every personal interaction.

Affiliation is essential, and I love that John includes it here.
The quality of our life and business is determined by the quality
of every one of our relationships. The people you affiliate with
both inside and outside your business will impact your business.
We become like the five people we spend the most time around,
so treating every minute of your time as precious helps leaders
make smart affiliations.

Achievement can be boiled down to a basic human need.
Success is much harder to come by if we are not actively growing,
hitting milestones, and achieving things. Small achievements are
stepping-stones to more significant achievements. But unless
we conquer the mountain we're on, we can never conquer the
next, bigger one. Achievements can be small or big, personal, or
related to business. All of it helps to keep leaders motivated and
focused despite outside turbulence.

Law #4: Go forward every day committed to worthy achievement, being altruistic, and building rewarding relationships with the people in your life.

John Mattone

Abundance has become a popular word in the coaching realm. When you hear *abundance*, your mind might jump immediately to money—the smell, the colour, the texture. But physical money is only one area of abundance. We can also have an abundance of innovative ideas, love and support, or even joy and play. When we feel abundant, we open ourselves to the expanse of ideas and limitless potential that exists within us all.

Mark C. Thompson

When I attended his session at CCMC, I found Mark to be exceedingly humble. He is one of America's top leadership transformation coaches. I was amazed by the story he told about being a schoolboy who landed in detention along with another boy, who happened to be Steve Jobs. Mark's business mentor (and partner) is, to my surprise and delight, Dr Marshall Goldsmith.

Mark's work is important to our discussion of Business As UnUsual because of his focus on humility, his dedication to learning from the best, and his four daily active questions (DAQs), which are the following:

1. Need to have people commit to change.
2. Don't see yourself as the expert.
3. Find something to love about the person you coach.
4. Don't take every client. Find the chemistry.

These DAQs help executives focus on the most important aspects of their roles as leaders in their organisations instead of seeing themselves as the "boss." These aspects encourage leaders to stay curious, humble, focused, and aligned with their mission.

Humility doesn't actually mean being humble.

Mark C. Thompson

Thompson asks us to recognise humility as a key trait in top-level leaders. But, as he notes, "Humility doesn't actually mean being humble." Humility is the ability to accept there are things you need to learn and commit to improving if you want to remain at the top. If we are willing to admit we don't know it all, we are humble. Hiring people who are smarter than you, for example, might threaten the ego of someone striving to be the smartest person in the room. Mark encourages leaders to hire people who are smarter than they are.

As a leader, hiring people who are smarter and more capable than you pushes you to innovate and focus on your own role and responsibilities instead of micro-managing others. Surrounding ourselves with the best people in our field makes our businesses grow stronger.

Dr. William Rothwell

Dr. William Rothwell's CCMC topic was about providing a coaching culture for sustainable growth. He's written a lot of books, about 150 of them, and I sense he's a walking encyclopaedia. His teaching style is a mix of intellectual and straightforward, and I like his systematic and formulaic approach to coaching because I think the same way.

Dr. William Rothwell's contribution to BAUU serves as a reminder that we can use many different theories and processes to create an aligned and successful coaching culture. It was

Dr. Rothwell who realised that different people have different needs in a coaching relationship, and just as each person needs a different type of motivation and support, they also need a variety of engagement strategies. Coaching styles can be visualised in the *Figure 14* below.

- The vertical axis ranges performance between the job and personal.
- The horizontal axis ranges from directive to non-directive:
  - Directive: this is pushing them/telling them what to do.
  - Non-directive: this is pulling them asking them what to do.
- In the centre, we have **collaborate** as the concept is to remain centred.

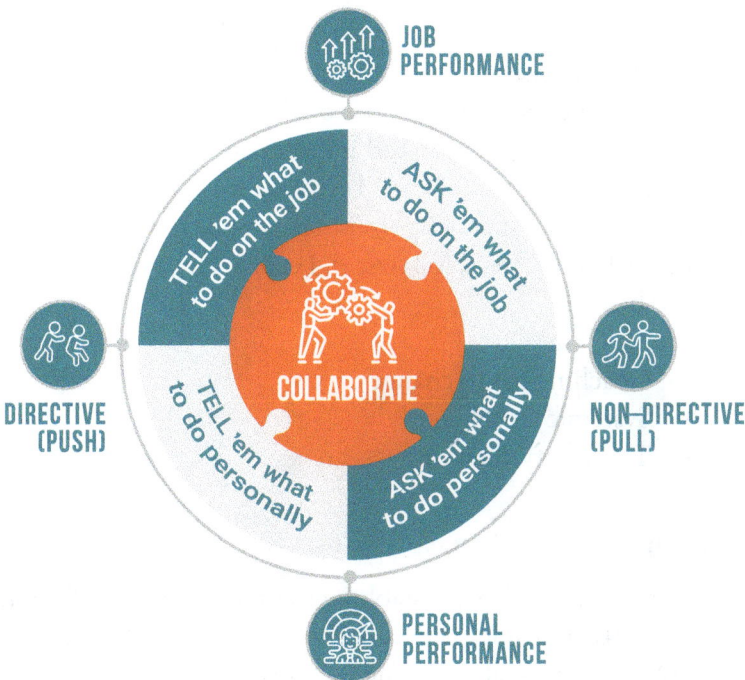

Figure 14. Coaching Styles

With these styles in mind, we can leverage the right cultural style, motivational type, and relationships with individuals to create larger cultural shifts within teams and enterprises.

Dr. Peter Hawkins

The biggest challenges lie not in the individual people but in the connections between them and between one team and another and the organisation and its stakeholders.

Peter Hawkins

Dr. Peter Hawkins CCMC topic was on group, team, and systemic coaching. He's also written a slew of books, and the one that especially captivated me is titled *Systemic Coaching: Delivering Value Beyond the Individual*.[74] In this book, Peter focuses on the connection between people and the positive ripple that happens when a person becomes aware of their current behaviours, beliefs, and impacts on stakeholders. This empowers them to make better behavioural choices because of this awareness. My most important takeaways from Peter in the context of BAUU are as follows, and explained in separate sub-sections below:

- Coaching has to change
- Systemic Coaching
- The empty chairs

Coaching Has to Change

Thomas J. Leonard first established coaching as a profession in the 1980s, and since then, coaching has achieved a lot with multiple professional coaching organisations being formed. Coaching is a field that moves quickly because we are constantly expanding our knowledge and methods as business and technology adapts. For this field to continue to grow, we need to provide new services and ground-breaking ideas that will allow the industry to continue to evolve along with the needs of the coachees it serves. The tools and techniques that got us to this point are already old and need to be reviewed, updated, and if necessary, replaced.

Two questions Peter poses are these: "What can coaching uniquely do that the world of tomorrow needs?" and "How do we gear up for tomorrow's needs?" These questions challenge coaches (and the coaching industry) to look beyond the current problem being coached and consider the future.

Peter shares that we must change from coaching twentieth-century leaders (individuals) to coaching twenty-first century collective leadership (everyone). Collective leadership refers to the process by which people come together to pursue change. It's a process aimed at accomplishing the collective (organisational) goals as opposed to individual goals and as such requires collective/coordinated action.

Systemic Coaching

Systemic coaching is the concept that coaches can and should deliver value that extends beyond the individual. Typically coaching involves two people, the coach and the coachee. In team coaching, a coach (can be more than one coach), coaches the team as a whole and as necessary, the individuals in the team.

Systemic coaching works with individuals, teams, groups, organizations, or systems on their interdependent relationships. It's working beyond the one-to-one coaching. Systemic coaching reinforces the notion that a company can't have a bunch of hard-working, highly motivated people who are all independent of each other. It helps align everyone's goals and bring groups closer to the company's mission, vision, and goals.

Peter and co-author Eve Turner argue that "coaching needs to step up to deliver value to all the stakeholders of the coachee, including those they lead, colleagues, investors, customers, partners, their local community, plus the wider ecology."[75]

The Empty Chairs

The Empty Chairs is a visualisation technique Peter coined to help coachees gain perspective outside their current lens. This activity involves closing your eyes and imagining that there are empty chairs in front of you. Now imagine your children/ grandchildren/partner/customer/co-worker, sitting in that chair. When we want to look at things from different viewpoints, we use the empty chairs as a prop to visualise a situation or problem from another person's perspective.

To get a lighter, more playful lens on a situation, I might sit in my daughter's chair. Suddenly, my problems seem to melt away and the only thing that matters is that my family and I exist right now. Sometimes, this lens helps me see a problem as a fun challenge or as a chance to connect with another person.

To get a practical lens, I might take the seat of my partner or co-worker. To get a creative lens, I might take the seat of an innovator or genius in my field. Whatever chair I imagine myself in, I always make sure that I do, in fact, carry those perspectives into my professional and personal experiences.

Peter Bregman

> *To get the right things done, choosing what to ignore is as important as choosing where to focus.*
>
> *Peter Bregman*

Peter Bregman's focus at CCMC was on strategic business coaching. He made it clear that his commitment is to impact, not to coach; consequently, he's not wedded to any particular coaching methodology. This appeals to me and my Dungeon coaching, which is an evolving collection of tools used to impact and get end results. My big *aha* moment was his Big Arrow process.[76]

In any organization, one of the biggest challenges is to make sure everyone is aligned and moving in the same direction. Instead of having several groups moving at their own rate and in their own direction, the Big Arrow encourages everybody to move in the same general direction (that is, towards similar or aligned goals). When people get off course, you make them aware of the Big Arrow, which helps people redirect themselves.

You start by defining the Big Arrow, which is the overarching direction of your enterprise. Next, you must identify the people in your business who will have the biggest influence in urging everyone to follow the direction. Once your key people understand their respective roles, they can create alignment by ensuring others are moving in the right direction. You'll need to provide some coaching here to ensure your key people have the tools they need to reach goals and overcome any obstacles.

Figure 15. Peter Bregman's Big Arrow

Figure 15 above is based on Peter's 2017 HBR article.[77] In the image example, you can clearly see that on the left, people (represented by arrows) are going in all sorts of directions. The Big Arrow on the right represents a company that is aligned and moving in the same general direction. When represented visually, the concept seems obvious. But as with so many obvious things, we need to experience that *aha* moment for ourselves.

To help align individuals with the larger direction, vision, and goals of the company, leaders can do the following:

1. Define or identify the Big Arrow, typically for the upcoming twelve-month period.
2. Identify the key people who are likely to have the biggest impact on the Big Arrow.
3. Create alignment. Each key contributor must understand their individual key contribution towards the Big Arrow.
4. Coach contributors, helping them overcome any obstacles and providing support.
5. Utilise the Bregman Acceleration Model (BAM)™ to identify gaps and obstacles and work with the team to overcome them.
6. Achieve the Big Arrow outcome and celebrate it.

Peter also leaves us with the sage advice that in leadership coaching, it is not so much about the techniques or skills we employ, but rather the intentions we hold as a coach that impact our coachee the most.

We shouldn't be rigid or get too attached to our models, philosophies, and coaching strategies because, ultimately, people just need to be supported and validated. Coach the real person sitting in front of you instead of trying to flex your coaching muscle and you will get a lot further in your coaching relationships.

CHAPTER 5 KEY TAKEAWAYS

- Coaching comes in many different forms and styles, all are based on the basic principles of trust, asking great questions, and empathetic and active listening.
- A coach guides the coachee's journey, while mentoring becomes a role model to teach, advise, and uplift the mentee.
- Coaching and mentoring are bound by rules and guidelines from certifying bodies.
- Sports coaching allows for a blend of coaching and mentoring without needing permission.
- Dungeon Coaching leverages pain and pleasure for growth.
- Empathetic listening and laddering build trust between coach and coachee.
- Discover the top coaching gurus around the globe and stand on the shoulders of these giants.
- Feedforward is a non-judgmental tool that helps achieve behavioural change and can transform cultures.
- "I Need Your Help" is about admitting you don't know everything and seeking help.
- Authenticity is a necessary trait for a perfect leader. Leaders should lead, motivate, and support their team, not necessarily be experts in every field.
- The Situational Coaching Model (SCM) comprises six patterns that can be used to navigate a coaching conversation.
- Reflective inquiry combines questions with reflective statements to create transformation through conversation.
- Living an abundant life means adopting an abundance mindset and creating abundant value for others.

- Hiring people who are smarter and more capable than oneself pushes leaders to innovate and focus on their role and responsibilities instead of micro-managing others.
- By leveraging the right coaching style, motivational type, and relationships, teams and enterprises can create larger cultural shifts.
- Coaching needs to deliver value to all the stakeholders of the coachee, including those they lead, colleagues, investors, customers, partners, their local community, and the wider ecology.
- The Empty Chairs is a visualisation technique to help coachees gain perspective outside their current lens.
- The Big Arrow process encourages everyone to move in the same general direction towards similar goals.
- Download Chapter 5 resources from RickYvanovich. com/BAUU/.

CHAPTER 5
REFLECTION PROMPTS

What's your **one** key takeaway from this chapter?

```
_____
_____
_____
```

And what else?

```
_____
_____
_____
```

What action will you take right away because of something you read in this chapter?

```
_____
_____
_____
```

And what else?

```
_____
_____
_____
```

CHAPTER 6
THE GREAT HALL

THE GREAT HALL

It's not what you know or who you know, its who knows you.

Susan RoAne

In medieval times, the Great Hall functioned as the social hub of the castle and its surroundings. It was here that the Lord and Lady of the Castle (that's you!) entertained the community. They created, strengthened, and maintained their connections with society by gathering, meeting, conversing, laughing, and cooperating with one another.

The Great Hall in our Castle metaphor depicts these:

- **Community**—where people connect.
- **Culture**—which nurtures the community and builds trust, friendships, and skills, enabling the people and the community to grow.
- **Leadership**—what type of leader do you wish to be?

Community

I alone cannot change the world, but I can cast a stone across the waters to create many ripples.

Mother Teresa

Family

The golden way is to be friends with the world and to regard the whole human family as one.

Mahatma Gandhi

Arguably, the family, as a social institution, has declined since the beginning of history. In decades past, multiple generations lived in the same household. However, today increased mobility, instant communication, and affordable housing makes this moment in time something for the history books, as families and households become more fragmented, especially with the advent of the nuclear family.

During the pandemic, some of us found ourselves locked down in the same household with our family, whilst others were kept apart by extreme restrictions on mobility. This has created an interesting dynamic and a dawning realisation for many that, yes, family *does* matter and thus multigenerational has been much renewed. Regrettably, many of us needed a global pandemic to open our eyes to this truth.

Family doesn't always mean blood relations. These could be people who supported you during challenging times, were loyal to you, protected your interests, made time for you, or even made you soup when you couldn't taste anything because you were sick with COVID. Just as you cultivate your other relationships, it's important to appreciate and nurture your relationships with the people in your family.

Friends

Good friends make us better people. They cheer us on when we hit bottom and keep us humble when we reach the top.

Simon Sinek

You remember friends, right? Those were the folks you used to go out to happy hour and dinner with before the lockdowns. The pandemic has given us time to rethink our relationships with our friends and how we have been showing up for them. Who have we missed? Who haven't we missed? Who have we forgotten? Who was there for us when we needed them?

As you grow, it can be hard to navigate the space of adult relationships due to shifting societal expectations. It's harder to meet people (are we relying on an App to connect us to a human?).[78] Remember that all relationships take time and energy to cultivate. Old friendships need just as much energy to stay strong and connected as new friendships, and both are worth the investment.

Network

Networking is not about just connecting people.
It's about connecting people with people, people with ideas,
and people with opportunities.

Michele Jennae

As your network grows larger and your impact spreads, you will be able to help more and more people. Your value and contribution to the world increase when you provide a product or service to increasingly larger numbers of people. In BAUU, we don't grow our networks the old-fashioned way by making connections over Scotch. Today, we join networks and associations that help us level up in life and business. So, get involved with organisations such as your local Chamber of Commerce to meet people, network, and share interests. I've had excellent first-hand experiences with the British Chamber of Commerce in Vietnam,[xvi] the American Chamber of Commerce in Vietnam,[xvii] and Eurocham Vietnam,[xviii] all of which have opened new communities to multiple people who turn into friends and business partners. Start with local events and grow outward from there.

Professional groups are another way to meet like-minded peers. As an accountant, I belong to multiple professional bodies. As you gain qualifications and certifications, be sure to join those associations and alumni groups, too. LinkedIn is

---

[xvi] The British Chamber of Commerce Vietnam: https://britchamvn.com/.

[xvii] The American Chamber of Commerce Vietnam: https://www.amchamvietnam.com/.

[xviii] The European Chamber of Commerce in Vietnam: https://eurochamvn.org/home-page/.

another growing platform where you can join relevant groups and discuss topics with industry peers.

Paid mastermind groups are full of growth-oriented and innovative thought leaders. For example, I belonged to Executive Global Network (EGN) whilst they were in Vietnam. Later, EGN exited and the Business Executive Network (BEN) emerged, where I continue to be an advisor and contribute to their magazine C-Vietnam as a columnist.[79] The connections I make through these organisations easily tripled my company's ROI, as they have helped me meet many interesting people.

Community Service

*Unless someone like you cares a whole awful lot,
nothing is going to get better. It's not.*

Dr. Seuss

We learnt before in the Tower of Purpose (Chapter 1) that it's not about us, but rather, what we can do for others. Community service is one way to make it about others and give back. Try serving your community a few different ways and see what resonates. Don't be surprised when you meet other like-minded individuals who are doing the same thing. Before you know it, a group of you will be working together.

When you have a good attitude and put some time and energy into helping others and providing valuable advice, you will naturally grow a community that values you and your work.

Growing Connections

Every person is a bridge to someone or something else.

Bobby Umar

Growing your connections is vital for expanding The Great Hall. However, as our pandemic-tainted world was primarily virtual, we needed to find new ways to connect and make new connections.

Before COVID, we used to meet for lunch, chat over coffee, and gather around the water cooler at the office. In today's WFA (Work From Anywhere) world, even though we now meet virtually, we can still get together for lunch, coffee, or a group chat. Activities such as these are critical for building a virtual network, and we should do all those things with *video on*.

Remember your first day of school? You walked into the classroom, and no one in the room knew each other. As you walked in, some people looked up and turned away, others looked up and smiled, and yet others beckoned you to take the seat next to theirs. And then, there was that person hidden behind a screen. You knew someone was hiding there, but you couldn't see who it was.

Questions:

- How did you feel when people looked away? Happy, annoyed, sad, relieved, anxious, uncomfortable?
- How did you feel when people smiled at you? Happy, annoyed, sad, relieved, anxious, uncomfortable?
- How did you feel when people invited you to sit beside them? Happy, annoyed, sad, relieved, anxious, uncomfortable?
- How did you feel when that person was hiding behind the screen? Happy, annoyed, sad, relieved, anxious, uncomfortable?
- With so many empty seats in the room, where do you decide to sit?
- Next to someone who turned away?
- Next to someone who smiled?
- Next to someone who invited you to take the seat next to theirs?
- Next to the person hidden behind the screen?

Whether you are the new kid in school or a newbie entering a company, that's what happens in face-to-face life, although I'm pretty sure no one will be hiding behind a screen at the office. The real questions then become, if you are in the room and someone walks in, how do you want to behave and how do you want to be perceived?

- Do you want to turn away and be seen as unfriendly?
- Do you want to return the person's smile and be seen as friendly?
- Do you want to invite the person to sit next to you and be seen as open, friendly, welcoming, and inclusive?
- Do you want to hide behind a screen and be regarded as odd?

There is no right or wrong, and it's up to you how you wish others to see you. I've posed this question to over one hundred virtual interns in the last year, and none of them wanted to be the person who looked away or the one who hid behind a screen. They all want to be the smiling person, and many were happy to invite the newbie over to sit with them.

In a hybrid virtual world, how do we do this, exactly? With camera and video on! You can't see anything with the camera and video off, and we lose the benefit of being able to see each other's body language and facial expressions.

Imagine logging on to meet your co-workers on your first day, only to discover they can't see you or you can't see them. It's awkward, at best, and disrespectful at worst.

We shouldn't focus only on seeing one another's faces. We also need to socialise with our work peers. That is where virtual coffee comes into play. Virtual coffee is simply the act of reaching out and inviting at least one person you do not know to meet you virtually for coffee. Do this every day for at least one month. It's helpful in a new organisation or mastermind group to network with thirty new people each month.

It's one of those skills you don't realise you need, but sooner or later, some bright spark will call this a "best practice." Just remember you read it in BAUU *first—and* you have already made it a habit. You're awesome, remember?

Team building is another component of growing connections and building trust. To trust each other, the individuals on a team need to know each other. So how, exactly, do you go about doing that in WFA? One idea is to start with an ice breaker, which is like those warmup exercises they do at the start of a workshop to help people engage in small talk. The idea is that small talk builds rapport between people. When you conduct virtual ice breakers every week, people begin to uncover some commonality with others.

A virtual ice breaker comprises two steps:

1. Introduce yourself to the participants. Tell people your name, where you're from, where you are located right now, what team you're on, and what your role is.
2. Ask fun, random ice-breaking questions, e.g., "Name something that amazes you?" or "What have you always wanted to learn?"

At virtual icebreakers, we ask questions we normally wouldn't ask each other. It's a BAUU best practice to get used to asking and answering even the most random or unrelated questions. In addition to building rapport, this exercise helps you develop your public speaking skills and helps bolster your confidence when speaking with strangers.

Another way to help build connections is by taking a cultural journey. During this weekly virtual event, someone volunteers to be the cultural ambassador, and they share with other participants information around a cultural theme—for example, the seasonal festivals in Vietnam. Then others share about festivals in their respective home countries and in the areas where they are right now. It's a fun way to learn about other cultures, revel in the group's diversity, and help drive connection and inclusion.

Growing connections comes down to being open-minded, diverse, and inclusive. Connect people whenever you can. Leverage the friends and colleagues you trust to continue expanding your network, and always remember to pay it forward.

Culture

Culture eats strategy for breakfast.

Peter Drucker

Culture, or more correctly organisational culture, refers to an organisation's beliefs and behaviours. It also includes the values the company has adopted and expects its employees to follow. Typically, the corporate culture statement is framed on a wall, posted on the company website, or tucked away in an employee handbook.

Traditional business cultures may feel like a way to keep people in line. Sometimes, they're thrown to the wayside the second the workday begins. But people in the workforce today aren't interested in the hollow promises of positive company culture.

Today's workers know an organisation's corporate culture isn't necessarily found in the words inside a frame on the wall, no matter how beautifully crafted they may be. Rather, corporate culture is defined by what the people within the organisation do and how they do it.

It's not enough simply to say your company is going green to gain more customers who are interested in the same initiative. Sometimes, the company that touts green initiatives on their website may not recycle the large amounts of paper and cardboard they use daily, make toxic products, or leave a hugely irresponsible carbon footprint.

The words only matter when they are true. Corporate culture is not what you say you're about; it's what your people do every day that defines your organisation's culture. When a business doesn't fully embody its values, I call this a lack of alignment. Failing to operate congruently with the values you hold affects the culture of your organisation, its teams, and the dynamics between leaders. I've seen first-hand how this misalignment can threaten seemingly stable industries.

I recently coached the team at a start-up company, helping them form their purpose, mission, and collective values. The entire ten-person company collaborated to identify the defining points of their business. Most were excited to have a clearly defined brand identity when the exercise was finished.

When I spoke with the founders after that initial coaching, I reminded them that when their headcount grows to one hundred, not everyone will be on board with the mission that was created by the initial group of ten, but not the other ninety. And, as new people join the company, the culture may change.

We added some cultural notes to capture the feelings and thoughts of the team so that future employees would better understand. Failing to prepare and manage cultural shifts will lead to a business with differing objectives and directions, i.e., not following the Big Arrow. For example, when each hiring manager is looking for a different type of person to fill their team, or a team leader reinforces a different culture, executives start having problems.

Instead, planning for growth and tying every decision to your mission, vision, and purpose will help each section of your business push forward in the same direction, even as you need to pivot during a global pandemic.

Culture Is Changing

A culture is not invented. A culture constantly evolves...
which is why it must be nurtured.

꙳

Simon Sinek

Shifts in business have been coming for a long time, and then came the black swan curveball of a pandemic. Businesses wobbled or collapsed and are still transforming. The world's economy and culture is still shifting to accommodate the unprecedented conditions. With so many curveballs coming our way, organisations need to look very, very carefully at how they're controlling their company culture.

Culture is the unwritten way people behave. However, as business models shift, it's becoming clear that organisations are not keeping up with how these changes affect their overall culture. Instead of uprooting the old systems and trying something new, they are making 180-degree turns to put a Band-Aid over the cultural issues.

Now is the time we need leaders to be coaches, who actively listen with empathy, help communicate and clarify the organisation's direction, and reinforce the key behaviours of high-performing teams. We need leaders who coach others to embody the company values and work hard to keep the connections with their people open, strong, and inclusive. It's time to open the doors rather than shut them and welcome ideas (remember Feedforward?) to make things better.

That's not to suggest that maintaining control of corporate culture in an era of Zoom meetings is easy. It's not—and I don't mean to imply any criticism of leadership on this point. It's simply a fact that any group of people determines group culture: what they think, what they believe, and how they behave. That means that you—yes, you—shape culture.

Anything can happen if the group is left to run its natural course. Diverse values would emerge if there were enough people in the mix, and people would congregate in their various cliques. This sort of model would perpetuate chaos in the current system. To ensure your business is moving in an aligned direction, it's worth rooting your culture in everything you and your people do.

Mind the Gap

Mind the gap—it's the distance between life as you dream it and life as it is.

Cate Blanchett

A key weakness is that most businesses are now moving to a hybrid work situation where people are unintentionally unaware of how hybrid is supposed to work. They don't know what they don't know. Shifting the corporate culture means businesses must identify the weaknesses in the current culture and provide the tools and skills needed to close that gap.

When business leaders don't know how to communicate virtually, messages get lost, and teams aren't on the same page. When managers don't know how to manage their teams in a virtual world and lack guidelines, teams begin to manage themselves. It's not enough to alter the old playbook. We need to throw it out and start from scratch.

Traditionally, business communications were primarily non-verbal and subconscious. We saw people, gestured to them, smiled at them, and said hello when we walked past them in the corridor. All these physical cues aided our communication, and we took them for granted until they were gone.

In a hybrid work situation, we have only a handful of opportunities during the week to make meaningful contact with other people. Most of the small talk we used to build relationships is gone. Over time, we have found that our peer-to-peer and internal team connections have also weakened because of our weakened communication.

Weak communication can lead to unclear expectations amongst individuals, teams, and peers. The exploding profusion of communications channels can lead to confusion and misunderstandings regarding which channel to use. The next thing we know, the same message is being parroted on multiple channels, which only adds to the confusion. Further, just because a message has been received doesn't mean it's been understood. Thus, we need to communicate with comprehension in mind.

Do these specific challenges apply to you, your team, or your business? Perhaps you need to take inventory of where your communication gaps may lie. For example, maybe you don't have enough people walking the talk or perhaps there's misalignment between personal, team, and organisational values. Whatever the gap, first identify it, be heedful of it, then choose to improve it or not.

Shaping Organisational Culture

If you do not develop your corporate culture it will develop itself.

Monique Winston

We must be cautious about the assumptions we make about the culture of an organisation. One belief is that businesses create a culture and values, stick them up on the walls, and then expect everyone to embrace them. In this type of environment, businesses assume that everyone will continue to understand and believe in those original values; even as teams grow, leaders change and thoughts about culture shift.

Businesses can overlook the fact that people come and go. Teams change over time, and it's the businesses responsibility to plan for those shifts. So, it's not only about creating a culture for now, but also for five or ten or more years down the line.

Businesses can use the ten dimensions of high-performance teams (see below) as levers to change corporate culture drastically in their existing business or use these dimensions to create a solid foundation to build a culture in a new industry. These dimensions aren't typical management skills, but rather, values and priorities you can use to guide your company culture proactively. By embodying these values and creating policies that enforce them, leaders within your enterprise can shift their focus, thoughts, and actions to these values as well.

What we give our attention and energy to grows, and these dimensions are positive. Here are the ten dimensions of high-performance teams that we also use for changing corporate culture that we'll be covering:

1. Unity
2. Clarity
3. Positivity
4. Connectivity
5. Integrity
6. Safety
7. Diversity
8. Agility
9. Accountability
10. Dependability

1. Unity

Unity is number one on our list of cultural dimensions because without it, a group of people could be working very hard, but the business might not be growing. Is the team united in values, vision, mission, strategy, direction, and decision? Do the people on the team share the same values as the business?

*Unity is strength...when there is teamwork
and collaboration, wonderful things can be achieved.*

Mattie J.T. Stepanek

Unity can strengthen the conviction of teams, but it also means that everything in your business is interconnected. Individuals know how their specific roles fit into the larger picture of the company, and everyone is united by a defining mission, vision, and values. These things help build community. Connecting everything you do as a leader to the threads that tie your company together will help create unity regardless of everyone's physical working location.

*We are only as strong as we are united and
as weak as we are divided.*

J. K. Rowling

Communication also helps to bridge unity. How often do you communicate outside your team? Do people from different teams ever have the chance to meet and interact? How often do you encourage unity and communication across leadership levels and projects?

Without unity and trust, team members may feel they cannot rely on one another, communication may falter, productivity and engagement may stagnate, innovation may stop, and the entire workplace might begin to unravel. Improve unity and trust by leading by example and demonstrating your belief in others. Work on communicating openly, allow yourself to be personable, and actively bond with your team.

Looking at unity holistically will drastically shift your people's perspective from the individual *me* to the collective *we*.

2. Clarity

Clarity of vision creates clarity of priorities.

John C. Maxwell

In the past, leadership and business focused primarily on outcomes. Bosses concentrated on the bottom-line and results, but it was primarily up to people working at the company to drive those results.

These days, we (thankfully) know much better. We know that while systems and outcomes are essential to any business, clarity is key to achieving them. Without clarity, people can work very hard and yet fail to achieve tangible results. Does the team have clarity of goals, roles, responsibilities, and expectations? Does each person in the team know the goals, for their own role *and* those of others?

In the book, *21 Irrefutable Laws of Leadership,* John Maxwell wrote that having a clear vision will naturally improve leaders' outcomes in business.[80] In other words, the more you can clarify a person's role and goal, the more defined their daily activities will be. Bringing clarity to the strategy, tactics, objectives, actions, and key results drives each person towards their goals.

With the clarity that comes from having a defined *Why* and plan of action, each person can focus on their respective responsibilities. This helps take any guesswork out of the equation. Focusing on goals and building good habits and work stamina inevitably drives results. When everyone knows their role and goals, the execution of day-to-day tasks becomes easier to manage.

It's far easier to go to the gym every day when you don't need to think about programming the workout (setting up the weights and timing every movement). For example, when you go to a CrossFit® gym, coaches clarify everything before you begin.[xix] Then, they write out a plan, assign a specific workload, and keep track of time and output. This way, all you need to do to improve your physical fitness is to show up and execute their program.

It works the same way for business professionals. Clarity improves the team's ability to execute and change direction confidently, leading to greater overall satisfaction. People have more confidence that they're doing the most important work they can, and they understand why their work matters to the bigger picture. Clarity improves things for your people. Everyone will be happier and more connected in their roles.

3. Positivity

Choosing to be positive and having a grateful attitude is going to determine how you're going to live your life.

Joel Osteen

Positivity is an integral part of corporate culture, particularly in our post-pandemic environment. The world has seen a few bleak years with mental health issues on the rise as a consequence of our increasingly disconnected society. Does your team have positive, consistent, and effective communication with humour and fun? Are people positively communicating with each other, or is negativity putting strain on the team dynamic?

When they have a negativity bias, humans find positivity problematic. Science defines *negativity bias* as the human brain's tendency to skew our thinking toward negative outcomes or

---

[xix] CrossFit® is a registered trademark of CrossFit, LLC.

worst-case-scenarios.[81] As a result, to survive in the wild (and in our current world), humans must be vigilant about anything that threatens our emotional and physical safety. This bias colours the lens through which we view the world to keep ourselves safe from danger. Have you ever kept quiet and not spoken up whilst around a criticising co-worker? That criticising co-worker is like a hyena stalking, waiting to nip at you and laugh.

It is impossible to ignore news coverage of a sinking economy or read every article about how your industry is crumbling. We want to protect ourselves from failure, and consuming knowledge or news can help us prevent that possibility. Negativity bias is why we get caught up in pessimism regarding change and why we can't see anything good in a presentation that (by our standards) bombed.

> *Happiness is when what you think, what you say,*
> *and what you do are in harmony.*
>
> *Mahatma Gandhi*

It's fun to be part of a positive, highly motivated team. Such teams can accomplish more than those that struggle with negativity and low morale. For your team members to be delighted in their jobs, you must first eliminate the causes of dissatisfaction and then add the "motivators" that produce satisfaction (see Herzberg's two-factor theory in Chapter 4).

Positivity increases our ability to think creatively, progress in our careers, cope with challenges, and work with others. It can reduce absenteeism and staff turnover and lead to more satisfied and productive teams. In short, it's an essential ingredient for success!

Focus on a culture of positivity by celebrating hardworking employees, giving peers a chance to acknowledge and thank one another publicly, and assume the best in your people. Achieve positivity through coaching, mentoring, and training.

These are just a few ways you can start increasing positivity in your culture; there are many ways to be creative and co-create with your people, making them part of the process.

4. Connectivity

Individually, we are one drop. Together, we are an ocean.

Ryunosuke Satoro

When operating in the hybrid virtual world, we must behave differently. Each of us must change how we work as hybrid is different and find out where and how we fit into the new picture. To stay connected to our peers, work, and goals, we need to create an internal shift to support us as we navigate this new social and business network.

The number one thing that needs to change is how we connect. We're no longer physically together as in the old days. We have moved into a hybrid world. Now, instead of sharing the same office space, we are dispersed. The way we work has shifted and forced us to learn or relearn how to connect. If you join a new organisation and turn up at the office, you'll find yourself in physical proximity to strangers.

New hires might know the Human Resources person and the others who interviewed them. Aside from those people, the individual probably knows no one else. When you were still working out of a physical office, you might have had some onboarding processes that involved HR or new co-workers taking a new hire to lunch or out for a coffee. Before you knew it, within their first week, the new person had connected with multiple people.

Those were the old days. Now, fewer people go to a physical office. Instead, they are hired over a video conferencing call and their first day is entirely virtual. After that, their entire work life may be virtual for as long as the office remains closed or working in the office remains an option. It's all new territory. Sure, having lunch in front of the computer can be strange if you're not accustomed to it, but we want people to be as connected as they used to be in a physical environment. So how do we achieve that? Is it possible in this hybrid environment? What needs to change? The best way to do this is to treat connection and communication as a package deal integral to modern working culture.

There is likely to be resistance to change. People don't like change in general; and they especially dislike rapid change that happens outside the realm of their control. For example, people may notice resistance to new meeting schedules or policies that require people to turn on video cameras during Zoom meetings. What does that mean for people and connections?

Maybe people are not comfortable turning their cameras on because their hair is messy or they haven't showered, shaved, or put on makeup. Regardless of the resistance, we must find ways to encourage people to appear on camera and speak. Sure, you might come to an internal meeting in a t-shirt. We need to make more of an effort to learn, leverage, and master these new means of connection and communication which are becoming essential tools. We have to find a way to make it work.

The opportunity for random meetings with your co-workers in the halls or break room no longer exists because we're taking breaks at home in our kitchen. Organizations must rethink how connections will work on multiple levels of business. What are the best practices for something new? Nobody seems to know yet. It's so unique; there is no standard practice yet.

5. Integrity

If you have integrity, nothing else matters.
If you don't have integrity, nothing else matters.

Alan K. Simpson

Integrity across all your team members is a defining factor that influences your culture. Do you maintain a high level of inter-personal trust and integrity through your intentions, words, and actions? Do your people do what they say and say what they do?

Lack of integrity can include major things such as waiting until the last minute to let your supervisor know a major presentation won't be ready on time or small things such as volunteering to lead the next meeting and then forgetting to prepare an agenda.

Integrity means having strong ethical and moral principles. It promotes a professional culture in which individuals can depend upon one another and treat each other with respect. As a result, people are typically more productive and motivated at work.

When you are able to maintain your own highest standards of integrity—regardless of what others may do—you are destined for greatness.

Napoleon Hill

Improve integrity by refraining from sharing confidential information with others, remaining honest with others, avoiding gossip, following through on promises, and admitting when you are wrong. People who possess the ability to be gracious, respectful, candid, responsible, and hardworking are often of high integrity and make fantastic team members.

Integrity means that no matter who's watching, you always follow through. Building a culture of integrity will, without a doubt, help propel your business farther than you ever imagined. Maintaining integrity in your corporate culture means always following through as a leader and as a coach and holding others to their word and the same high standard that you hold for yourself.

6. Safety

Psychological Safety is a belief that the context is safe for interpersonal risk-taking—that speaking up with ideas,

questions, concerns, or mistakes will be welcomed and valued
even when I'm wrong. It's a sense of permission for candor.

Amy Edmondson

Safety is a psychological need which, when met, helps motivate us towards accomplishing our goals. "Safety" typically pertains to physical safety and means keeping yourself from harm. But safety isn't limited to physical issues.

Do people feel safe when communicating? Does your organisation perpetuate respect for differences and understanding when resolving conflicts? Do people feel safe, even though they are all different? Can they talk about their problems?

Amy Edmondson, Novartis Professor of Leadership and Management at Harvard Business School, introduced the theory of team psychological safety in 2021 and defined it as "a shared belief held by members of a team that the team is safe for interpersonal risk taking."[82] Psychological safety is a shared feeling that it's OK to be open and honest in a group setting.

When building psychological safety within a team, speaking up and learning from mistakes are encouraged—even celebrated. Employees who feel empowered to engage with others are more likely to act. In a safe environment, individual opinions are heard, valued, and challenged. Having a high level of safety can positively impact a team's ability to innovate by integrating ideas.

Questions are really powerful in creating safety—they
indicate to someone that you actually want to hear their voice.

Amy Edmondson

Edmondson gives five steps for leaders wishing to build psychological safety in the WFA hybrid model.

Step 1: Set the scene. As a leader, you need to make your team aware of challenges and help them recognise any shared challenges. The discussion aims to share ownership of the problem and get your people equally invested in finding solutions.

Step 2: Lead the way. Far too many managers demand more emotional vulnerability and authenticity but don't protect people or make them feel comfortable when they do share. Lead with the values you want to instil in your culture, and others will follow your lead. Be candid about your own challenges of this new reality, but tread lightly.

Step 3: Take baby steps. Before you can run, you need to walk and crawl first. Take time to build authentic trust, and don't be surprised if employees don't bring up their most significant challenges right away. Start by making small, candid disclosures yourself, and encourage others to share, as doing so will build confidence in understanding that sharing will not be penalised. Establishing psychological safety might take time. By working with your people intentionally and incrementally, you will see lasting changes to your company's culture.

Step 4: Share positive examples. Some people at your company will need to be convinced before they can feel psychologically safe. We don't know everyone's history or comfort level with candour, so market the appeal of psychological safety by showing social proof that it helps and provides transparency, but do not force others to conform to the new standard.

Step 5: Be a watchdog. Psychological safety takes time to build but only moments to destroy. Watch the language you use around your team and encourage contribution without pressure. For example, instead of saying, "We could really use you" or "We want to see more of you" or "How about another six a.m. meeting?" try saying, "We miss your thoughtful perspective and understand you face constraints. Let us know if there is any way we can help." Which do you think is more likely to prompt engagement or response?

In short, admit when you are wrong, ask for the team's input, respond positively to questions and doubts, and forgive employees' mistakes without passing emotional judgment. Safety helps increase trust within teams and gives leaders a unique ability to see what is going on under the surface. Having a safe environment enables executives to manage the nuances of this new corporate environment because they know that if a problem should arise, they will hear about it before it becomes something that detracts from a happy and healthy workplace.

7. Diversity

Strength lies in differences, not in similarities.

Stephen R. Covey

We live in a world that's connected by the internet, opening us up to new potential hiring candidates who have a wide range of lived and professional experiences. But *why* the push for diversity? As Covey wrote in his book *The 7 Habits of Highly Effective People*, "We think we see the world as it is, when in fact, we see the world the way we are."[83] If this is true, it means our narrow lens on the world can only see problems or challenges from one angle—ours.

Does your team embrace the diversity of expertise and strengths available for innovative, high-value creation or to gain a competitive advantage? We need to leverage diversity because it is our differences that drive innovation!

Diversity refers to differences between people, such as age, nationality, religious background, functional background or task skills, sexual orientation, and political preferences, among many others. Different types of diversity include demographic, personality, and functional.

When we open our ranks to people who carry their own unique experiences and ways of viewing problems and solutions, we will be more likely to have a variety of problem-solvers engaged in finding the best solution. It's like asking a roomful of artists to draw the same bowl of fruit—each will have a different perspective, depending on where they're sitting *and* their internalized experiences with the fruit. Diversity in business works the same way.

Improve your culture of diversity by hiring diverse individuals! First, seek people whose lens of the world is different from yours. Next, constantly rethink and revisit diversity prioritisation in your company culture. Third, check your biases and train your staff to identify and actively overcome their respective biases. Finally, drive inclusion by seeking out and valuing diverse people and opinions.

> *Diversity is being invited to the party; inclusion is being asked to dance.*
>
> *Verna Meyers*

Having a diverse staff opens leaders to various perspectives that might lead to a new solution for an old problem. In addition, engaging leaders at all levels to leverage their personal experiences and professional backgrounds in their current roles allows them to bring their whole selves to the table. Reinforce their unique personal views by enthusiastically seeking their candid opinions.

Diversity in people results in diversity of thoughts and ideas and that helps improve creativity and innovation, leading to better returns on investment.

8. Agility

> *Agility is the ability to adapt and respond to change. An agile organization views change as an opportunity, not a threat.*
>
> *Jim Highsmith*

I was never much for athletics as a youth. I was short, with a more diminutive stature than most, so the idea of tiptoeing around players twice my size as they ran and collided at full speed was never attractive to me. However, the good news was that I could learn to be agile in ways that didn't involve a football (also known as a soccer ball to you Americans out there).

Agility in Business As UnUsual means anticipating or confronting personal, societal, environmental, or business disruption by treading lightly and having tenacious drive. Agility is the ability to move around and through challenges in a corporate culture without compromising your mission, vision, and goals. In the simplest definition, agility lets you move quickly and easily through obstacles. Agility is also a concept related to our thinking capacity—that is, the ability to draw quick and accurate conclusions under stressful circumstances.

Does your team have agility to improve continuously and learn quickly? Do you have the agility to change as new things come up? Do you make things happen?

Success today requires the agility and drive to constantly rethink, reinvigorate, react, and reinvent.

Bill Gates

We must acknowledge that people will undoubtedly worry about the future in the face of economic challenges and uncertainty. Some might even panic. Agile people focus on the solution rather than the problem or challenge.

Creating agility in your culture can look like encouraging innovation and seeing future adjustments as new and exciting problems or puzzles to solve. Start posing *what-if* questions to practice thinking and feeling your way through challenges that might arise in the future.

Drive agility by identifying this trait in people when you see it in action. Most of us need to be agile to solve minor problems and adjust our sails a bit every day. Make sure those moments don't go by unnoticed within your team. People are more apt to use skills that are applauded, so encouraging agility will empower everyone to embody this trait more often.

9. Accountability

Accountability is the glue that bonds commitment to results.

Will Craig, Living the Hero's Journey

I don't know about you, but I never learned about proper accountability in my business classes. There was certainly no "accountability training manual" that came with my company formation paperwork.

Accountability is the obligation of an individual or organisation to account for its activities, accept responsibility for them, and transparently disclose the results. It's simple: to be accountable to a team, a person needs to be clear about what they plan to do, execute on it, and let others and the team know when it's done. Does your organisation have a similar culture of accountability?

Teams that are not accountable may miss deadlines, encourage mediocrity, and ultimately create resentment among team members who have different performance standards. Accountability means you hold people to a certain standard of integrity and follow-through. We need accountability because relying on integrity alone isn't enough to drive action.

How many times have you told yourself you'd get up before dawn for a workout or sworn that you'd eat more salad? If you're like me, you've probably had similar internal dialogues many times. You commit to your routine for a few days, then the moment the external action stalls, you lose momentum. You hit the snooze button a few extra times, making you miss your workout. Then, you decide to grab a bite at the local burger spot with your co-worker after work. No one is holding you to your commitments, making it easier to slip up.

Accountable teams make sure members feel pressure—to improve, to identify problems quickly by questioning each other, to establish respect among team members who are held to the same high standards, to avoid excessive bureaucracy around management and corrective actions, and so on. Accountability might not mean texting an employee to remind them of their 5:00 a.m. workout, but it might mean checking their presentation a week before it's due to ensure it includes all the necessary information and facts. Accountability means giving people the reins to take on projects that inspire them, holding them to deadlines, and regularly checking on their progress. Accountability also means not calling an employee into your office to interrogate them about why a report was late to ensure it never happens again. We want to be calling people *forward* (again, Feedforward is of the utmost importance!) instead of calling them out.

Within a culture of accountability, leaders cannot shy away from being held accountable themselves. Of course, just because you're at the top doesn't mean you're immune to procrastination, perfectionism, and project overwhelm. Letting others hold you accountable in a supportive way shows a willingness to take uncomfortable feedback if it means bettering yourself and the business—which doesn't go unnoticed.

10. Dependability

Ability is important in our quest for success,
but dependability is critical.

Zig Ziglar

You can have a team of the most brilliant and the most experienced people working for your company, but if they aren't people you can count on to show up in the face of challenges and trials, it could mean the downfall of your business.

Can you depend on your team to deliver consistent results and provide mutual support, recognition, and celebration? Can you depend on each other and celebrate each other's achievements?

Dependability isn't something you can screen for during an interview. Frankly, people grossly overestimate their dependability. Therefore, it needs to be a value you integrate into your corporate culture.

When a team member isn't dependable, they aren't likely to be trusted or well-received by the group. A single undependable team member can upset the entire team dynamic, forcing others to take on more responsibilities to compensate, which leads to working extra hours, and ultimately, to feeling dissatisfied.

Dependable employees have a strong work ethic, are motivated to complete their assigned tasks satisfactorily and take pride in accomplishing their work assignments. In addition, dependability means your team members can count on one another to do their jobs. The Sales team can depend on Payroll to get their pay on time. Companies can depend on the Web team to make sure the company's website looks professional. Dependability requires people to focus on their own roles and responsibilities whilst trusting that their colleagues will execute on theirs as well.

These ten dimensions of corporate culture help shift the organisation's core values to increase the satisfaction and investment of the employees. These values and dimensions become the best influence on people when one commits to adopting them personally, which inevitably ripples throughout the rest of the organisation.

The Losada Ratio

The Losada Ratio is a tool you can use to measure the value of interactions with others. Specifically, this tool helps ensure that we offset any previous negative interactions by making a higher ratio of positive interactions in the future.

An example of a *positive interaction* is when you compliment your colleague on their new outfit. The compliment will likely make your colleague smile for a while, maybe even all morning. That's a *positive*.

An example of *negative interaction* is when you laugh at your colleague's new outfit. Laughing will make your colleague scowl, and the insult may sting for days, if not longer. That's a *negative*.

Whilst small jabs and digs disguised as humour or sarcasm are considered negatives, people can perceive other types of messages as negative too, depending on the tone used to deliver the message and the internal state of the person who receives it.

Barbara Fredrickson and Marcial Losada proposed the critical positivity ratio in 2005 after they researched how groups work.[84] First, they studied teams of eight people as they developed strategic plans and catalogued all their interactions. Then, they classified each interaction as positive or negative and found that they could predict the success of each team based on their ratio of positive to negative interactions. Shawn Achor's book titled *The Happiness Advantage* popularised the concept, which is now commonly known as the Losada Ratio or Losada line.[85] The Losada Ratio is defined as the sum of the positivity in a situation divided by the sum of the negativity. A score between 3.0 and 6.0 is considered high performance, which is in the target range. If the ratio is less than three, you're in a toxic environment, a ratio of three to six is a sign that you're in an uplifting work environment. It is possible for the ratio to be higher than six. In theory, there is no limit, though I'd be curious to learn if such nirvana exists.

Many positive actions need to occur to offset a negative state. If anyone has ever made fun of your new outfit, you know it takes a lot to turn that around. Sometimes, you need an apology from the person who insulted you to make things right.

The Losada Ratio helps ensure we have more positive interactions than negative ones. Ideally, the ratio of positive to negative should be three-to-one or even six-to-one.

Tone from the Top

Where there is great power there is great responsibility.

Winston Churchill

The best leaders are those who boldly embody the values of their business. For example, Ed Catmull valued creativity so much that he let all his Pixar employees (and I'm sure his current Walt Disney Animation Studio employees) decorate their desks any way they wanted. Nothing was too wacky or personal, from chandeliers and beanbag chairs to shiplap and Legos.

In meetings, Steve Jobs valued courage and was known for openly opposing people, even and especially his own people. Why? He wanted to see if they would stick to their guns when he challenged them. Jobs' desire to work with brave and confident people led to Apple's innovation and courage in the tech industry.

Leaders and the values they embody are critical to any cultural shift. Tone and culture start at the top and cascade down. If we, as leaders, aren't clear about the culture of our workplace in this hybrid world, how can anyone else have clarity about it either? Once we have identified company culture and values, we must have employee buy-in. Habits will slide back into the familiar if people don't invest in the cultural changes.

To stop the cultural backslide before it starts, we need the genuine buy-in of key opinion leaders in their business. A key opinion leader (or KOL) is someone whose opinions matter to others. Others notice when the KOL says or does something. The more a KOL resonates with other people, the more the

KOL will influence your people and the more likely they will be to mirror the KOL.

In marketing, KOLs are called influencers. We see them cropping up everywhere as increasing numbers of people monetise their influence on social media. In Business As UnUsual, we look at influence in the context of work and in the qualities KOLs possess, so you can identify them in your organisation.

Not all KOLs influence others deliberately (although marketing influencers do). However, whether they do or don't, the result is the same. In my mind, if an individual is helpful, dependable, and makes good choices, then yes, they will probably be seen as a KOL.

KOLs are trustworthy and credible. Therefore, they influence people by inspiring trust. KOLs tend to be the go-to people for gaining trust and cooperation, for solving problems or dealing with challenges because their opinions are highly valued. However, with great power comes great responsibility. When an individual becomes a KOL, they need to be cognisant of their ego, lest it turn them into more of a prima donna than a KOL with integrity.

KOLs can be at any level in an organisation. They are not necessarily the people with big job titles. The go-to person in any environment, whether it's work-related or not, is probably a KOL. KOLs can just as quickly hinder as much as help corporate culture, strategies, tactics, and actions and as such can be like a double-edged sword. It can cut both ways.

Whenever leaders are looking to change something in their business—in this case, we're looking to shift corporate culture—having immediate buy-in from people is vital. It's known as the First Follower effect.[86] Once the first person, the first follower, buys in, others are more likely to follow, as they know they won't be alone.

It takes guts to be a First Follower! You stand out and brave ridicule, yourself. Being a First Follower is an under-appreciated form of leadership.

The First Follower transforms a lone nut into a leader. If the leader is the flint, the First Follower is the spark that makes the fire.

Derek Sivers

When the First Follower is a KOL, other followers are attracted even faster, and new policies receive more buy-in across the organisation. When the First Follower is not a KOL, it takes more effort to persuade others. I'm not a fan of giving special attention to any individual KOL per se, as I believe in diversity and inclusiveness; thus, everyone's ideas and opinions merit being heard and considered.

To be a leader who people want to follow, you must be inspirational and vision-oriented. We must paint a clear picture of where we're going and clarify how it aligns with the organisational/team/individual's purpose to strengthen engagement and belongingness and give people autonomy and agency. It's up to the follower to follow. It's their choice, so ensure that the followers have the right skill set for the job. If not, help them acquire the necessary skills and communicate in the way your followers understand and prefer. Your people will then follow you anywhere.

Coaching Culture

A coach is someone who tells you what you don't want to hear, who has to see what you don't want to see, so you can be who you always known you could be.

Tom Landry

To enhance performance, we need to have high-performing teams. If we have those, then the individuals within them will also be high performing. If all our teams are high performing, we'll have a high-performing organisation. We'll need a coaching culture to help teams fulfil their potential and operate at the highest level possible.

One way to set the tone of a coaching culture is by defaulting to the Feedforward (see Chapter 5 Feedforward) model of communication. No matter what sort of leader you are (or imagine yourself to be), you won't be able to lead or coach people effectively if you struggle to communicate with them.

In traditional work relationships, you might receive feedback on areas you need to improve to continue climbing the ladder at the company. Sometimes this is a benchmark you need to meet or a production cost-cutting target. If you are struggling, you might be told that you're deficient in a particular area and are sent to a training seminar or have you shadow another employee. Worse yet, you might be threatened to be fired. All these behaviours and feedback directed towards you can be handled in a different and more supportive way. The Feedforward model helps people put on their coaching hat and provide non-judgemental support.

Instead of offering criticism, the Feedforward approach is more open-ended. It might sound like, "Let's do some Feedforward. Steve, you're up first. Give me one or two ideas about how we can convert more clients to reach our numbers." I would then collect Steve's ideas and ask each of the other team members to provide one or two ideas. We could collect ideas every month and implement one strategy each week to see which, if any, work. When one idea doesn't work, we move on to the next. When an idea works, we might implement the initiative company-wide. In this way, we change behaviours whilst shaping the future.

The fundamental basis of trust is that people must be able speak to one another without being judged. That's why I say Feedforward is a foundational building block for enhanced communication, collaboration, connection and, yes, even coaching.

The Feedforward model is an excellent way for new leaders to build their coaching skills. It removes the superior and subordinate position titles and allows for the free exchange of candid ideas without making people feel guarded. It's a way to encourage free thinking without taking your employees by the hand and fixing things for them (which is often counterproductive to authentic learning).

Today leaders need just as much support with coaching, active listening, and driving connection as they do with other nuanced areas of businesses. These are the foundations for being a good coach and establishing a coaching culture within your company.

I believe in and evangelise Feedforward. At TRG International, it's a daily habit. New hires join our monthly Feedforward webinars, which are now public.[xx] I also teach Feedforward at RMIT (Royal Melbourne Institute of Technology) University, Vietnam campus,[xxi] to business networking groups, and to anyone else who's interested.

Leadership

I want to clarify that not every coach is a good leader, and not every leader is a good coach. However, to run a successful business and support your employees in becoming as satisfied and motivated as they can be, you need to be both a coach *and* a leader.

Some business managers think they are coaching employees when all they're doing is telling people what to do. Leadership without coaching is like a manager who focuses on achieving outcomes—that is, a boss who gives instructions without listening to their people. In contrast, coaching without

---

[xx] Feedforward workshops are available at trginternational.com/events-overview/ and as a Masterclass and at RickYvanovich.com/BAUU/.
[xxi] RMIT Vietnam: https://www.rmit.edu.vn/.

leadership means having good ideas, but lacking the influence needed to bring them to fruition. Leadership skills help you get buy-in. You can be the greatest coach, but you won't get very far without a strong *why* and a mission that people want to get behind.

To have a holistic and synergistic business, you need both coaching and leadership skills in your new corporate culture toolbox to be fully equipped to understand and effectively address challenges that arise.

5 Levels of Leadership

According to John C. Maxwell, authentic leadership isn't about title or position. In his book, *The 5 Levels of Leadership*, Maxwell does a thorough analysis of the levels that differentiate leaders and their circles of influence.[87] *Figure 16* below depicts Maxwell's 5 Levels of Leadership. Each level is described in more detail in the sections that follow.

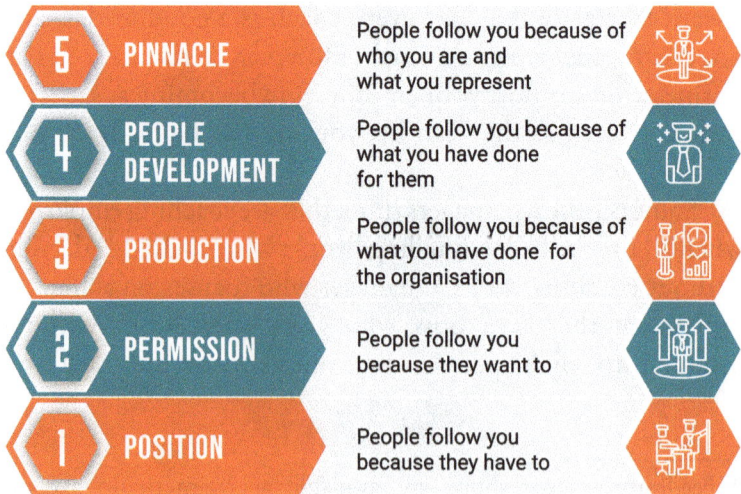

5	PINNACLE	People follow you because of who you are and what you represent
4	PEOPLE DEVELOPMENT	People follow you because of what you have done for them
3	PRODUCTION	People follow you because of what you have done for the organisation
2	PERMISSION	People follow you because they want to
1	POSITION	People follow you because they have to

Figure 16. John C. Maxwell's 5 Levels of Leadership

Level 1—Position

Position is when people follow you because they have to. You are their supervisor/manager/leader, and your approval pays their expense claims, paycheck, etc. Your job title gives you influence over others. Whilst there is nothing wrong with having a lofty title, there is everything wrong when a person uses their position to force people to comply. Wielding your position to influence people in your business makes you a boss, not a leader. It makes your people subordinates and not team members.

Here are some ways leaders at this level can grow and improve:

- Empathise with employees to show you care about them beyond their role in the business.
- Encourage and motivate employees by passing on and supporting the employees' ideas or praising them for a job well done.
- Focus on Feedforward and deliver feedback without passing judgment.
- Communicate with individuals about how their personal goals align with the business.

Level 2—Permission

Permission is when leadership is based entirely on relationships. When leaders treat people as a valued part of the team, they build trust and influence. Of course, people can like you without letting you lead them, but you can't lead them if they don't like you. The best coaching relationships, though, are those that are cultivated when coaches and coachees like and trust each other.

KOLs naturally start at this level of leadership because they have a warm and welcoming personality backed by knowledge of the company and role competency.

To develop at this level of leadership, remember to the following:

- Consider both the intention and impact of any decision affecting your people.
- Encourage your people to initiate new projects.
- Encourage collaborative and solution-oriented team discussions.
- Practise accountability within your team.
- Learn how to communicate and motivate your team members.

Level 3—Production

In addition to the levels that precede this, people follow others because they have contributed to an organisation. Good leaders are impactful by moving the needle on projects and achieving meaningful goals.

Leaders at the Production level can tackle challenging problems quickly without second-guessing themselves. They make difficult decisions and see their decisions through. Their actions make a difference to the people working in a company because no one wants to follow a wishy-washy leader.

Leaders at this level shouldn't be overly resistive to change course in the face of changing circumstances or new information. They should be thoughtful about making decisions and carrying out plans.

Leaders at this level can leverage their skills by doing these:

- Connecting with people to determine what makes them feel engaged and empowered.
- Actively listen and pose questions for reflection.
- Welcome people's input on decisions.
- Share their personality, charisma, and technical skills to help others learn and grow.

Level 4—People Development

At the People Development level of leadership, people follow you because of what you have done for them. Leaders become great not because they have power but because they have the ability to *empower* others.

In the 5 Levels of Leadership, we aim to develop leaders up to Level 4 (minimum) because Level 4 is the most influential stage of authentic leadership.

Performance increases, and more leaders on the team help improve everyone's performance. As a result, teamwork and collaboration increase because of the high level of investment in people. Investing in people deepens relationships, strengthens loyalty, and helps teams get to know each other. Level 4 leaders change the lives of the people they lead, and people follow them as a result. Relationships can be lifelong.

Level 4 leaders can continue to grow by focusing on the following:

- Embodying the Ten Dimensions of Corporate Culture and leading by example.
- Communicating expectations clearly and holding people accountable.
- Taking a coaching, person-first attitude.
- Providing the tools and wisdom people need to achieve upward leadership mobility.

Level 5—Pinnacle

At the Pinnacle leadership level, people follow you because of who you are and what you represent. Pinnacle leadership is the highest and most challenging level of influence leaders can achieve. You can learn to climb from Level 1 to Level 4, but Level 5 requires high talent.

Pinnacle leaders help the leaders below them reach Level 4. Developing and inspiring people to become able and willing leaders who desire to develop and strengthen others is the most challenging leadership task.

You achieve Level 5 leadership when all the leaders at your company have the tools, education, and support needed to help every employee make lasting habit and mindset changes that will support everyone in achieving their goals. Level 5 leaders give more to the people who need it and work on developing rising talent until their pupils are confident enough to support others and build their teams.

Pinnacle leaders do these things:

- Increase productivity by driving the success of teams using a variety of motivational techniques.
- Create environments that contribute to the success of individuals and teams.
- Respect, value, and seek the feedback of everyone in their organisation.
- Lead corporate culture by ensuring business decisions align with the company's mission, vision, and values.
- Allow other leaders to make independent decisions and take the initiative whenever possible.
- Communicate effectively and influentially.

VUCA Leadership

VUCA (volatility, uncertainty, complexity, ambiguity) has become a very trendy acronym in the world of business leadership, but it's been around since the late 1980s. You can thank its recent popularity to the growth of business coaching culture and the need for a fresh take in response to a coaching culture. *Figure 17* below depicts the meaning of each of the elements of VUCA.

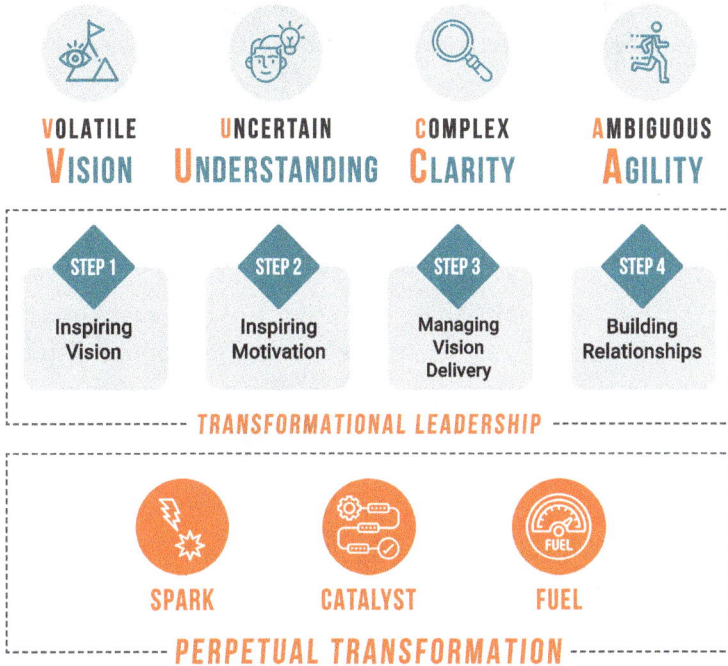

Figure 17. VUCA Defined

Do you feel energised when working for a company that's skating by on thin ice, waiting for the most delicate layer to crack? I don't. I want to be part of an organisation that manages challenges effectively and harnesses the intellect and collective energy of the entire company.

As the world continues to be turbulent in the wake of coronavirus, trying to put together an effective business strategy as a leader can feel like you're swimming upstream. With the disruption of business as usual, we find that struggling businesses have at least one of the four VUCA problems.

VUCA leadership is the ability to shift/change (be agile) in spite of things being volatile, uncertain, complex, and ambiguous (VUCA).

The role of leadership today is to bring clarity in uncertain times. The more uncertain things are, the more leadership is required. There is no job description for what you are facing, no rule book... Today's leaders need to thrive in the face of this uncertainty.

Satya Nadella (CEO, Microsoft)

VUCA leadership is very relevant for Business As UnUsual as it's a framework for the mindset needed for coping with the unknown. Ask yourself things like: "What can we see on the horizon? What's around the corner? What's going to hit us?" When we're able to predict situations in the future, we become better at leading others simply and straightforwardly. As Miguel de Cervantes said, "Forewarned, forearmed; to be prepared is half the victory."

Imagine, for a moment, that you're driving, and your eyes are on the road. If it's a road with many twists and turns, you need to focus on what's right in front of you. That way, you don't need to wonder what is coming your way. You can see or sense when something is approaching because your sight and focus help prepare you for the unexpected. The alternative would be *not* to pay attention to the road. But then don't be surprised if you get sideswiped or make a wrong turn down a ditch.

New developments happen so routinely in business and the world that we often don't take time to understand them. The key is to understand what's happening now and what's sitting on the horizon. Then, look at each development and its consequences to prepare a plan for each, whilst keeping a keen eye out for opportunities and gaps.

Because forecasting and preparing for the *what-ifs* in business is complex, we need to seek clarity. Clarity brings awareness, which enables your comprehension. The more uncertain and complicated our business becomes, the more we need to impose a trusting style of leadership. As a leader, you need to exemplify the attitudes and behaviours you expect from your people. You need to keep a calm head to guide people through uncertain challenges instead of letting the fear overtake you and your company.

Back when technology was just starting to develop new ways of conducting business and automating processes, the idea of AI and robots sent the business world into a panic. People were afraid they would lose their jobs to robots! It was all very uncertain and massively complex. So, how do you handle that uncertainty and complexity? What is your plan?

We might think we know what developments will hit us and when, but we can never be 100 percent sure. *Maybe* this and *maybe* that, but the overarching point is that leaders must be agile and prepared for what comes next, as do their people. If you don't know, they won't know, and it will cause ripples of uncertainty and volatility throughout your company's culture.

VUCA leadership is all about understanding and being comfortable with pivoting your business and strategies. You must have an agile mind that can see challenges as opportunities and see things from different perspectives. Your view may not be the only one, nor even the correct one, and there may be things just outside your lens that would greatly help. Swap your narrow lens for a wider one, so you're not missing significant opportunities as they pop up.

The good news for leaders Is that each of these challenges can be reframed with a more desirable outcome, an antidote to each of the VUCA elements that helps leaders lift the haze around these challenges.

- **Volatility** we reframe and overcome with **Vision**.
- **Uncertainty** we reframe and overcome with **Understanding**.
- **Complexity** we reframe and overcome with **Clarity**.
- **Ambiguity** we reframe and overcome with **Agility**.

This reframing I call transformational VUCA as I feel it's important to highlight that it's not going to happen overnight and it's something we must work hard on, persistently and consistently to bring to reality. *Figure 18* below shows the visualisation of transformational VUCA, where we have transformed each of the letters of the VUCA acronym. It's depicted as a cycle as the elements are linked and impact each other. For example, if we have Vision, we drive Understanding, which helps drive Clarity, and helps us be Agile.

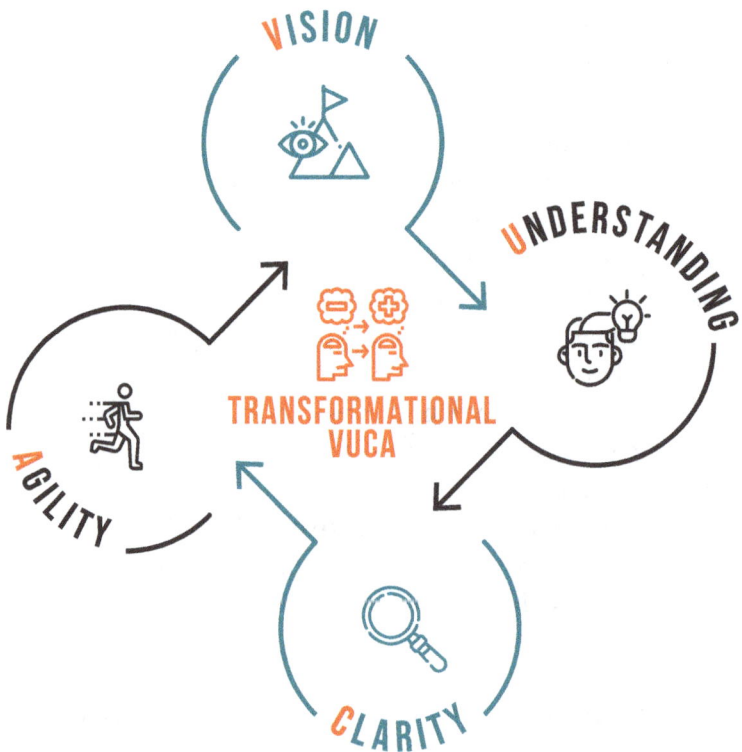

Figure 18. Transformational VUCA

Transformational vs. Transactional Leadership

Transformational leadership is an approach that elicits change through inspiration, motivation, and encouragement. It creates valuable and positive changes in people and thus drives company success. The VUCA framework encourages leaders to adopt a transformational leadership style to improve a company and its people.

Transformational leadership differs from more traditional transactional leadership. Transactional leaders motivate others using rewards, punishments, supervision, and oversight. These leaders value consistency, predictability, routine, and structure. They believe that if they can control the people, their schedules, and the business's organisational structure, they will eliminate chaos and inefficiency. These leaders also focus more on the process than the people, which results in a more centralised management system. Transactional leaders view people as either insider or outsiders.

Do you think you would find it exciting and energising to work for a transactional leader? If you're like me, your answer is an unequivocal *no* because transactional leaders focus on business outcomes and analytics at the cost of building trust, encouraging people to try new things, and driving teams to success.

The opposite of a transactional leader is a transformational one. The 1–7 numbering in the bullets below refer to *Figure 19* below depicting the contrast.

- **1**—Transactional leaders use carrots and sticks. Transformational leaders invest in coaching and mentoring their people.
- **2**—Transactional leaders tend to micromanage. Transformational leaders value independence and diversity, as they know that diverse teams can provide better solutions to complex problems.

- **3–4**—Rather than punishing people for their mistakes, a transformational leader encourages innovation by focusing on improvement in the next go-round, and people learn more as a result. They learn about themselves, and about which processes worked, which didn't, and why. This learning is integral to honing a person's potential and gives them the confidence to handle challenges more effectively in the future.
- **5**—Transformational coaches see failure as less risky to individuals and the business because we learn from failure. The lessons empower people to get to the root of the problem or failure and gives them the tools and encouragement they need to try again.
- **6**—Transformational coaching is people-driven. The best leaders know that the people working for them are the company's lifeblood. Without employees, most Fortune 500 companies would cease to exist. A leader who puts people first knows that running a business smoothly means that people need to be satisfied, fulfilled, and driven by purpose. That is the focus of a transformational coach, and that's why their businesses have greater sustainability, resulting in longevity that reaches far beyond a particular industry or sector.
- **7**—Transformational leaders know they're not experts in everything related to their businesses. To best support their people and themselves, they make a distributed leadership team accessible to everyone. Each designated leader specialises in a certain area or a skill, and people can go to them for support when they feel stuck or disengaged. Having leaders spread across different teams and locations helps promote cross-company collaboration and a positive culture.

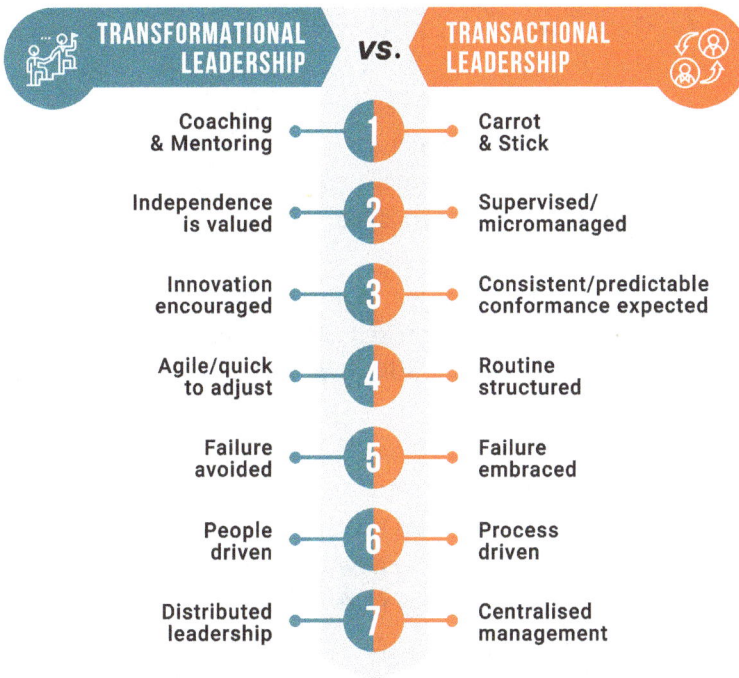

TRANSFORMATIONAL LEADERSHIP	vs.	TRANSACTIONAL LEADERSHIP
Coaching & Mentoring	1	Carrot & Stick
Independence is valued	2	Supervised/ micromanaged
Innovation encouraged	3	Consistent/predictable conformance expected
Agile/quick to adjust	4	Routine structured
Failure avoided	5	Failure embraced
People driven	6	Process driven
Distributed leadership	7	Centralised management

Figure 19. Transformational vs Transactional Leadership

Transformational Leadership and VUCA

We've touched on the meaning of transformational leadership and VUCA, and I wanted to give another perspective of VUCA for you to reflect on. So, here's a reverse psychology/negative way of looking at each part of VUCA:

- Do you want to be perceived as a **Volatile leader** where your changing and erratic behaviours drives good people away?
- Do you want to be perceived as an **Uncertain leader** where your changing directions will frustrate people and lead them to question your capabilities?

- Do you want to be perceived as a **Complex leader** where no one will get to know you or your expectations? Or you appear aloof?
- Do you want to be perceived as an **Ambiguous leader** where your procrastination over taking action prevents people from being engaged?

It's your choice how you want to be perceived. And if you wish to transform yourself, then you need to answer wholeheartedly yes to the following two questions, then the change can begin:

- Do you want to do better?
- Are you willing to feel the discomfort of putting in more effort and trying new things that will feel weird and different and may not work right away?

A caterpillar must want so much to fly that it must give up being a caterpillar to become a butterfly.

Pivoting

A pivot is a change in strategy without a change in Vision.

Eric Ries

The path to enduring success is never a straight line. Pivoting in a business is often necessary, as ambitious entrepreneurs wade into deeper and darker waters. Changing direction can be a good thing. It can provide the clarity and conciseness needed to attract investors and make sales, however pivots can sometimes go a little awry and create less than desirable result if mismanaged.

In Business As UnUsual, we've seen the absolute necessity to pivot, be agile, and flexible when dealing with the unknown, applying VUCA and infinite mindset, along with coaching leadership to help us keep moving forward.

The pivot is a change in direction, which likely means that you need to change your mindset or lead and coach others to help them change their mindsets.

Pivoting to WFA

*Pivoting is not the end of the disruption process,
but the beginning of the next leg of your journey.*

Jay Samit

In recent years, many of us have pivoted from commuting to and from the office every day to working from home (WFH) because we were suddenly locked out of the office due to the pandemic.

Many years prior to the pandemic we already had a Work From Anywhere (WFA) policy, as the growth of so many digital warriors scattered around the globe resulted us in closing most of our offices around the world. We still had a handful of offices, and despite WFA, some (maybe a lot) of people still felt they had to come into the office, and many leaders also (silently, and not so silently) expected their teams to be there. Arguably, we were not embracing WFA properly.

The pandemic changed how we all perceived WFA. In 2020 we closed all TRG Vietnam offices just to test what would happen if there was a lockdown. One week into that test, Vietnam was in compulsory lockdown, and a one-week test turned into multiple weeks and months. After years of resistance, mindsets about WFH and WFA began to change. This included mine. I've tried WFH a few times when I lived in Switzerland and Singapore, but it didn't work well for me. Maybe it was because I had babies at home, and they didn't follow company policy.

Today, two years into the pandemic, we're in full WFA mode. WFA really means anywhere—it can be your home, the beach, a coffeeshop, and if WFA means the physical office, that's okay, of course.

I'm finding for myself, TRG, and most companies and businesspeople I speak to, that we must continue to change our mindsets and work practices, focusing specifically on connections. In a world where some people are in the office and others are remote, trying to build connections virtually with strangers (who could be new work colleagues) is more challenging than doing it face-to-face, and if the techniques we use when we're face-to-face do not work so well in the hybrid world, it means we need to find new ways.

One way we learnt how to deal with the switch to WFA was to pivot from 100 percent in-house internships to 100 percent virtual internships at scale. I suggest you try it if you haven't yet. Pre-pandemic, we typically had six to twelve interns at any one time most of the year, and they're from all over the world. They tended to come to our Vietnam offices, as Vietnam is a fun place for a young person to see, experience, and travel (and maybe party a lot). It's part of our diversity and inclusion program and our desire to help young folks skill up to enter the world of work successfully.

The virtual internships—which we'd hardly ever done before the pandemic—also allowed us to learn how to build relationships, connections, and teams. So, we scaled all the way up to forty or fifty at one time, and as a result, we've hosted hundreds of interns from a dozen countries within the last eighteen months. As we were allowed to reopen physical offices we reintroduced in-office internships as well as hybrid internships. It's been a roller coaster learning ride, and we now have a better working formula for internships as well as working WFA and hybrid. We've made a lot of mistakes and have learnt from them. Throughout, we made it clear we are stepping into the unknown and thus sought ongoing feedback and feedforward from both interns and employees on how we can make it better. We've benefitted from hundreds of ideas so much so that I'd guess that more than 50 percent of the current internship program is based purely on all those ideas from interns.

Pivoting the business

If we're not moving the drivers of our business model, we're not making progress. That becomes a sure sign it's time to pivot.

Eric Ries

The 2018 Global Reinvention Survey Research revealed that 79.7 percent of businesses need to reinvent themselves every two to five years if they hope to survive. That means the business you are in today is not (cannot be) the business you'll be in three years from now.[88] You need to adapt or find refuge in a new one entirely.

Whenever leaders need to pivot their business, they're less likely to receive pushback from stakeholders if the change seems to be in line with larger aims. The link between the new strategic direction and the initial vision isn't always obvious. So, to continue receiving support and appearing a competent leader, you need to make the connection clear.

Besides keeping the goal and message consistent, leaders must show empathy to the stakeholders in their business. Too often, entrepreneurs think empathy is a sign of weakness or that stakeholders will lose faith if leaders apologise for pivoting and thus they procrastinate and delay or don't pivot. However, empathy and remorse are a part of the leader's role when informing people of changes, especially if the changes aren't welcome. People are far more willing to remain loyal when they're told how changes will affect them and when leaders genuinely care about their situation.

When leaders are clear about their purpose, mission, values, and vision during a pivot, they encourage trust, confidence, and clarity, even in the face of the uncertainty that accompanies change.

CHAPTER 6 KEY TAKEAWAYS

- Leaders can change company culture simply by aligning themselves with the cultural expectations and embodying them in every interaction with others.
- Corporate culture has changed in the wake of the global pandemic. The old culture can't adapt to the new environment and must be completely overhauled.
- How do we change corporate culture?
  - Get the support of key opinion leaders in the company.
  - Align any new cultural expectations with the mission, vision, and values of the company.
  - For every correction or shift that's needed, ensure you give people ample positive encouragement.
  - We can use the ten dimensions (Unity, Clarity, Positivity, Connectivity, Integrity, Safety, Diversity, Agility, Accountability, Dependability) of high-performance teams to help changer culture.
- Keep the Losada ratio between 3 and 6.
- Establishing a coaching culture means moving away from traditional business methods that value results more than people. Adopting a people-first culture will change the entire lifeblood of an organisation.
- Feedforward workshops are available at trginternational.com/events-overview/ and as a Masterclass and at RickYvanovich.com/BAUU/.
- VUCA leadership is the ability to shift/change (be agile) in spite of things being volatile, uncertain, complex and ambiguous (VUCA).
- Focus on Transformational over Transactional leadership.

- Transformational leadership is an approach that elicits change through inspiration, motivation, and encouragement.
- Transactional leaders motivate others using rewards, punishments, supervision, and oversight.
- Your business needs to reinvent itself, so don't be afraid to pivot your business or your corporate culture.
  - Pivoting is most successful when leaders can tie the changes into the company's mission, vision, and values.
  - Showing empathy without apologising for having to pivot helps leaders maintain authority and influence during a pivot.
- Download Chapter 6 resources from RickYvanovich. com/BAUU/.

CHAPTER 6
REFLECTION PROMPTS

What's your **one** key takeaway from this chapter?

```
_____
_____
_____
```

And what else?

```
_____
_____
_____
```

What action will you take right away because of something you read in this chapter?

```
_____
_____
_____
```

And what else?

```
_____
_____
```

CHAPTER 7
THE STABLES AND THE TREASURY

THE STABLES

THE TREASURY

We keep moving forward, opening new doors, and doing new things, because we're curious and curiosity keeps leading us down new paths.

Walt Disney

The Stables represent looking forward to the future, evolving, transforming, and searching for satisfaction. The Treasury represents your finances, both how you generate income and what you retain it. The Treasury is necessary to finance your goals.

Darwin's theory of evolution is a common topic amongst schoolchildren to pique the curiosity of our origins. Today, Netflix, BBC, National Geographic, Discovery Channel, and others have helped fuel this curiosity with documentaries such as Planet Earth narrated by Sir David Attenborough. Knowing our origins as a planet or species is evolving helps us predict the future and our evolving needs.[89]

We all understand that the Earth is changing, and as humans, we must evolve and adapt to continue to survive. In science, the process of change is known as *natural selection*. It shouldn't be hard to understand because, as humans, it's our nature to undergo constant change—we are evolving right now, as we live and breathe on this planet. The science of evolution shows us that animals make biological and social changes in response to changes in their environment. Those animals that make advantageous adaptations have greater longevity and more extensive social networks.

Change, however, is something most people consciously resist. Because humans can think rationally and logically and interpret our environment, we tend to overthink change. We hold on to the old ways with an iron-clad grip because "it's worked before" or "that's how we've always done it." We are scared to let go of things even when they are no longer working because they are familiar. Have you heard the phrase, "The devil you know is better than the one you don't?" Well, it's a load of nonsense. To grow, we must also change. We cannot have one without the other.

If you're like most high achievers, the challenge of change isn't so much with the ability to change. You've made it this far by adding skills, habits, and structuring routines that have enabled you to grow. The challenge is knowing *what* we need to change, and the even more substantial challenge is knowing *how* to change it. These two aspects can feel daunting at times, but change doesn't have to be overly complicated.

Identifying and adapting for the future starts with taking an inventory of where we are now and where we want to end up in the future, and then aligning our skill sets with the end results to prepare us for achieving those future goals.

Looking Forward to There

Life is like riding a bicycle, to keep your balance, you must keep moving.

Albert Einstein

Many business practices that leaders use are dated and no longer apply in today's pandemic, (or post-pandemic) world. In *What Got You Here Won't Get You There: How Successful People Become Even More Successful*, Marshall Goldsmith points out that "people often do well in spite of certain habits rather than because of them and need a 'to stop' list rather than one listing what to do."[90] We tend to favour several character habits that can be obstacles to our own success. These habits can be divided into two types: information related and emotional related habits. Informational related habits are either sharing too much when it's not needed (adding too much value) or sharing too little, resulting in withholding of information. Emotional habits are sharing when it isn't appropriate and communicating too much or too little in your message. Thus, to get to where you want to be, one needs to have identified any flaws we have and put into action a plan to correct those flaws step by step.

Similarly, adjusting your business to succeed in the future requires careful consideration of where you are now and where you want to be. You don't want to make random guesses about the future and risk creating a plan for conditions that do not—and might never—exist. Such an approach would be like a headless chicken that's running around sightless and directionless. Instead, we need to be proactive, and predictive and avoid reactionary measures. The goal is to forecast the future without drastically having to overhaul your business processes and risking that it might be rendered useless in a year or less.

To build resilience, sustainability, and agility in business, we need to have a mindset looking towards future planning and analysis rather than focusing only on the here and now. As leaders of ourselves, and maybe of teams and businesses too, we need to know where opportunities are evolving in our industry and always look forward to "there."

Industry 4.0

You cannot stop the Fourth Industrial Revolution, but you can influence its direction and impact in your life.

Nicky Verd

The First Industrial Revolution (1760–1840) brought steam and waterpower to mechanise production. The Second Industrial Revolution (1870–1914) brought electricity. The Third Industrial Revolution (1970–2000) or Digital Revolution brought electronics. Today we are in the Fourth Industrial Revolution (2011), IR 4.0, or Industry 4.0. Klaus Schwab, executive chairman of the world Economic Forum (WEF) made it more visible in a 2015 article and "Mastering the Fourth Industrial Revolution" was the theme of the 2016 World Economic Forum Annual meeting in Davos-Klosters, Switzerland.[91]

In Business As UnUsual, the pandemic has greatly accelerated digital transformation, exacerbating the need for change. Industry 4.0 is all about digital transformation, including technology like Artificial Intelligence (AI) and machine-to-machine interaction, and it has triggered the debate that the machines or robots could replace human jobs.

Now, I'm a baby boomer. I finished school in the UK in 1980, the same year the PC was born. Growing up pre-'80s meant we did not have computers in school. An electronic calculator was considered high-tech and wasn't always allowed in the exam room. Those of us who struggled with an abacus used a slide rule, and if you had neither, you had to count on your toes (just kidding). All that said, I didn't grow up with much technology and I can empathise that the task of learning all about technology can sound daunting.

The good news is that just because technology is the future of business doesn't mean you need to re-enrol in university and get a degree in business technology. So, if that's the case, what needs to change?

Because Industry 4.0 heralds new digital technologies, we will need to learn new skills and look to reskill people who *might* soon be replaced by machines. Whilst no one is expecting you to be an expert in every new technology, you might need to hire a top tech professional who is fully versed. As a leader, it's good to be knowledgeable about technology and business operations, but you don't need to be the sole company expert.

Industry 4.0 has also brought us the need to learn multiple digital technologies that will impact how work is done and, consequently, how we will work as human beings. For example, what interpersonal skills do we need to cultivate because of the technological changes affecting our business? What systems (technological, business, and processes) need to change to continue to support the people who support our technology?

In 2006, Dr Carol Dweck, in her book, *Mindset: The New Psychology of Success,* taught us all that we do is governed by one of two mindsets—fixed or growth. That mindset impacts our success. We can make ourselves more successful if we have a growth mindset and concerted efforts can lead to a change in mindset.[92]

To me, the growth mindset helps trigger and reinforce the desire to learn and to grow.

Changes to our systems, skills, and workforce need to be deliberate. We need to watch trends carefully so we can predict what might happen beyond this year or the next and stay relevant for generations.

Future Readiness of Leaders

The World Economic Forum's (WEF) "Jobs of Tomorrow: Mapping opportunity in the new economy" report outlines emerging jobs and the top skills associated with them.[93] As more people become aware of current job needs, and organisations look at what jobs and skills are required, it's become increasingly apparent how significant the skills gaps are. For example, WEF's "Future of Jobs Report 2020" says 50 percent of all employees will need reskilling by 2025, and for those workers set to remain in their current roles, 40 percent of their current core skills are expected to change within the next five years.[94] So, regardless of which generation you belong to, with numbers this high, you are likely to be affected.

Leaders at Level 4 on the leadership development scale (People Development) are preparing the next generation to take over departments and carry more responsibility in a growing enterprise. But it's not enough to gift them our knowledge and skills alone. It's also vital to equip emerging business leaders with the skills they'll need in the future.

We need a different mindset to build resilience, sustainability, and agility, so we're constantly improving and always skilling up. By doing this, we narrow any gaps.

It has often been debated which skills are more important—hard, or soft skills. Hard skills relate to your technical ability and specialised knowledge gained through education, practice, and repetition. Soft skills are general characteristics and behaviours linked to personality traits. The WEF report just talks about skills and does not segregate hard and soft skills. This highlights that people need a range of skills, and yes, they are a mix of hard and soft skills.

Soft skills, which are much more marketable in a rapidly advancing business environment, are the key to setting us up for future success, as hard skills are forever changing. The Top 5 skills I recommend prioritising are these:

Curiosity. Future leaders need to have a curious attitude and the ability to get to the heart of the matter by asking *why*? When something went wrong on a production line in the '80s, the floor manager could be seen stomping around, looking for someone to blame. Who did the job incorrectly? Who made a mistake, and how can we discipline them?

Leaders should know that blaming employees who make mistakes doesn't make the errors stop; it only creates distrust between leaders and their teams. Having a curious attitude means we look to understand *why* something happened instead of placing blame. By listening and understanding why mistakes happen and challenges occur, leaders can fix the root cause of an issue instead of treating the symptoms.

Kaizen. I know we've covered kaizen a lot in this book (see Chapter 3), because it genuinely reflects excellent leadership potential. Kaizen means lifelong learning and constant self-improvement. Leaders should never stop seeking knowledge and improvement because the moment we stop growing, our business starts to die. Therefore, growth and knowledge are the keys to sustainable success and relevance.

Critical thinking. Leaders are defined by the choices they make and, often, how quickly and confidently they make them. Critical thinking means making logical, well thought out reasoned judgments. It's an attitude involving questioning things. A good example of critical thinking would be a triage nurse in Accident and Emergency in a Hospital deciding the order which patients should be treated.

*It is better to debate a question without settling it than to
settle a question without debating it.*

~~~

Joseph Joubert

Design thinking. As you develop the next generation of
leaders, look for people who excel at design thinking (creative
problem-solving). You want leaders with diverse skills and a
different way of looking at challenges. People with design-
oriented thinking can solve abstract problems and transfer
knowledge or experience from one area of expertise to another.
People with a design thinking mindset adopt a beginner's mind.

*In the beginner's mind there are many possibilities,
in the expert's mind there are few.*

~~~

Shunryu Suzuki

Communication. Leaders who are looking to develop
others need to develop clear and effective interpersonal
communication skills. Funnily enough, despite the myriad new
ways of connecting digitally, we appear to have weakened our
ability to communicate and connect effectively, thus making it
harder for us to collaborate. There are several reasons for this:

- Having to communicate more virtually, which
  removes the non-verbal cues that are critical for face-
  to-face communication. This was made worse during
  the pandemic when a person had to wear a mask or
  cameras were off.
- Technology is removing the need for us to communicate
  with a human. When you go to the supermarket do you
  use the self-checkout and speak to a machine, or do you
  queue up to for the human checkout?

When communicating virtually, according to Erica Dhawan, in her book *Digital Body Language: How to Build Trust and Connection, No Matter the Distance*, there's a digital body language we need to overcome the miscommunication we're experiencing because of the lack of non-verbal body language we're used to in face-to-face communications.[95]

A bonus skill, is, unsurprisingly, coaching! Experience first-hand how incredibly life-changing it can be to have a coach in your corner. Whether helping you deal with life or business, the ability to coach others (and be coached yourself) is an excellent sign of a future leader who is ready for the next step in their career.

I refer to the act of preparing future leaders as *knowledge sharing*. It's about transferring knowledge from one person to another. A good practice in any team is for each team member to focus on one new bit of knowledge, acquire it, and then do a knowledge sharing session with others. Then, the rest of the team can do the same thing. Each person learns and teaches others and has the opportunity to be taught by others. It's a good habit that I've found helps accelerate knowledge acquisition of individuals and teams.

Preparing future leaders also means cataloguing and retaining organisational knowledge. As an organisation, we need to convert what we all collectively know into online learning to help ensure (organisational) knowledge is not lost, as well as to allow everyone in the organisation the opportunity to access all that knowledge.

Where Is Change Leading?

Looking at the list of the waning top ten jobs and positions, many are data entry roles that can be automated using new technologies. The incumbents in these roles must be upskilled and transformed into new roles.

Businesses are moving toward softer skills. Leaders and innovators know that soft skills equip us to be agile and deal with change. Additionally, soft skills invite leaders to be more progressive, self-reliant, and self-aware of their own development. This is critical because, by adopting this model, we as humankind can become capable of achieving even more and building a better world.

What Skills Are Needed?

The future belongs to those who learn more skills
and combine them in creative ways.

Robert Greene

So, you've come around to the idea that people need to be in a constant state of forward progress and evolution. The trouble is that, without a magic crystal ball, there is no way to determine with certainty where business or industry will take us in the future. It can feel daunting trying to predict every outcome or scenario and how it may (or may not) evolve as you grow.

One way to identify the skills necessary for the future is to refer to the WEF "Future of Jobs Report 2020" report, they have already done the research and analysis and the top 15 skills for 2025:[96]

1. Analytical thinking and innovation
2. Active learning and learning strategies
3. Complex problem-solving
4. Critical thinking and analysis
5. Creativity, originality, and initiative
6. Leadership and social influence
7. Technology use, monitoring, and control
8. Technology design and programming
9. Resilience, stress tolerance, and flexibility

10. Reasoning, problem-solving, and ideation
11. Emotional intelligence
12. Troubleshooting and user experience
13. Service orientation
14. Systems analysis and evaluation
15. Persuasion and negotiation

The skills listed above could all be classified as soft skills. What makes these soft skills so valuable is that they are easily transferrable. A person who possesses these traits and abilities is likely to succeed in a wide range of different businesses or industries because these skills are so widely applicable and sought-after.

If these above listed skills don't resonate with you, think about the skills and areas of business or life that currently interest you the most. Then ask yourself: if I had this skill, what could I do with it? Where could it take me? How would I feel when I got there or achieved that? This exercise can help people look to the future in a way that aligns with their personal interests and desired vision. As we know, congruency is crucial if we're motivated to acquire the knowledge and skills needed to achieve our goals.

Another way to start thinking about the skills and knowledge you might need in the future is to visualise. Close your eyes and imagine yourself in the future. What do you want to achieve in the next year and five years from now? Ask yourself what skills you will need to learn to accomplish those things. Then ask yourself: if I have that skill five years from today, what will I be doing, and how will I feel about it?

Hold that future positive feeling. Visualise it. Now, when the going gets tough and you find yourself struggling to find the motivation and commitment to learn new things, recall that future visualisation and imagine all the benefits the new skills will bring to your life, relationships, and business.

When considering new skills, how compelling is it for you to think of skills such as being a better coach, partner, leader, and businessperson? And if you were to learn these new skills, how would they impact your future job prospects? Whilst it's essential to consider the future and our plans, we also don't want to just live in the future. Focusing too much energy on future possibilities can be overwhelming. To keep progressing, I suggest you keep track of your skills, and here are some tips for doing that:

- List the skills you want to learn.
- For each, identify on a scale of 1 (low) to 10 (high):
  - Where you are now.
  - Where you want to be.
- What are the gaps?
  - What are the biggest gaps?
- What's the impact of each skill on you?
- Then, prioritise which skills you will work on and put an action plan together.

Humans are creatures of comfort, and learning new things not only tests our skills and abilities, but our egos too. We don't like changing our ways, and we certainly don't enjoy feeling like a beginner, especially when we're at the top of our field in other capacities. However, resistance to acquire knowledge can quickly lead to pain, even more pain than starting out as a beginner. So, consider how your future job prospects will be impacted by acquiring and developing new skills, or not.

If you have read this far, you already understand the importance of life purpose and life goals and learning new skills can support your purpose and goals.

The Jobs of Tomorrow

"The Future of Jobs Report 2020" predicts the top 10 roles for which demand is expected to increase over the next few years.[97] According to WEF, the fastest-growing jobs expected to continue their upward trend are:

1. Data Analysts and Scientists
2. AI and Machine Learning Specialists
3. Big Data Specialists
4. Digital Marketing and Strategy Specialists
5. Process Automation Specialists
6. Business Development Professionals
7. Digital Transformation Specialists
8. Information Security Analysts
9. Software and Applications Developers
10. Internet of Things Specialists

To the above list, I'd like to add the eleventh: Project Managers. There is already a high demand for agile project managers, and the need for Project Managers in general is unsurprising given the amount of change that needs managing.

Whilst some of these jobs require hard skills and academic study, most will require a combination of hard and soft skills in the future. For example, at first glance, you might think AI learning specialists wouldn't need strong social skills; however, they will need to communicate clearly and effectively when explaining how AI works or when troubleshooting as part of a team.

Soft skills, such as effective communication—even though taught in many schools—remains to be required by employers across all industries and jobs. I mentioned this skill specifically as I have found that when I ask interns and graduate entry folks what skills they would like to be trained on, effective communication is always one of the top skills mentioned and is usually the #1 when I speak to hiring managers of interns and graduate entry.

Top 10 Waning Jobs

Just as it's crucial to analyse the jobs for which demand is growing, it's also essential to look at which jobs are on the decline. Taking an inventory of growing and declining industries will help you spot trends over time and allow you to predict what might lie ahead in the future.

By examining both sides of the spectrum, one can see which areas of business or industry are being phased out and *what is taking their place*. Industries and positions rarely vanish; instead, old roles and industries are replaced with newer ones requiring updated skills.

"The Future of Jobs Report 2020" gives the top 10 waning positions in 2020:[98]

1. Data Entry Clerks
2. Administrative and Executive Secretaries
3. Accounting, Bookkeeping, and Payroll Clerks
4. Accountants and Auditors
5. Assembly and Factory Workers
6. Business Services and Administration Managers
7. Client Information and Customer Service Workers
8. General and Operations Managers
9. Mechanics and Machinery Repairers
10. Material-Recording and Stockkeeping Clerks

As you can sense, many of the above roles involve data entry. Today, many data entry tasks are already being partially replaced by some form of digitalised automation. Systems are being updated and integrated, and the need for manual data entry is declining. Whilst it might be an unpopular opinion to some people, I say leave data entry to the computer systems and let people work with other people. Ultimately, the incumbents in these declining roles will need to be upskilled so they can grow into new roles and rediscover their place within the company and the transforming business landscape.

Utilising AI to help people and industries focus on the human element of business is a beautiful oxymoron, isn't it? With aspects of business being automated, people can be assigned to more human responsibilities such as client support, teamwork, and creative problem-solving—activities that make humans feel happier, more confident, and more fulfilled. So, instead of competing with AI, we can accept its growing role in business and use it to propel our personal progress. You can't help but love it!

Where Is There?

In this chapter so far, we've looked forward. How did it make you feel? Do you feel that there are some skills you need to acquire? Do you feel you are going in a specific direction? Do you feel you are going in the right direction? Do you feel you need to change where "there" is?

Now is the time to pause and reflect. Like the mall map, get clarity on where you are heading and identify where "there" is.

Transforming (from Here to There)

Every success story is a tale of constant adaption, revision, and change.

Richard Branson

With the mall map, you need to know where you are right now, the red dot says you're "here," and you need to get "there," where you want to go. First, there is going to be a gap. Next, you need to work out how to close that gap. Finally, you need to be committed to closing that gap. Wherever the gaps are, you must have a plan to close them. If you are stuck and feel overwhelmed, ask yourself, what's *one* thing I can do to close the gap *today*? And then do it. Tomorrow, ask yourself the same question, and the day after, and the day after... If you need help, find yourself an accountability buddy or a coach!

KASH

KASH is an acronym for Knowledge, Attitude, Skills, and Habits. In terms of current and future performance, looking at your KASH can show you where you might need to grow to fill the gap and innovate in your given industry. Using KASH, we can clearly see what our strengths and weaknesses are.

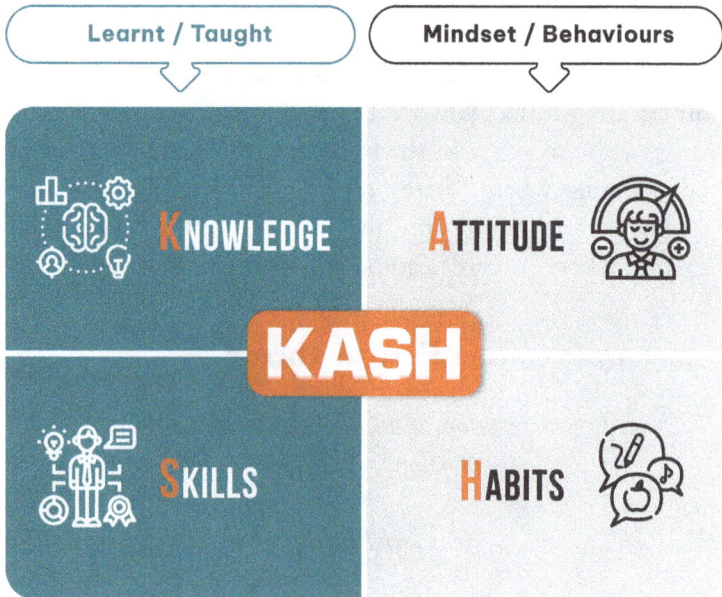

Figure 20. KASH Model

Knowledge. We must invest in acquiring knowledge. Whether it's knowledge of self, knowledge of industry, or knowledge of a new hobby, we need to be focused on learning and expanding our minds.

Attitude. Do you have an infinite mindset or a fixed one? When we have an infinite mindset, we are perpetually transforming and growing. Choose to be aware of your attitude for all that you do, be deliberate.

Skills. Having hard skills in technology and business and soft skills such as people management and leadership are invaluable for the future. If we lack the skills and resourcefulness to make our goals a reality, we risk failure.

Habits. Habits are the foundation of successful people. Habits are actions, emotions, and thoughts that we engage in unconsciously. Practicing positive and healthy habits every day will lead to positive action towards accomplishing your goals. With supportive habits, the road to success will be less frustrating and tiresome. Additionally, Knowledge and Skills are acquired through learning (self-learning and through training), and Attitudes and Habits are mindsets and behaviours. We use coaching and mentoring if we need help in changing them.

Figure 21 below can be used to document your KASH.[xxii]

	Knowledge	Attitude	Skills	Habits
Strengths	1– 2– 3–	1– 2– 3–	1– 2– 3–	1– 2– 3–
Weakness	1– 2– 3–	1– 2– 3–	1– 2– 3–	1– 2– 3–

Figure 21. KASH Template

[xxii] The KASH and other templates can be downloaded from RickYvanovich.com/BAUU/.

We don't always develop our KASH evenly as we may prioritise one area more than another. One way to help create a prioritisation is to give each of the strengths/weaknesses in the KASH a target score (from 1-low to 10-high) of where you want it to be, and a current score (from 1-low to 10-high), then calculate the gap and prioritise the biggest gaps.

As Alice said to the Cheshire Cat...
Alice: "Would you tell me, please, which way I ought to go from here?"
Cheshire Cat: "That depends a good deal on where you want to get to."
Alice: "I don't much care where."
Cheshire Cat: "Then it doesn't matter which way you go."

Lewis Carroll, Alice in Wonderland

Sometimes, our growth can feel random, and that's also OK. I learn whatever strikes my fancy at the time. Knowing the information will be useful at some future point.

The Psychology of Success

What did you learn today? What mistake did you make that taught you something? What did you try hard at today?

Carol S. Dweck

Dr. Carol Dweck covers the psychology of success in her book, *Mindset: The New Psychology of Success*. She proposes that our internal mindset determines which behaviours we choose to achieve success.[99] When you think success relies on talent alone and you don't believe you have talent, you are more likely to give up on your goals and aspirations. This attitude differs greatly from the belief that effort determines success. If you think you can achieve success through hard work and by applying skills and resources, you are much more likely to succeed. Whilst the former belief places a person in a box, effectively giving them a glass ceiling, the latter encourages unlimited thinking. Indeed, it ignites hope and determination within our minds and hearts because people who have a growth or infinite mindset know that success will eventually come if they keep working hard and refining their systems.

Leverage the psychology of success by *investing in your ability to achieve through effort and learning*. When you believe you can improve and grow in any area you put your mind to, there is nothing you can't achieve.

Searching for Satisfaction

Human satisfaction must ultimately come from within oneself.

Dalai Lama

When the COVID-19 pandemic hit, many businesses and their leaders went into panic mode. I had CXOs and prominent business leaders calling me, their voices on the other end of the phone terse and upset.

"We *can't* let our people work from home."

"Our company won't survive."

"The industry is completely gone."

Owning a business and having the responsibility of carrying that business through something like a global pandemic, forced lockdowns, and a near-complete halt of the global economy, is a beast of a challenge. Not to mention things like company retention rates and the satisfaction of the people now forced to adopt new living, working, and business conditions literally overnight.

Those who had been sensing or experiencing disruption in the evolving business world know that COVID-19 was simply the straw that broke the camel's back. There's been a quiet renaissance in the last decades that necessitates leaders, CXOs, managers, supervisors, and other business decision-makers to move away from more traditional business methods and models. This shift invites leaders to step into something more modern and newer, and something more unusual as well.

I'm sure you know the old carrot-and-stick culture that's too often tarted up as pigs with lipstick to make it look better. Leaders used to lead exclusively from the top, passing down new rules and expectations like a game of telephone. People working for big businesses have long felt disconnected from their leaders, and the conditions forced onto companies by their respective governments have only pushed people to become further disconnected.

The pandemic radically changed the way we do business and, thus, changed the way we go about our lives. People have been thrust into a digital work-from-anywhere (WFA) culture that has shaken many companies to their core. People who once relied on the structure and accountability of the physical office are now left to manage their own time and work on their own schedule. Not to forget the counterintuitive result that people are also coping with their home responsibilities whilst at work, which is now also home, making balancing work and life even more challenging. The digital gap created between teams and companies has been noticeably felt by all in the business world. The uninitiated are still forcing their old business rules and standard motivational techniques on dissatisfied, disconnected, and intrinsically unmotivated people. These outdated practices are even more ineffective under these new conditions.

Now more than ever, dissatisfaction is growing like a weed. Extended lockdowns, ever-changing regulations, and massive upheavals to entire industries and communities have people focused on the negatives. We're so caught up in things we've lost, enforced sacrifices, and waning connections that we can't see we're trying to fit our circular peg lives into shape-shifting holes. It no longer makes sense; it doesn't fit.

Many people feel they've lost the sense of meaning in their work and personal lives. The pandemic forced many to focus on surviving instead of leaning harder into their purpose and passion. Our emotional brain is working overtime, trying to classify the tsunami of stimuli into threat or reward, and our amygdalae are screaming, *danger, danger, danger!* Without even knowing it, our nervous system is triggered into a fight, flight, or freeze, and our stress levels automatically rise. Try explaining that to your ancient emotional brain that's triggering whatever your default fight, flight, or freeze mode response is. Evy Poumpouras, in her book *Becoming Bulletproof*, says, "If it's a threat we think we can overpower, we go into Fight mode. If it's a threat we think we can outrun, we go into Flight mode. If it's a threat where we think we can do neither—we Freeze. People may have a different response to the same stimuli."[100]

We're all feeling it: the siren song of a riptide carrying us further away from the shore. It's lingering all around us. Pulling, pushing, tugging, and sucking us deeper into the depths, we're swept up and fighting to survive. It's relentlessly sapping our strength, wearing us down, ever threatening to overwhelm. For some, it's even defeating us.

Riptides are not new. To survive in this new world, you need to understand the signs of the changing tides. Paradoxically, leaders need to keep calm and relax. We can't expend all our energy fighting the inevitable and must learn how to change course and start swimming parallel to the shore.

Some people can spot the shift in the tides. The pandemic that began in 2020 created more profound dissatisfaction with work and life than we have seen since the Great Depression. Dissatisfaction has permeated everything we experience as work-life balance becomes a redundant concept, heralding work-life balancing challenges as WFA blends our homes with our workplaces and as lockdowns combined everything else.

We work where we live, and we live where we work.

❧

Rick Yvanovich

We work where we live, and we live where we work. Without physical face-to-face connection with other people, bosses, and colleagues, our work becomes subject to the three-year-old in the other room and what sort of tantrum they decide to have today. Our work feels increasingly meaningless as we become disembodied heads on Zoom, Teams, and various screens. The dissatisfaction we feel daily has seeped in and flooded every aspect of our lives.

What only serves to drive our dissatisfaction is the hope that we can return to the "new normal" soon. But what is this new normal? A traditional nine-to-five cube with daily status meetings? Spinning that familiar wheel and going nowhere? If this is your idea of work and business, I hate to break it to you, but there is no more normal, and there's no new normal, and it will forever remain that way. There's only Business As UnUsual (BAUU).

Companies holding out for a return to regular business are approaching this opportunity all wrong. You can't fight a changing tide, and companies can't ignore the massive changes that are already happening to our workforce. Entire industries have shut down, millions of people have lost their jobs, and many are being forced to start new businesses from scratch or completely reimagine existing institutions and themselves.

As these waves of change come crashing down, many companies have focused solely on survival, numbers, and bottom lines to keep their business open and operating. For this reason, questions about employee's satisfaction haven't made their way to the top of the priority list.

And in the end, it's not the years in your life that count;
it's the life in your years.

❧

Abraham Lincoln

This new direction for business needs to consider all these nuances to create a completely new and different system that works to manage and motivate people (employees). What it takes to keep people satisfied is constantly evolving. Digitalisation makes us more impatient and seeds cravings for instant availability and gratification.[101] The world is instantly accessible: material goods from everywhere are routinely delivered anywhere with a few clicks and a bit of plastic (your credit/debit card). We want it all, and we want it now. Our dissatisfaction is fuelled when our immediate demands are not instantly fulfilled.[102] And even when instantly fulfilled, material things never bring us the satisfaction we really crave and need to feel. The hit of dopamine we get from mindlessly scrolling, tapping, clicking, and getting a "like" on social media will never compare to the profound feeling of satisfaction we receive when doing meaningful work. Work we enjoy, which serves our life purpose, allows us the freedom to live our lives rather than just exist.

Leaders and managers can't leave their employees to be self-sufficient and expect them to transform their dissatisfaction with work and life into satisfaction. Leaders and managers must do much more to keep people satisfied and engaged at work and maintain a positive company culture.

Satisfaction and Dissatisfaction

There are two primary choices in life: to accept conditions as they exist or accept the responsibility for changing them.

Denis Waitley

I'm a baby boomer, so the things that animate me with passion and excitement might differ from those that excite younger people. The goal of this book is not to force my passion or purpose onto people; that's not my way, style, or philosophy. Instead, it's essential to choose to recognise that your employees are human and entirely unique. Each has different needs that contribute to their feelings of satisfaction. Getting in touch with your true purpose in life will start you on the path to true satisfaction and allow you to coach and lead your people in the same way.

Assumptions are dangerous things.

Agatha Christie

The multi-generational workforce isn't new; however, for the first time in history, we have five generations in the workforce. It means people have a vastly different set of needs, expectations, and motivators for their careers. It's essential to address these differences explicitly and directly. Workers no longer only want fifteen-minute smoke breaks or yearly bonuses; they want a sustainable living wage and diversity among their peers. Do workers even want to be called workers? (Starbucks calls them partners.) Addressing the expectations and needs of the people who work for you means asking for their input and actively listening. *Figure 22* below depicts the five generations at work today and their differences.

As a leader, you must ensure the expectations held by you, your business, and your people are clear and in alignment with each other. What baby boomers (like myself) might consider a "no brainer" might need more explicit clarification with other generations in your workforce and teams. Remember the adage, "When you assume, you make an ass out of you and me!" (Note to Rick: stop being a silly ass.)

GENs at Work

	Experienced / Characteristics	Work attitude / Aspirations	Job changing / Career path
1928 1945 **SILENT GENERATION** *Traditionalists*	**Experienced:** Great Depression WW2 Social security **Characteristics:** Dependable Straightforward Loyal	**Work attitude:** Follow established rules & policies **Aspirations:** The same loyalty from their employer	**Job changing:** Unwise **Career path:** Slow & steady
1946 1964 **BABY BOOMERS** *Boomers*	**Experienced:** Civil/Women's rights Cold war Moon landing **Characteristics:** Risk-taking Ambitious Work-centric	**Work attitude:** Strong sense of company loyalty **Aspirations:** To be valued & needed **6%** workforce*	**Job changing:** Sets me back **Career path:** Upward mobility
1965 1980 **GEN X** *MTV Generation*	**Experienced:** Fall of the Berlin wall Computer revolution September 11 **Characteristics:** Flexible Informal Independent	**Work attitude:** Prefer freedom to manage their work **Aspirations:** Work-life balance & independence **35%** workforce*	**Job changing:** Necessary **Career path:** Need to know options now
1981 1996 **MILLENNIALS** *Gen Y*	**Experienced:** New Millennium Dot-com bubble 2008 recession **Characteristics:** Civic & open-minded Achievement-oriented Digital savvy	**Work attitude:** Work collaboratively Socially engaged **Aspirations:** Seek order in world & meaning in work **35%** workforce*	**Job changing:** Part of my daily routine **Career path:** Switch frequently & fast
1997 2012 **GEN Z** *iGEN*	**Experienced:** COVID-19 2008 recession Social networking **Characteristics:** Progressive Entrepreneurial Tech reliant	**Work attitude:** Technoholics **Aspirations:** Security & stability **24%** workforce*	**Job changing:** What's a job? I have gigs **Career path:** Career "multitaskers"

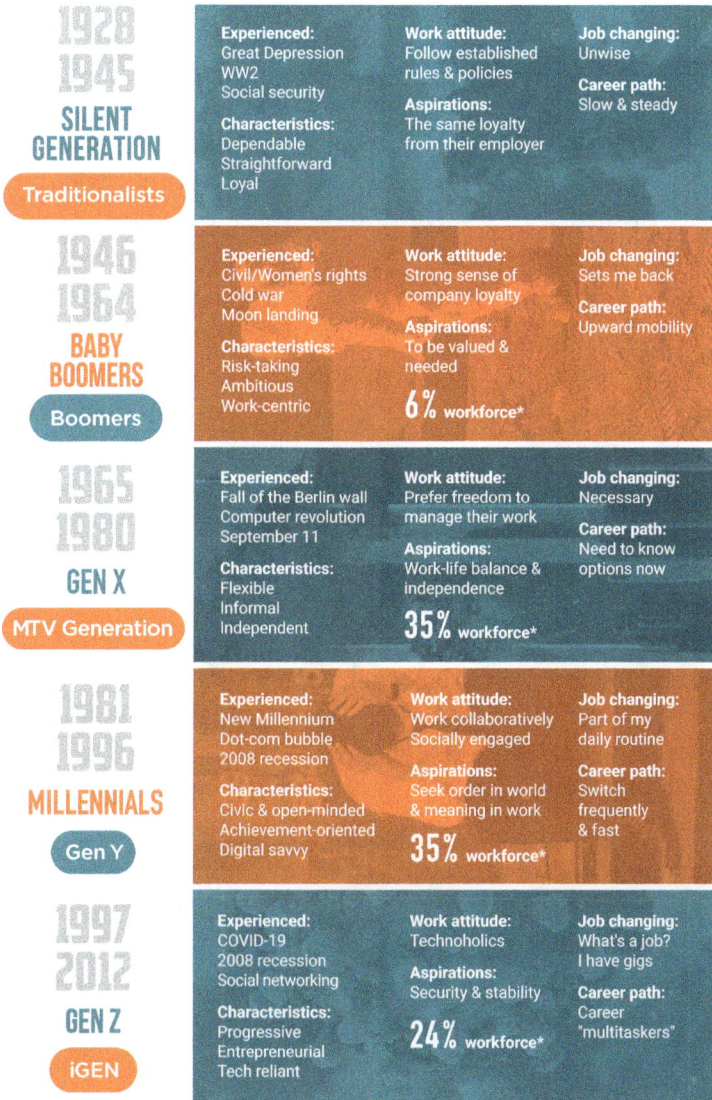

Source: Employment Worldwide by 2020, by Generation, Statista Research Department (2016)

Figure 22. Multiple Generations at Work

Some aspects of business may never truly improve across the board. For example, in-house training. People will still be dissatisfied with the announced day and time in advance, no matter where and in how many places we offer the training. It's not the best feeling, but I can't accommodate every person's schedule. (I guess that's an accepted aspect of a diverse and global team.) Even if I could, I'm sure some people would still be dissatisfied with the continuing education we require as a company. Kaizen[103] is one of the core values of our company (see *Figure 5* Kaizen in Chapter 3 of the book) and we interpret it as lifelong learning which is also one of my core values. We need to accept that some factors, such as employee complaints, will never improve no matter what changes we make.

To have satisfaction is to have a purpose, and our purpose then becomes our North Star, guiding our actions and fuelling our motivations. When we lose our way, we return to our purpose repeatedly to keep us moving forward on our goals because it's no longer just about us. It's about what we can achieve when we work together. It's about who we can become individually and as a unit when our purpose is achieved.

But purpose alone isn't enough to fuel our motivation, especially in our current conditions. Purpose can quickly be overshadowed by an unexpected illness or other duties that need to be picked up at home or can become clouded by too many decisions or decision-makers. We can get muddled by all the choices at our fingertips and easily overwhelmed, which often results in not acting on our purpose at all. This is the case for far too many people. They might know what they want to achieve and the purpose they're after, but they don't know how to bridge the gap between where they are now and where they want to be. This is why managers, leaders, and people, in general, give up most of the time. They don't know how to get themselves unstuck so they can move forward.

*Without knowledge, action is useless, and
knowledge without action is futile.*

~~~

Aku Bakr

It's not enough merely to discover your purpose; you must act on it. As a leader, you help your people bridge the gap between where they currently are and where they need to be. We achieve this by taking inventory of where we are right now and putting action steps in place for us to move forward and actualise those goals.

You can easily set goals for yourself and for others, but should you? You can't hold people's hands and micromanage them; that's not leadership. This is where my I AM OK TO FLY model comes in, and it can be used to help organisations, teams, and individuals set goals and act for increased satisfaction. I'll show you how to build your coaching skills and motivational techniques so people will be banging your door down, trying to discover how you cracked the code.

I AM OK to FLY

Be happy but never satisfied.

~~~

Bruce Lee

The reality is that there are many factors that pull us down and sink us—bad rules, bad policies, clock watching, wrong or late pay—they S(T)INK, making us dissatisfied. (I call issues that pull you and your organization down "S(T)INKers"—they stink, you sink.) Managers and leaders try to remove these dissatisfiers and try to motivate us and we all know that rarely works. Yes, we no longer sink, we just FLOAT and that brings us to no dissatisfaction; however, we still have No Satisfaction either.

But what if we could FLY? That's all very well believing that it's possible, but can we turn this belief into a reality? Fortunately, we can! The I AM OK to FLY coaching model helps people become passionate, fully engaged, thrive, and shine and become Satisfied, and of course, Fly. *Figure 23* below depicts the stages of S(T)INK, FLOAT, and FLY.

Personal perception, expectations, and individual beliefs all impact satisfaction. Without being too demanding or imposing, businesses can leverage these to help dissatisfied employees become satisfied. The I AM OK to FLY model works with people's perceptions and expectations to get to the root of dissatisfaction, enabling CXOs, leaders, executives, and managers to implement a clear and actionable plan for improvement and move from dissatisfaction to satisfaction.

S(T)INK
=
DISSATISFACTION

FLOAT
=
NO DISSATISFACTION
+ NO SATISFACTION

FLY
=
SATISFACTION

Figure 23. I AM OK to Fly Model

The I AM OK to FLY model aims to help employees and leaders formulate the vision for their lives that aligns with personal dreams or desires, decide upon the goals they want to achieve, and implement the plan of action that supports them in getting closer to their purpose by moving forward personally and professionally. We cannot sustain our people unless we know what they want to achieve and how we can help.

The first barrier that must be overcome is the barrier of personal perception. When we perceive something as unfair or unjust, it leads to dissatisfaction. For example, if we had been waiting in line at the bank for over an hour and someone were to waltz in and sit down at a teller's desk without saying a word, we would rightly be annoyed. I mean, *we're* the ones who had been waiting. From our perspective, the other person would be disrespectful to us by jumping the queue.

Now, if we had been told that other people had appointments that day and that the wait for us without an appointment would be over an hour, our perception of the events might different. Or, with this explicit information, we could choose to make an appointment and return at the appointed time instead. In both instances, clarity of the entire situation influences our perception of the events, resulting in different options and choices and outcomes.

Perceptions go hand in hand with our expectations, and expectations are particularly tricky. Why? Because they can be so different, depending on who sets them. The company must set the correct expectations by ensuring that they are clear, understood by employees, and aligned with the company purpose and goals. People who work for a company want and deserve to know what to expect and when to expect it. They can also reflect on how well they personally align with the company expectations.

Clear expectations enable the business to know what to expect as well. The relationship is symbiotic. Unfortunately, most business owners and managers see it as parasitic. Your people are not leeching off the enterprise. They are gaining and contributing to the business as much as the industry should be contributing to them. Therefore, everyone needs to know precisely what they can expect from each other and when they can expect it. Expectation alignment is key.

The I AM OK to FLY model helps guide us to the root of employee dissatisfaction. Even though some things may never improve across the board, it's essential to address the whole person in these meetings. As I mentioned before, challenges and issues in our personal lives tend to bleed into other areas of our lives.

There are five systematic steps to the I AM OK to FLY model:

- Step 1 is **I**nvestigate
- Step 2 is **A**nalyse
- Step 3 is **M**otivate
- Step 4 is **O**perate
- Step 5 is **K**aizen (explained in detail in Chapter 3 – Kaizen)
  And FLY is the feeling we get when we get it all right, that feeling of being so in the zone we can fly. I liken it to what psychologist Mihály Csíkszentmihályi in 1975 called a state of "flow,"[104] the psychology of optimal experience, a highly focused mental state which is conducive to greater productivity.

Implementing this framework helps uncover underlying problems in an organisation that may have remained purposefully or mistakenly disguised and hidden. It helps give leaders the information needed to get to the root of employee dissatisfaction, even if that dissatisfaction isn't directly related to work or the business. Any issues related to business can be addressed more effectively when leaders welcome feedback from their people and do their best to make changes to support them. This process also teaches leaders how, in their own unique way, to validate and motivate the people who work for them.

Although individuals can follow the model themselves, I recommend that it be performed as a team exercise, and it's best facilitated by a coach as there will be a lot of discussion and differences of opinion, which is the point of gaining greater awareness of people's feelings and perspectives of the issues and factors identified.

It's easier to understand the model by referring to the worksheet example in *Figure 24* below. This template is also available for download.[xxiii]

Step 1: Investigate—Where Are We Now?

> *The important thing is not to stop questioning; curiosity has its own reason for existing.*
>
> *Albert Einstein*

The first step is to establish the current state, finding where you are now, exactly. It's the proverbial "you are here" dot on the map at the mall. The **Investigate** step has two phases: Identify issues/factors and Classify issues/factors.

[xxiii] I AM OK to FLY template and other resources can be found at RickYvanovich.com/BAUU/.

	A	B	C	D	E	F	G	H	I	J	K	L	M	N	O
			We are here		Where we Plan to be			Benchmark Gap							
	Ref #	Whats the issue / factor?	Classification	Severity	Classification	Plan	Plan Gap	Benchmark Target	Benchmark Gap	Benchmark-Plan-Gap	Months to close Plan Gap	Priority ranking	Who controls it?	Budget Control?	Budget to close Gap
	1	Can pay salary up to 1 week late	S(t)ink	-7	Float	0	7	0	7	0	3	1	Payroll	CFO	
	2	20% of the time there are pay calculation errors especially overtime	S(t)ink	-6	Float	0	6	0	6	0	3	2	Payroll	CFO	
	3	No parking in office	S(t)ink	-2	S(t)ink	-2	0	0	2	2	n/a	n/a	Admin	CFO	
	4	No free lunch	S(t)ink	-1	Float	0	1	0	1	0	3	3	CHRO	CFO	
	5	Coaching available to everyone	Fly	4	Fly	8	4	9	5	1	24	5	L&D	CFO	
	6	Some managers micromanage	S(t)ink	-5	Float	0	5	0	5	0	9	4	CHRO	CHRO	
	7	Training available with training bond	Fly	3	Fly	7	4	8	5	1	6	7	CHRO	CEO	
	8	Mid level employees have IDPs	Fly	2	Fly	7	5	8	6	1	9	6	CHRO	CHRO	
	9	Employee of the quarter	Fly	1	Fly	3	2	7	6	4	3	8	CHRO	CHRO	
	10	13th month Annual Bonus	Float	0	Float	0	0	0	0	4	n/a	n/a	Payroll	CFO	

B - Investigate + Motivate (Explanation of the factor / issue)

C - Investigate + Motivate (Classification as S(t)ink, Float or Fly)

D - Analyse (Severity level. Float/S(t)ink (-10 to 0) & Fly (0 - 10))

E - Analyse (Classification as S(t)ink, Float or Fly)

F - Analyse (Plan level. Float/S(t)ink (-10 to 0) & Fly (0 - 10))

G - Analyse (Gap between F - D)

H - Analyse (Benchmark Target)

I - Analyse (Benchmark Gap H - D)

J - Analyse (Benchmark-Plan-Gap H - F)

K - Analyse + Operate (Estimated time in months to close the Plan Gap)

L - Analyse + Operate (Priority ranking)

M - Analyse (Who controls the issue, the PIC accountable to solve it)

N - Analyse (Who controls the Budget to this issue / factor)

O - Analyse + Operate (What Budget has been allocated to close the Gap)

Figure 24. I AM OK to FLY Template

Step 1 Phase 1: Identify Issues/Factors

Step 1 Phase 1 is to identify all factors related to the current level of satisfaction or dissatisfaction. List every single obstacle and issue—whether existing or missing, seen or unseen—that could be preventing satisfaction. This relates to column B in *Figure 25* below. This phase is about raising everyone's awareness of the current challenges that employees are facing. Where is the company experiencing dissatisfaction and satisfaction? You don't know what will aid or detract employees in being more satisfied unless we ask!

It's always better to ask than make an assumption.

Miguel Angel Ruiz

A	B
Ref #	**Whats the issue/factor?**
1	Can pay salary up to 1 week late
2	20% of the time there are pay calculation errors especially overtime
3	No parking in office
4	No free lunch
5	Coaching available to everyone
6	Some managers micromanage
7	Training available with training bond
8	Mid level employees have IDPs
9	Employee of the quarter
10	13th month Annual Bonus

B - Investigate + Motivate (Explanation of the factor / issue)

Figure 25. I AM OK to FLY Step 1 Phase 1: Identify Issues/Factors

Below are some suggested guiding questions you can use as a coaching tool in Phase 1 when assessing individuals, teams, and organisations. You don't necessarily need to use all the questions.

They're here to help uncover the current underlying issues and increase awareness. Depending on the answers given, you can use additional coaching questions to get to the root of the problem. In my mind, one of the best coaching questions is "*and what else*" (AWE) from *The Coaching Habit* by Michael Bungay Stanier. AWE is like the Swiss Army knife of coaching questions.[105] The following questions are open ended and will facilitate a conversation to uncover issues, as they require answers that go beyond a simple yes or no:

1. What comes to mind when I say *I can't get no satisfaction*?
2. What are you, your team, and your organisation satisfied with right now?
3. What are you, your team, and your organisation dissatisfied with right now?
4. What's demotivating you, your team, and your organisation right now?
5. What's motivating you, your team, and your organisation right now?
6. Walk me through what your, your team's, and your organisation's funnest day at work would be like.
7. What are the top three challenges you, your team, and your organisation face right now?
8. What are the top three opportunities you, your team, and your organisation face right now?
9. If you, your team, and your organisation could change one thing right now, what would it be?
10. If I could wave my magic wand and fix one thing in your life, your team, or your organisation, what would that be?

Step 1 Phase 2: Classify Issues/Factors

Step 1 Phase 2 is to classify each of the issues/factors identified in Step 1 Phase 1 into one of three categories: Sink, Float, or Fly. This relates to column C in *Figure 26* below. Whilst some might not actively drag you down, they also don't excite you or propel you forward. They're likely taken for granted and you only notice them when they don't happen. These factors simply allow you to float; hence, we aptly call them Floaters.

Both S(t)inkers and Floaters tend to be more extrinsic and environmental. They are the outside events that slide by unnoticed to trigger feelings of dissatisfaction. In contrast, factors that make people feel deeply valued, successful, and confident tend to be intrinsic, and we call them Flyers because they allow people in the company to Fly.

A	B	C
		We are here
Ref #	Whats the issue/factor?	Classification
1	Can pay salary up to 1 week late	S(t)ink
2	20% of the time there are pay calculation errors especially overtime	S(t)ink
3	No parking in office	S(t)ink
4	No free lunch	S(t)ink
5	Coaching available to everyone	Fly
6	Some managers micromanage	S(t)ink
7	Training available with training bond	Fly
8	Mid level employees have IDPs	Fly
9	Employee of the quarter	Fly
10	13th month Annual Bonus	Float

C - Investigate + Motivate (Classification as S(t)ink, Float or Fly)

Figure 26. I AM OK to FLY Step 1 Phase 2: Classify Issues/Factors

Below are suggested guiding questions, along with examples that will help classify the factors you identified as S(t)inkers or Floaters or Flyers.

These questions tend to be help classify S(t)inkers and Floaters:

1. Which issues/factors, when **not** resolved, will make you feel unhappy? (S(t)inkers)
    Examples:
    ▪ Your working hours are miscalculated this month, and you get paid less than you expected. Similar

mistakes happen next month, and the next, and the next. (S(t)inker)
- Your salary is again paid late this month. That's the third month in a row. (S(t)inker)
- Your payslip shows different amounts to what you were paid. (S(t)inker)

2. Which issues/factors, when resolved, will **not** make you feel happy? (Floaters)
   Examples:
   - Next month, you get paid for the hours you were short-changed for last month. (Floater)
   - Your pay slip shows the correct pay calculation and matches what you were paid. (Floater)

3. Which issues/factors, when they don't happen, make you feel unhappy? (S(t)inkers)
   Example: Some of the lifts in the bustling building you work in are out of order today. You end up waiting an extra twenty minutes, and you're late for a meeting. (S(t)inker)

4. Which issues/factors, when they happen on time, do you overlook? (Floaters)
   Examples:
   - Your salary is paid on time. (Floater)
   - Your train arrived on time. (Floater)

5. Which issues/factors are used as threats to get someone to do something? (S(t)inkers)
   Examples:
   - You're told your leave will not be approved unless you get the report out in time. (S(t)inker)
   - You can't go home until your work is one hundred percent complete. (S(t)inker)

6. Which issues/factors are used to stop someone from doing something? (S(t)inkers)
   Examples:
   - Company restriction on overtime hours. (S(t)inker)
   - Compulsory brown paper bag working lunch today stops you from going out to lunch with your friends and relaxing. (S(t)inker)

7. Which issues/factors affect the physical working environment? (S(t)inkers or Floaters)
   Examples:
   - WiFi remains spotty and slow in your area of the office. (S(t)inker)
   - WiFi always works normally on the other side of the office. (Floater)

8. Which issues/factors affect the organisational working environment? (S(t)inkers or Floaters)
   Examples:
   - Your office is in the middle of nowhere with no shops nearby. (S(t)inker)
   - Working hours are nine to five with no flexibility. (S(t)inker)
   - The company policies are clear and easy to understand. (Floater)

9. Which issues/factors affect interpersonal relationships? (S(t)inkers or Floaters)
   Examples:
   - Your boss micromanages you. (S(t)inker)
   - You have supportive co-workers. (Floater)

10. Which issues/factors are extrinsic/environmental in nature? (S(t)inker or Floater)
    Examples:

- No parking close to the office. (S(t)inker)
- The buildings elevators are fast and never crowded. (Floater)

11. Which issues/factors are transactional in nature? (S(t) inkers or Floaters)
    Examples:
    - The company trip was cancelled at short notice in 2020 due to the pandemic. (S(t)inker)
    - The company trip was not cancelled in 2022. (Floater)

Now, here are some suggested guiding questions, along with examples, that will help differentiate between Floaters and Flyers but watch out for S(t)inkers as they have a nasty habit of popping up.

1. Which items/issues, when resolved, will make you feel happy? (Floaters or Flyers)
    Examples:
    - The broken elevators are fixed. (Floater)
    - The coffee machine is fixed. (Floater)
    - The aircon works today. (Floater)

2. Which items/issues, when they happen, will make you feel happy? (Floaters or Flyers)
    Examples:
    - Your salary is paid early. (Floater)
    - You are awarded the Employee of the Month. (Flyer)

3. Which items/issues won't you miss if it doesn't happen all the time? (Likely to be Floaters)
    Example:
    - Doughnuts at the Friday morning meeting. (Floater)
    - You deliver a lunch and learn. (Flyer)

4. Which items/issues are intrinsic in nature? (Typically Flyers, but could end up being Floaters)
   Examples:
   - You complete your daily active goals for the fifth time this week. (Flyer)
   - You come up with new personal goals to achieve. (Floater for some, Flyer for others)

5. Which items/issues relate to personal growth? (Flyers)
   Examples:
   - Your company sponsors you for the CCMP certification course.[106] (Flyer)
   - Your company sponsors you for an executive MBA. (Flyer)

6. Which items/issues relate to achievement? (Flyers)
   Examples:
   - You are awarded the CCMC certification upon completion of the course.[107] (Flyer)
   - You complete your MBA and graduate with distinction. (Flyer)
   - Your team wins the team of the year award. (Flyer)

7. Which items/issues relate to advancement? (Flyers)
   Example:
   - You're promoted to Project Manager upon passing your Project Management Institute (PMI) certification. (Flyer)
   - You completed your traineeship. Your job title changes from trainee to junior accountant. (Flyer)

8. Which items/issues relate to recognition/appreciation? (Flyers)
   Example:
   - Your boss drops a note to thank you for the excellent brochure design you created. (Flyer)

9. Which items/issues relate to the work itself? (Flyers)
    Examples:
    - You are invited and join a project because of your knowledge, attitude, skills, and habits. (Flyer)
    - You are invited to attend a prestigious conference to share your project success story. (Flyer, though could be a S(t) inker if you hate being in the spotlight)

10. Which items/issues relate to responsibility? (Flyers)
    Examples:
    - You are assigned an important project to lead. (Flyer, though could be a S(t)inker if you've been set up to fail)
    - You are assigned a fast-track management trainee to mentor. (Flyer)

11. Which items/issues are related to autonomy? (Flyers)
    Examples:
    - You are empowered to attend any accredited coaching certification course of your choosing. (Flyer)
    - You are empowered to select the members of the project team. (Flyer)

12. Which items/issues are associated to relatedness? (Flyers)
    Example:
    - You become an ambassador on the company's employer branding team because you walk the talk. (Flyer)

Step 2: Analyse—Where Do We Want to Be?

Without a standard, there is no logical basis for making a decision or taking action.

Joseph M. Juran

Step 2 begs the question: *where do we want to be?* When conducted collaboratively, these first two steps—Investigate and Analyse—enable your organisation to uncover the underlying issues, classify them, assign severities, and come up with a benchmark for each issue. Once we know the differences between where people are and where they want to be, we can help them. Getting clear about the goals opens the door for innumerable opportunities to workshop, greenlight, brainstorm, and apply design thinking (creative problem solving) to transform and overcome barriers to satisfaction.

When figuring out where we want to end up, we must reflect on every issue/factor uncovered listed in Step 1 Phase 1 (*Figure 25*, column B) and Step 1 Phase 2 (*Figure 26*, Column C) then allocate each issue with a severity level (*Figure 27*, column D). For S(t)inkers and Floaters, we use the range -10 to 0. For Flyers, we use 0 to +10.

A	B	C	D
		We are here	
Ref #	Whats the issue/factor?	Classification	Severity
1	Can pay salary up to 1 week late	S(t)ink	-7
2	20% of the time there are pay calculation errors especially overtime	S(t)ink	-6
3	No parking in office	S(t)ink	-2
4	No free lunch	S(t)ink	-1
5	Coaching available to everyone	Fly	4
6	Some managers micromanage	S(t)ink	-5
7	Training available with training bond	Fly	3
8	Mid level employees have IDPs	Fly	2
9	Employee of the quarter	Fly	1
10	13th month Annual Bonus	Float	0

D - Analyse (Severity level. Float/S(t)ink (-10 to 0) & Fly (0 - 10))

Figure 27. I AM OK to FLY Step 2: Analyse – Where Do We Want To Be?

Next, we reconsider the classification from Step 1 Phase 2, and we set a plan to what classification we want it to be. For example, a current S(t)inker we'd likely plan to make a Floater (*Figure 28*, column E). Whether we reclassify it or not, we give it a plan severity level (*Figure 28*, column F). So how do you select what the plan level should be? That's the result of continuing dialogue about the issue. In our example, in Step 1, we identified an issue that salaries are regularly paid one week late, and this was classified as a S(t)inker with a severity of -7.

Our plan may be to resolve this issue by paying on time per the payroll calendar and thus turn it into a Floater with a severity of 0 (it's no longer negative as we pay on time, it's not a Flyer as people expect to be paid on time and only notice when this does not happen). So, we're planning to change this S(t)inker into a Floater and improving its severity from -7 to 0 (*Figure 28*, the plan gap column G). You may be wondering who would plan to *not* pay salaries on time? Well, what it you were a start-up strapped for cash or the pandemic has severely impacted your business, in such extreme cases maybe the plan is to pay late. Presumably it's going to be a temporary thing and as it's reframed as the survival of the company, you keep it as a Floater and give it a bit of a negative score, say -2.

A	B	C	D	E	F	G
		We are here		**Where we Plan to be**		
Ref #	Whats the issue/factor?	Classification	Severity	Classification	Plan	Plan Gap
1	Can pay salary up to 1 week late	S(t)ink	-7	Float	0	7
2	20% of the time there are pay calculation errors especially overtime	S(t)ink	-6	Float	0	6
3	No parking in office	S(t)ink	-2	S(t)ink	-2	0
4	No free lunch	S(t)ink	-1	Float	0	1
5	Coaching available to everyone	Fly	4	Fly	8	4
6	Some managers micromanage	S(t)ink	-5	Float	0	5
7	Training available with training bond	Fly	3	Fly	7	4
8	Mid level employees have IDPs	Fly	2	Fly	7	5
9	Employee of the quarter	Fly	1	Fly	3	2
10	13th month Annual Bonus	Float	0	Float	0	0

E - Analyse (Classification as S(t)ink, Float or Fly)
F - Analyse (Plan level. Float/S(t)ink (-10 to 0) & Fly (0 - 10))
G - Analyse (Gap between F - D)

Figure 28. I AM OK to FLY Step 2: Analyse – Where Do We Want To Be?

Continuing our example, we can set a benchmark if there is an industry or other internal benchmark or metric available. As far as paying salaries on time, the benchmark is to pay on time! In this example, the benchmark would be 0 (*Figure 29*, column H). The benchmark can be different to the plan, that's up to you. Then we calculate the two benchmark gaps. The Benchmark Gap being the difference between the benchmark and actual (*Figure 29*, column I) and the Plan-Benchmark Gap, the difference between the plan and the benchmark (*Figure 29*, column J). Next is setting a timeframe (months) to close the plan gap (*Figure 29*, column K). This can be changed to days or years depending on however long you think it's going to take.

A	B	H	I	J	K
			Benchmark Gap		
Ref #	Whats the issue/factor?	Benchmark Target	Benchmark Gap	Benchmark-Plan- Gap	Months to close Plan Gap
1	Can pay salary up to 1 week late	0	7	0	3
2	20% of the time there are pay calculation errors especially overtime	0	6	0	3
3	No parking in office	0	2	2	n/a
4	No free lunch	0	1	0	3
5	Coaching available to everyone	9	5	1	24
6	Some managers micromanage	0	5	0	9
7	Training available with training bond	8	5	1	6
8	Mid level employees have IDPs	8	6	1	9
9	Employee of the quarter	7	6	4	3
10	13th month Annual Bonus	0	0	0	n/a

H - Analyse (Benchmark Target)
I - Analyse (Benchmark Gap H - D)
J - Analyse (Benchmark-Plan-Gap H - F)
K - Analyse + Operate (Estimated time in months to close the Plan Gap)

Figure 29. I AM OK to FLY Step 2: the Benchmark Gap

As we analyse, we identify who controls the issue (*Figure 30*, column M) and who has budget control over it (*Figure 30*, column N). Use these prompts to help:

1. Which items are 100 percent within your control?
2. Which items are 100 percent within someone else's control?
3. Which items are outside of your organisation's control?
4. If the item is subject to a budget, who controls it?

In our example, salaries are controlled by the payroll team, and that's under the CFO who controls that budget. As there may be a financial cost involved in addressing some of the issues, undoubtedly Return on Investment (ROI) will come into play and some fixes may be deemed too costly to completely fix. When this happens, be warned there can be some heated debates! The resulting budget to close the gap should be agreed and authorised (*Figure 30*, column O). Finally, we need to rank them in priority order (*Figure 30*, column L).

A	B	L	M	N	O
Ref #	Whats the issue/factor?	Priority ranking	Who controls it?	Budget Control?	Budget to close Gap
1	Can pay salary up to 1 week late	1	Payroll	CFO	
2	20% of the time there are pay calculation errors especially overtime	2	Payroll	CFO	
3	No parking in office	n/a	Admin	CFO	
4	No free lunch	3	CHRO	CFO	
5	Coaching available to everyone	5	L&D	CFO	
6	Some managers micromanage	4	CHRO	CHRO	
7	Training available with training bond	7	CHRO	CEO	
8	Mid level employees have IDPs	6	CHRO	CHRO	
9	Employee of the quarter	8	CHRO	CHRO	
10	13th month Annual Bonus	n/a	Payroll	CFO	

L - Analyse + Operate (Priority ranking)
M - Analyse (Who controls the issue, the PIC accountable to solve it)
N - Analyse (Who controls the Budget to this issue / factor)
O - Analyse + Operate (What Budget has been allocated to close the Gap)

Figure 30. I AM OK to FLY Step 2, Who Owns the Issue?

There's a lot going on in this Step 2, so here's a bullet point recap that refers to *Figure 31* below.

Ref #	Whats the issue / factor?	Classification (We are here)	Severity	Classification (Where we Plan to be)	Plan	Plan Gap	Benchmark Target	Benchmark Gap	Benchmark-Plan-Gap	Months to close Plan Gap	Priority ranking	Who controls it?	Budget Control?	Budget to close Gap
1	Can pay salary up to 1 week late	S(t)ink	-7	Float	0	7	0	7	0	3	1	Payroll	CFO	
2	20% of the time there are pay calculation errors especially overtime	S(t)ink	-6	Float	0	6	0	6	0	3	2	Payroll	CFO	
3	No parking in office	S(t)ink	-2	S(t)ink	-2	0	0	2	2	n/a	n/a	Admin	CFO	
4	No free lunch	S(t)ink	-1	Float	0	1	0	1	0	3	3	CHRO	CFO	
5	Coaching available to everyone	Fly	4	Fly	8	4	9	5	1	24	5	L&D	CFO	
6	Some managers micromanage	S(t)ink	-5	Float	0	5	0	5	0	9	4	CHRO	CHRO	
7	Training available with training bond	Fly	3	Fly	7	4	8	5	1	6	7	CHRO	CEO	
8	Mid level employees have IDPs	Fly	2	Fly	7	5	8	6	1	9	6	CHRO	CHRO	
9	Employee of the quarter	Fly	1	Fly	3	2	7	6	4	3	8	CHRO	CHRO	
10	13th month Annual Bonus	Float	0	Float	0	0	0	0	0	n/a	n/a	Payroll	CFO	

Figure 31. I AM OK to FLY Step 2 Recap

- **Column D** = Allocate each item a severity level. Float/S(t)ink (-10 to 0), Fly (0 to +10).
- **Column E** = Set a target classification: S(t)ink, Float, or Fly, for where we want to be, which could be different from where you currently are, the initial classification you put in Column C. Consider what is the impact of each item if its status changes?
- **Column F** = Set a plan level of where we want to be: Float or S(t)ink (-10 to 0), or Fly (0 to +10).
- **Column G** = Calculate the gap (Column F minus Column D) between where we are now (Column D) and where we want to be (Column F).
- **Column H** = What should the performance benchmark be for each item? Set a benchmark target (best practice or industry benchmark): Float or S(t)ink (-10 to 0), or Fly (0 to +10).
- **Column I** = What is the gap between actual and ideal performance? Calculate the benchmark gap (Column H minus Column D), the difference between where we are now (Column D) and the benchmark target (Column H).
- **Column J** = Calculate the benchmark-plan gap (Column H minus Column F), the difference between the benchmark target (column H), and the plan of where we want to be (Column F).
- **Column K** = What's the timeline for closing the gap for each item?
- **Column L** = What's the priority of each item? Rank them in priority order.
- **Column M** = Identify who controls the issue. The Person in Charge (PIC) is accountable for solving the issue. For example, for the late payment of salaries, the PIC would be the head of the payroll department.
- **Column N** = Identify who has budgetary responsibility for each issue. For example, the facilities manager controls the budget for lift repairs and maintenance for the broken lifts.

- **Column O** = If closing the gap will have a cost, what should the budget be?

In some cases, this Analysis Step serves as a vehicle to transform the current issue from one state to another, such as S(t)inker to Floater and, more importantly, increases awareness of the state of each issue and provides the clarity to help make the hard decisions, whether to solve and transform issues completely or not.

Additionally, by identifying the effort and cost, we can see the expected ROI associated with fixing an issue. Collaboration and co-creation are keys to success between you and your people who need to help create and be part of the solution.

When looking at the ROI, you will likely notice the potentially poorer ROI for improving S(t)inkers and Floaters and the far greater ROI for Flyers.

Step 3: Motivate—I Believe I Can Fly

I believe I can fly
I believe I can touch the sky
I think about it every night and day
Spread my wings and fly away
I believe I can soar

R. Kelly, I Believe I Can Fly Lyrics

I believe *I* can fly. Do you believe that you and others can fly, too? For leaders, it's not just about making sure people are satisfied with their work. It's also our job to facilitate growth. In Step 3, we turn our attention to uncovering things that can create sustainable motivational experiences for our people. Optimal motivation means having positive energy, vitality, and a sense of well-being, as well as being in the flow and achieving meaningful goals—all of which allow your people to thrive, shine, and fly, both inside and outside of the corporate environment.

I've so far mentioned internal and external motivation, which is the simple duality that I believe many people are aware of. I'd now like to go a bit deeper to challenge that, though; I ask you to be open-minded about it, and I wonder if you'll be curious enough to read the following book I'm referring to, as it triggered me!

In her books *Master Your Motivation* and *Why Motivating People Doesn't Work and What Does*, Susan Fowler introduces us to the term *optimal motivation*.[108,109] Most people think of motivation as a feeling; you either have it, or you don't. In contrast, Fowler views motivation on a spectrum across the two dimensions of self-regulation (low quality to high quality) and psychological needs (low quality to high quality) which result in a range from disinterested to external to imposed to aligned to integrated and finally inherent.

Spectrum of Motivation

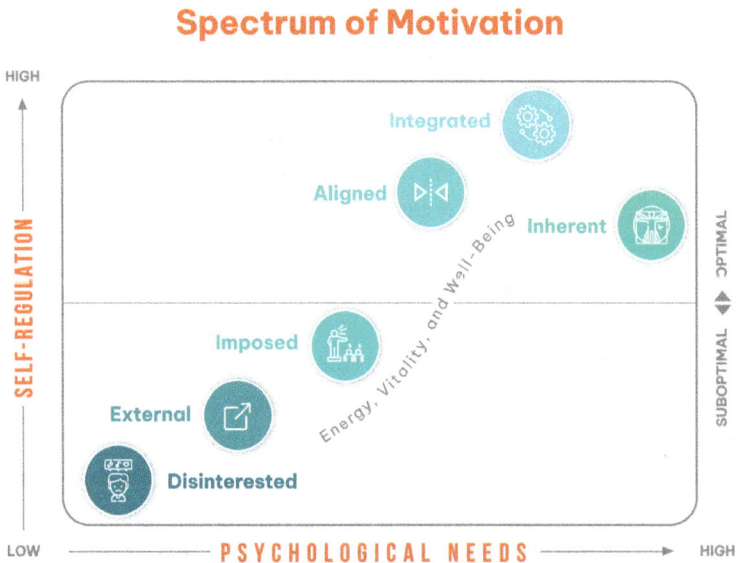

Figure 32. Spectrum of Motivation

Disinterested motivation is when self-regulation and psychological needs are low, your employees' needs are not being met, and from Fowler's model, that's the bottom half of both self-regulation and psychological needs. They're disinterested, external, and imposed. At the other end of the spectrum is *optimal motivation,* where self-regulation and psychological needs are high, your employees' needs are being met, and from Fowler's model, that's the top half of both self-regulation and psychological needs. They're aligned, integrated, and inherent. They're infinitely more satisfied at work because they can regulate their emotions, provide their own motivation, and meet their own psychological needs.

I recommend you read the book to get the full value and understanding of it. I'm hardly scratching the surface. To demonstrate the spectrum, let's imagine you just attended a weekly project status meeting and let's look at the six types of motivational attitudes:

1. Disinterested motivational attitude—"What a waste of time, zero value, and now I'm even further behind in my work."
2. External motivational attitude—"Cool, I demonstrated I'm ahead of schedule on my part of the project and everyone agreed I'm an asset to the team."
3. Imposed motivational attitude—"Peer pressure makes me attend, despite me having better things to do with my time. Don't people realise how stressed I am to keep up?"
4. Aligned motivational attitude—"I'm glad I attended, that presentation from Zara and Jim was inspiring. I'd never thought to do things that way and it just clicked. I'm gonna use that method moving forward!"
5. Integrated motivational attitude—"I reminded the team how this project aligns to the quarterly and annual objectives, not just of the division but the whole

company. Everyone agreed they'd lost sight of that and that really helped get everyone get pumped."

6. Inherent motivational attitude—"These project meetings are the highlight of my week, so much fun, I wish every day was like this!"

Motivated people always find a way.
Unmotivated people always find a way not to.

Ed Latimore

Motivation is a skill. Below are some suggested guiding questions to help leaders understand the motivation of their employees and create self-sustainable motivation:

1. Which of your company's core values most strongly resonates with you and your team?
2. What's your current life purpose? What's stopping you from achieving this through your team or organisation?
3. What's your current life goal? What's stopping you from achieving this through your team or organisation?
4. How can you, your team, and your organisation support personal growth?
5. How can you, your team, and your organisation help ensure everyone has a clear life purpose?
6. How can you, your team, and your organisation promote an infinite mindset? (see Chapter 3 Infinite Mindset)
7. How can you, your team, and your organisation equip people with the skills they will need in the future?
8. How can you, your team, and your organisation enable autonomy?

9. How can you, your team, and your organisation improve individuals' emotional intelligence? (See Chapter 3 How I Show Up)
10. How can you, your team, and your organisation create a high-performance team culture? (See Chapter 6 Culture)
11. How can you, your team, and your organisation create a coaching culture? (See Chapter 6 Coaching Culture)
12. How can you, your team, and your organisation foster greater relatedness/belonging to the team and organisation?
13. How can you, your team, and your organisation foster greater certainty and variety in a person's job?
14. How can you, your team, and your organisation foster a learning culture?

There are many ways to Fly. Motivational workshops, brainstorming, greenlighting (structured brainstorming where only ideas are generated with no comments, judgement, or questions asked about ideas given), and design thinking (creative problem-solving), are all tools executives can use to motivate people.[xxiv]

In Step 3, it's not uncommon to unearth individuals' life purpose or lack thereof. If that happens, you can use the tools from Chapter 1 Life Purpose Formulation. Remember, each person is unique, and this process supports a people-first culture.

As we work through this stage, we need to repeat the Analyse stage in Step 2, as new insights open new ideas about where we want to be. Because motivation is critical, we did a deep dive earlier in Chapter 4 Motivation, so one idea is to look at that section again.

[xxiv] Greenlighting resources can be found at RickYvanovich.com/BAUU/.

Step 4: Operate—Actions to Get There

There is never enough time to do everything, but there is always enough time to do the most important things.

Brian Tracy

We must act and improve how we conduct Business As UnUsual to transform the areas of employee dissatisfaction into areas of great satisfaction. In this Step, we need to put each of the prioritised items from Steps 2 and 3 into an action plan. We use **S**trategy, **T**actics, **A**ction, and **B**reakthroughs (a.k.a. the STAB model) to help us make the most impactful choices that yield the biggest cultural and personal transformations. Now I'm not suggesting you need to run around with a knife on Friday the 13th to make your point. But the STAB model has helped many radically transform their business and culture to promote a place of passion, purpose, and accountability and create the type of organisation where people want to work.

STAB Model – Strategy, Tactics, Actions, Breakthrough

Strategy without tactics is the slowest route to victory. Tactics without strategy are the noise before defeat.

Sun Tzu, The Art of War

People say they understand strategy, tactics, and actions, but the elements get mixed up all too often. When they're not in logical alignment, they are noticeably less impactful. I created the STAB model shown in *Figure 33* below to help address this challenge and keep each aspect in alignment.

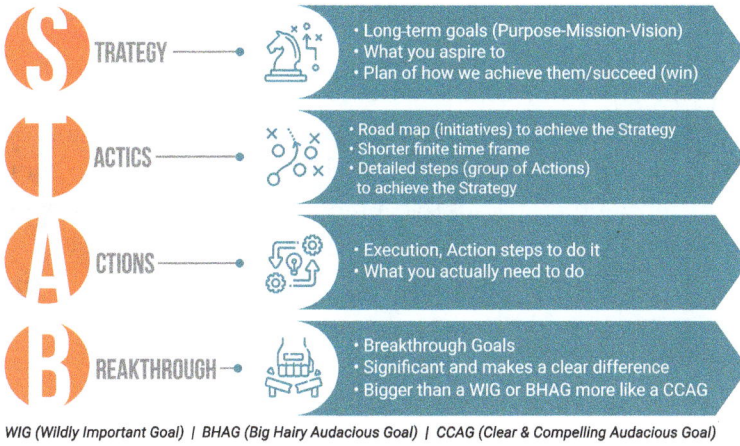

WIG (Wildly Important Goal) | BHAG (Big Hairy Audacious Goal) | CCAG (Clear & Compelling Audacious Goal)

Figure 33. STAB Model

What is strategy? What are tactics? People keep talking about them, yet struggle to define, differentiate, and achieve them. This model shows you how to take one or more STABs to ensure you succeed. STAB is a linkage from top to bottom and from bottom to top. It's designed to ensure alignment.

Strategy in this context refers to strategic plans, the long-term goals, what you aspire to, and the comprehensive plan for achieving them. We tie an employee's long-term goals to their personal life purpose, the purpose and mission of the company, and the vision that you and that person have for their tenure with the company.

Step 4 sets the expectations for taking into consideration what you as the business owner want your employee to aspire to and your employee's aspirations. Strategy also covers what the employee needs to do to achieve their goals and what the leader will do to support them. Typically, we aim for up to three top strategies. Any more than that, and we'll lose focus and fail to achieve them.[xxv]

[xxv] The Power of Focus and other resources can be found at RickYvanovich.com/BAUU/.

Tactics are the roadmap (initiatives) for achieving the strategy. They cover a shorter, finite timeframe. Tactics comprise detailed steps or groups of actions that need to be executed for each strategy. This ensures employees make small, sustainable progress on their goals without stalling or losing forward momentum. Remember, progress leads to happiness. Don't forget to celebrate achievements (we covered this in earlier Chapters).

Actions are the steps we need to execute to achieve the tactics, and thus, the strategy. The most crucial part of this work is the action. Without action, there is no progress, and therefore, no change in the level of satisfaction. The actions or habits are the steps to achieve the strategies and tactics. Actions need to be measurable as without measurement, we'll never know if the action has been reached or accomplished. Actions need to be achievable (we don't want to set up anyone to fail as that would be demotivational) and instantly understandable by whoever needs to do the action. The clearer an action is, the easier it will be to execute without misunderstanding. By clarity, we mean the clarity of the goals, roles, responsibilities, and expectations of the action.

Breakthrough goals are even bigger than Wildly Important Goals (WIGs) or Big Hairy Audacious Goals (BHAGs). They're more like Clear and Compelling Audacious Goals (CCAGs). To raise the bar, knock it out of the park, or even off the planet, we need to establish some breakthrough goals. So, look at the goals and challenge whether they are breakthrough or not, and if they aren't, then make them bigger.

Logically, one would think we should start with breakthrough goals because they come before strategies. However, have you ever smiled or laughed or leapt for joy when presented with the prospect of coming up with strategies, tactics, and actions? Probably not. Nor have I (unless a grimace can be misinterpreted as a smile). Contrast that with the STAB analogy that says: we gotta have multiple STABs at it until we kill it! Made you smile, right?

Referring to the STAB template in *Figure 34* below, there is a cascading relationship between the items:[xxvi]

- I recommend up to 3 breakthrough goals (B1–B3).
- For each breakthrough goal e.g. B1, I recommend there can be up to 3 strategies (S1–S3).
- For each strategy (B1–S1), I recommend there can be up to 5 tactics (T1–T5).
- For each tactic (B1–S1–T1), I recommend there can be up to 5 actions (A1–A5).
- Every item is given a priority, a target completion date, and a person in charge of completing the task.
- The template also allows leaders to track each task's status, marking it as not started, on track, ahead, or completed.

Overall Purpose:						
Priority (1-10)	Target Completion Date	Person in Charge (PIC)	Status	Reference*		Strategy Tactics Actions Breakthrough
						Breakthrough
				B1		
				B2		
				B3		
						Strategy
				B1 S1		
				B1 S2		
				B1 S3		
						Tactics
				B1 S1 T1		
				B1 S1 T2		
				B1 S1 T3		
				B1 S1 T4		
				B1 S1 T5		
						Actions
				B1 S1 T1 A1		
				B1 S1 T1 A2		
				B1 S1 T1 A3		
				B1 S1 T1 A4		
				B1 S1 T1 A5		

* References links & cascades STAB together = Breakthrough to Strategies to Tactics to Actions

Figure 34. STAB Template

[xxvi] The STAB template and other resources can be found at RickYvanovich.com/BAUU/.

Now that you have the gist of the STAB tool, let's return to the I AM OK to FLY worksheet in *Figure 31* above for each of the issues and factors prioritised in Steps 2 and 3. To promote a culture of passion and innovation, we need an action plan to realise these goals. Without a plan encouraging people to grow, action sputters and fizzles. Priorities, timelines, and budgets need to be reconfirmed and adjusted as required. Below are some suggested guiding questions to help come up with the Step 4 Operate plan and complete the STAB:

1. Which items are you, your team, and your organisation saying Yes to?
2. Which items are you, your team, and your organisation saying No to?
3. What are the top three strategies for you, your team, and your organisation?
4. What tactics are associated with each strategy for you, your team, and organisation?
5. What detailed action steps are required to drive each tactic for you, your team, and your organisation?
6. What are the breakthrough goals for you, your team, and your organisation?
7. What is the priority of each strategy, tactic, and action?
8. What is the target completion date for each strategy, tactic, and action?
9. Who is the Person in Charge of each strategy, tactic, and action?
10. Which observable behaviours need to change?
11. What habits need to change?

Step 5: Kaizen—Sustainable Satisfaction

Kaizen means ongoing improvement involving everybody, without spending much money.

Masaaki Imai

In Step 5, we return to Kaizen, the Japanese "change for the better" business philosophy that focuses on continuous improvement in work and life. It became popularised through the book *Kaizen: The Key to Japanese Competitive Success* by Masaaki Imai.[110] My definition is a slight adaptation of this original Japanese meaning. I see it as lifelong learning, primarily the continuous improvement of self and also of processes. We adopted this as one of our core values at TRG International, and literally hundreds of interns each year say it's the number one value they like and will follow even after their internship ends.

So, Step 5 in the I AM OK to FLY model is an opportunity to reflect, which goes hand in hand with kaizen's continuous improvement. We want sustainable satisfaction and continuous improvement. Striving for ongoing personal and professional growth means everyone's attitude and mindset needs to be better, starting with one idea at a time.

The following are some suggested guiding questions to help leaders navigate kaizen:

1. What progress can we celebrate?
2. What worked well?
3. What did not turn out as planned?
4. If we could rewind the clock and do it all over again, what would we change?
5. Which actions produced the biggest results?
6. How do we feel about the outcomes we achieved so far?
7. What are our emotions telling us about the current situation?
8. What's stopping you, your team, and your organisation from accelerating the breakthrough goal?
9. How are we doing on a scale of 1 to 10? What needs to happen or change to raise that to a 10? If we're already at 10, how can we get to 11?
10. What adjustments need to be made to the STAB?

This step in the model relies on leaders to set within their teams the cultural tone that trickles down to individual employees. It's the executives' or CEO's job to set the cultural precedent for leaders. The value of continuous progress, both for individuals and the collective, allows for innovative ideas, candour between employees, and open dialogue about the challenges we face as a business and a team.

Under this guiding principle, I know that I, as a leader in my business, am not the single decision-maker or forward thinker. This value makes it a priority to hear all the voices in an organisation and treat people like the intelligent and capable problem-solvers they are instead of like people who need to be "kept in line" or given extensive rules to continue making progress in business and life.

Step 6: Fly

The moment you doubt whether you can fly,
you cease for ever to be able to do it.

J. M. Barrie, Peter Pan

Flying in this framework is akin to (Mihály Csíkszentmihályi's) "flow," that feeling of being in the zone, when time just flies by without you noticing as you are so focused and being so productive, time just flies.[111] So in this model, Flying is when we help our employees to integrate all these different aspects of growth and purpose into their day-to-day work and personal lives. The more we eliminate S(t)inkers and fuel Flyers, the more satisfied people become personally and professionally, resulting in greater success for all. We're helping and we want people to be in the zone.

Every person in an organisation sees things differently because we all have different perceptions, experiences, and beliefs. We're all unique and pack our own work and personal experiences into who we are, both inside and outside of our professional roles. As business leaders, we want to help make as many people as possible satisfied in the workplace. In business, just as in life, we need clarity, direction, and clear goals for satisfaction.

However, you cannot achieve things for others. You can't make anyone do anything, no matter how important it is to you or how much you believe it would increase their job and life satisfaction. You have a business to run, and you can't be there to hold everyone's hand along the way.

That's why these tools are helpful, but they're not helpful on their own. It's important to balance the sources of motivation for your employees. Internal motivation comes from the employee's internal desire to do more and achieve. External motivation comes from the validation or acknowledgement shown by peers and supervisors.

Understanding and implementing the different models and tools in this book that leverage both internal and external motivation in the workplace help increase overall employee satisfaction and the clear and direct expectations, goals, and systems already in place.

Does the Job Fit?

The only way to do great work is to love what you do. If you haven't found it yet, keep looking. Don't settle.

Steve Jobs

Businesses need to have a strategy for people placement that addresses both internal and external hiring. When searching for the right candidate to place, a company uses multiple assessments to find that rare but crucial combination of job fit and job sculpting. Let me explain.

Job fit is about matching a human (a peg) with a job (the hole) and seeking the best possible fit. People who fit into their roles well will perform well without the need for constant supervision and management. As new people join a team, the culture and performance of the team change. Thus, the job performance pattern (the hole) also changes, which makes finding the right fit an ongoing and dynamic process.

Job sculpting is slightly different to job fit. Sometimes, candidates are the perfect fit for a job that isn't available or doesn't even exist. However, if a candidate has the right attitude, skills, experience, and energy, we often sculpt a job around their strengths and passions.

> *If we get the right people on the bus, the right people in the right seats, and the wrong people off the bus, then we'll figure out how to take it someplace great.*
>
> *Jim Collins*

By assessing each person, we can identify the right people for the different seats on the bus (using Jim Collin's analogy above) and identify the wrong people for the bus. This includes how people behave and what makes them tick. Do the same for the job we want to fill, by assessing the best performers in that role and finding more like them. We find the best people for that job. This process makes it easier for leaders to match the right candidate with the right job and team—just stick the right peg in the right hole.

People have moved away from working in an office and towards working remotely. A distributed remote workforce has presented all sorts of problems. How we communicate and interact with each other remotely is a far cry from how we interacted when we were sitting next to each other at the office. The skill sets people need to thrive in this new working model have changed. The way we behave has changed, as have the behaviours we need to adopt, but no one is teaching us where to go next.

Behaviour tests and competencies enable people to get deeper knowledge of themselves and gain insight into their own behaviours so they can adjust for their well-being. These tools help us become more aware of our internal states and external behaviours so we can become aware of our preferences and adjust our habits and behaviours.

The world of work has changed. People, organisations, and business owners are coping with it in different ways. What should a business owner do? What should an individual do? What is this world of work that we now live in? All the assessments available to us can measure that.

Let's get the right peg in the right hole. If you stick the wrong peg in the wrong hole, it's not going to work. Even toddlers know you cannot stick the triangular peg in the round hole; it won't fit. It's the same with jobs. When people underperform, it's often because they weren't placed in the right position. Sometimes the job isn't a good fit for the person. Taking the time to go through this process saves your organisation time and energy.

If the sales team is made up of ten people, they're not all going to be A-list performers, right? Statistically, following a normal (bell curve) distribution, at the top end of the scale you'll have one, two, or, if you're lucky, three top A-performers on that team. At the bottom end, you'll also have some bottom performers, and if you've ever inherited a team you may wonder why they were ever hired in the first place as well as why they're still employed! These people might wonder what value they contribute and wonder how long they'll remain employed. The rest of the people will fall somewhere in the middle. It's easy for lower performers on the team to become dissatisfied and question their worth, value, and abilities.

This team has three types of performers (top, middle, and bottom). That's the hole in our analogy. We can use assessments to determine the shape of each hole. What's the shape of the top/A-list performers, the mid-level performers, and the bottom performers? By using assessments, I know what shape (peg) you are, and all I need to do is find which role (hole) you best fit into—whether you a top, middle, or bottom performer. It's that simple, although it may seem that complicated.

Over the years at TRG, we've tried, tested, used, sold, and consulted on a plethora of assessments and surveys from multiple vendors. Our main go-to tool is from Great People Inside (GPI).[xxvii] They are customisable right out of the box and have hundreds of dimensions (behaviours) to choose from, making them more comprehensive and flexible than anything else we've seen (and we've looked at literally hundreds of competing solutions). These tools give us the shape of people and allow us to see our starting point (red dot on the map), making it easier to work out the road map to bring them to satisfaction and success. We use the tools to select the right people and get them into the right seats and, more importantly, to develop them further. Additionally, we use the Genos Emotional Intelligence (EI) tools when we need an Emotional Intelligence focus.[xxviii]

Job Satisfaction

> *True motivation comes from achievement,*
> *personal development, job satisfaction, and recognition.*
>
> *Fredrick Herzberg*

[xxvii] Great People Inside (GPI) is the award-winning Cloud-based "Next Generation People Intelligence Platform." https://greatpeopleinside.com/.
[xxviii] Genos International helps professionals apply core emotional intelligence skills that enhance their self-awareness, empathy, leadership, and resilience. In our world of "do more with less," applying emotional intelligence at work is fundamental to success.

Understanding motivations for work is important. Barry Schwartz, in his book *Why We Work*, dispels the widespread belief that we work to earn a paycheck and reveals that our reasons and motivations go much deeper than that.[112] According to Schwartz, when work is a calling, workers are more engaged. He examines the factors—such as autonomy and investment—that act as triggers in causing this heightening sense of satisfaction with work. Autonomy gives employees independence and responsibility and results in more deeply invested employees. Why? Most people don't like being micromanaged. They don't want the boss breathing down their necks. They want to say, "I know what I'm doing. Give me the ability to do it. Empower me. I'll have the responsibility. I'll go off and do it."

This means that businesses must invest in their people. This is truer now, in our WFA world, more than ever before. We may have hired people with a good education and a lot of experience, but things change faster than our past education and experience. We must all adapt, and organisations need to take the lead in facilitating the way we prepare ourselves for change.

Schwartz also stresses how important it is for everyone within a company to believe in the mission. What are we doing, and why does it matter? If the employees align with the organisation and believe in its mission, engagement will increase, and productivity will skyrocket.

When we apply Schwartz's writings to Business As UnUsual, we're saying we need to make workplaces better for everyone working there. We need to emphasise the positives and neutralise or mitigate the negatives to improve employee satisfaction. That sounds like common sense to me, yet it seems there's a lack of common sense in the world at present.

When turning negatives into positives, we should look to the work of Viktor Frankl. In his book *Man's Search for Meaning*, published in 1946, Frankl describes his experiences as a prisoner in Nazi concentration camps in World War II.[113] He developed a method of coping with his experiences by choosing a purpose in life to feel optimistic about and focusing his energy, so he could survive the horrific conditions around him. Without hope for the future, Frankl believed he and his fellow prisoners would be doomed. As he wrote, "Everything can be taken from a man but one thing: the last of the human freedoms—to choose one's attitude in any given set of circumstances, to choose one's own way."

Everything can be taken from a man but one thing: the last of the human freedoms—to choose one's attitude in any given set of circumstances, to choose one's own way.

Viktor Frankl

The same principle applies to this moment in history, when we are trying to navigate Business as UnUusual. There must be a point to everything we do, and we must choose to be in a state of gratitude and positivity despite our current circumstances. Instead of focusing on the negatives, we must do our best to find the positives or lessons that every moment or challenge is here to teach us. However, unless we are engaged in our day-to-day business and taking time to be aware of how we feel, it will be hard to feel satisfied with anything.

Earlier in our discussion of Business as UnUusual, we referenced this concept of engagement. By utilising the I AM OK to Fly model, key business leaders have one way to help ensure that everyone is engaged in the work as much as possible. That is a crucial element in the success of any business, and it's even more critical now. We need all hands on deck if we are not only to survive the effects of the pandemic but to thrive and fly.

Surface-level engagement is close to pretending. Go with the flow and don't rock the boat is the strategy, but you know they're kidding themselves and cheating others and the organisation. This shallow engagement leads to artificial harmony. Sure, co-workers can sit around the conference table and agree on everything. However, when the meeting is over, everyone will share their true feelings about what was discussed. This type of engagement is like barnacles on a boat. Unsightly, yes, and more importantly—it creates resistance against forward movement.[114]

Authentic engagement is obviously the preferred form of engagement. You need to go the extra mile at every step to ensure the organisation gets closer to the finish line. This form of engagement is for those who are passionate and "on board," as the expression goes. Conversely for those who are not on board, a choice can be made how they get on board or exit. True engagement, like all forms of positive thinking, is infectious in a good way. It creates enthusiasm and ensures increased productivity. Not only are individuals contributing to and driving wins, but they are simultaneously feeling fulfilled, which creates a cycle of repeating wins over and over. It's an excellent thing.

I know a quick way to determine which side you're on here. Think about your typical workday. Do the minutes tick by slowly in that painful march toward quitting time when you can sign out and go home? Or do you look at the clock at the end of the day and wonder where the time has gone? If the workdays glide by slowly, chances are you're in the trap of surface-level engagement. Conversely, if each day whizzes by and you can't wait for tomorrow to get back on task, you are in the grips of true engagement.

Finally, the last tip for leaders looking to increase job satisfaction is to ensure they are not comparing their direct reports to one another. This accidentally is a way to push dissatisfied employees deeper into dissatisfaction and increase feelings of lower value and worthlessness, which is not recommended for businesses trying to build trust, connection, and community with their employees! As a manager, you wouldn't want to be compared with other managers, so walk the talk. You must never do the same thing to your employees.

Comparing ourselves *only* to ourselves is key, and this same principle applies to our employees as well. Keep comparisons limited to the specific goals outlined in each employee's individual development plan and allow them to grow according to that plan. Looking at our own growth is *key* to purpose, passion, and motivation. Therefore, we track our progress of our clearly defined goals. We weigh these against other areas of life satisfaction to ensure we are growing in a way that feels good to our employees and in alignment to allow the company to grow so we all grow.

Comparing people to others is a trap that damages self-worth, leading to a downward spiral that turns positive, productive members of the team into energy drains on themselves and those around them.

How do you avoid falling into the comparison trap? By looking inward. The only comparison that is worth your time is the one you can affect yourself. So, compare yourself to yourself. Ask yourself: What can I do to be better? How can I achieve my personal best? Think like an athlete and improve your personal best.

Maybe this is one gift the pandemic has made possible. Each of us has more time to focus on ourselves. As our work structures have changed, we can spend time thinking about changes we can make to be prepared to meet the current challenges and the ones we suspect are coming in the not-too-distant future.

There's a reason why forward-thinking organisations always pay attention to employee retention rates. If you start to lose employees to this "grass is greener on the other side" mentality, you must look at what you can do to brighten the turf in your own organisation. When a business doesn't need to brag about high retention rates, it's a sign good things are happening within.

Another true victory in this scenario is when the organisation wins back *boomerang employees*. These people bought into the whole "grass is greener" idea and left the company, only to return when they discovered they preferred the grass at the company they had just left. In some countries e.g., Vietnam, there is a concept that you never return to a company you have already left, and this acts as a barrier to doing so; it's like an urban myth. We suggest you help dispel such concepts as you can return to a company you left, and companies should keep doors open to those boomerang or multiple boomerang employees.

Once we have a solid understanding of where we and our teams are, we can create a coaching plan and provide the coaching to get everyone where they want to be. Once we have a plan and goals in place, one thing that can stop continuous individual improvement is ourselves, when doubts of self-confidence and worth creep in made worse by comparing to others.

This comparison trap really relates to our larger discussion about Business as UnUusual in this pandemic world. If things have gone wrong and you've lost your job, you'll find yourself in a funk because it's easy to compare where you are now with what you had before the pandemic. We must escape that trap. We must still believe that we can fly. We can still believe that we can do it. We must keep building that self-confidence, keep building that self-efficacy, keep building that self-worth, keep building that self-value—these are all upward spirals to build a taller stronger Tower of Self (Chapter 4).

Coming from a coaching perspective invites managers and leaders to see satisfaction as an inside job and improvements that can be made as coaching opportunities. It also draws the best out of your employees because it asks how you, as a manager, can be more precise, concise, and supportive to help employees reach their goals.

The tools laid out in this chapter can help broaden your mindset and the mindset of your employees through greater awareness, persistence, and motivation. Businesses that take care of their employees are taken care of by their employees. Putting employee satisfaction and people first helps open employees up to shift their internal mindset and narrative required in the face of massive change and internal growth.

THE TREASURY

THE TREASURY

Too many people spend money they haven't earned
to buy things they don't want to impress people they don't like.

Will Rogers

The Treasury is the part of the Castle that deals with finances and consists of money generation (income) and total wealth (net worth). Money from the Treasury is needed to finance all areas of the castle. In the Tower of Purpose (Chapter 1), we established our life purpose, goals, and legacy, and some of these activities need financing. From those that do, first establish a financial goal (income or net worth or a mixture of the two). I'm going to say very little in this section as it's your choice how you wish to look at the importance of money. In my castle, it's something needed to achieve some goals and enable my life purpose, and it's not a measure of either happiness or success.

Maro Up

Be thankful one thousand times a day.

Wahei Takeda

Money may not grow on trees. However, what if we could attract more of it? If we "maro up," maybe we can. The term *maro* is short for *magokoro*, which means "sincere heart" in Japanese.[115] The book *Maro Up: The Secret to Success Begins with Arigato: Wisdom from the "Warren Buffet of Japan"*[116] tells the story and the term popularised by Wahei Takeda, a wealthy investor in Japan who attributes his fortune to the philosophy of saying arigato (thank you) consistently and applying maro. It's hard to pin down an exact translation for the phrase, but *maro* is akin to a state of selflessness.

Those who are in touch with *maro* always look for the positive in every situation, seek ways to serve, and strive to provide maximum joy and happiness to others. It's the belief that if you have a true heart of sincerity and kindness, others will treat you with kindness in return. The exchange of kindness and positive energy allows you to feel supported by the Universe. Inviting *maro* into your life invites miracles, and as your maro increases you "maro up."

Arigato for reading this book, arigato for buying it too, and arigato for just being you.

Net Worth

When your self-worth goes up, your net worth goes up with it.

Mark Victor Hansen

When planning personal and/or business financial goals for five and ten years down the road, we can use net worth to measure our progress relative to these goals.

It's a useful exercise to get to the root underlying reason why we have selected whatever the financial goal is as this helps to drive clarity of the goal. Maybe you want to achieve a level of personal financial security that will allow you to do volunteer work; use your time, effort, knowledge for some other activity; or donate to a worthy cause.

The *Five Whys* technique is a helpful tool to reveal the true root reason for whatever financial goal we have set. The *Five Whys* technique was developed by Sakichi Toyoda, who stated that "by repeating *why* five times, the nature of the problem as well as its solution becomes clear."[117] Interestingly, it's one of the many tools we also use in design thinking.

Income

> *It is literally true that you can succeed best and quickest by helping others to succeed.*
>
> *Napoleon Hill*

In order to increase Net Worth, we need to generate income and hold on to some of it; i.e., don't spend it all. Income is not only monthly salary, but also your investments. How much income you need is determined by how much net worth you wish to accumulate as well as monthly expenditures and the cost of achieving your goals, if there is a monetary cost involved.

When your life purpose fosters a commitment to serving and bettering others, you will see your personal income increase faster as you create joy, abundance, and excitement.

A people-first business will see more consistent bottom line growth. And if there is alignment between an individual's (employee) life purpose and goals and the business's, then income for the business also increases faster.

CHAPTER 7 KEY TAKEAWAYS

- Identifying and adapting for the future starts with taking an inventory of where you are now and where you want to end up in the future, and then aligning your skill sets with the end results to prepare for achieving those future goals.
- Changes to our systems, skills, and workforce need to be deliberate.
- WEF's "Future of Jobs Report 2020" says 50 percent of all employees will need reskilling by 2025.
- The Top 6 skills I recommend prioritising are:
  - Curiosity
  - Kaizen
  - Critical Thinking
  - Design Thinking
  - Communication
  - Coaching
- A good practice in any team is for each team member to focus on one new bit of knowledge, acquire it, and then do a knowledge sharing session with others.
- The WEF "Future of Jobs Report 2020" identified the top 15 skills for 2025:
  1. Analytical thinking and innovation
  2. Active learning and learning strategies
  3. Complex problem-solving
  4. Critical thinking and analysis
  5. Creativity, originality, and initiative
  6. Leadership and social influence
  7. Technology use, monitoring, and control
  8. Technology design and programming
  9. Resilience, stress tolerance, and flexibility
  10. Reasoning, problem-solving, and ideation
  11. Emotional intelligence

12. **Troubleshooting and user experience**
13. **Service orientation**
14. **Systems analysis and evaluation**
15. **Persuasion and negotiation**

- **The WEF "Future of Jobs Report 2020" identified the fastest-growing jobs expected to continue their upward trend:**
  1. **Data Analysts and Scientists**
  2. **AI and Machine Learning Specialists**
  3. **Big Data Specialists**
  4. **Digital Marketing and Strategy Specialists**
  5. **Process Automation Specialists**
  6. **Business Development Professionals**
  7. **Digital Transformation Specialists**
  8. **Information Security Analysts**
  9. **Software and Applications Developers**
  10. **Internet of Things Specialists**
  11. **Project Managers**

- **KASH, which is an acronym for Knowledge, Attitude, Skills, and Habits, is an individual development tool. Using KASH, we can clearly see what our strengths and weaknesses are.**
- **Leverage the psychology of success by investing in your ability to achieve through effort and learning.**
- **The I AM OK to Fly coaching model helps people become passionate, fully engaged, thrive, and shine and become satisfied, and of course, Fly.**
  - **S(t)inkers pull us down, sink us, and make us dissatisfied.**
  - **Floaters are S(t)inkers we have removed and bring us no dissatisfaction or satisfaction.**
  - **Flyers bring us satisfaction.**

- Ensure the right person is in the right seat on the bus.
- Say Arigato (thank you) consistently and Maro up to attract more money.
- Arigato for reading this summary.
- Download resources for Chapter 7 at RickYvanovich. com/BAUU/.

CHAPTER 7
REFLECTION PROMPTS

What's your **one** key takeaway from this chapter?

```
_____
_____
_____
```

And what else?

```
_____
_____
_____
```

What action will you take right away because of something you read in this chapter?

```
_____
_____
_____
```

And what else?

```
_____
_____
_____
```

CHAPTER 8
BUILD YOUR CASTLE

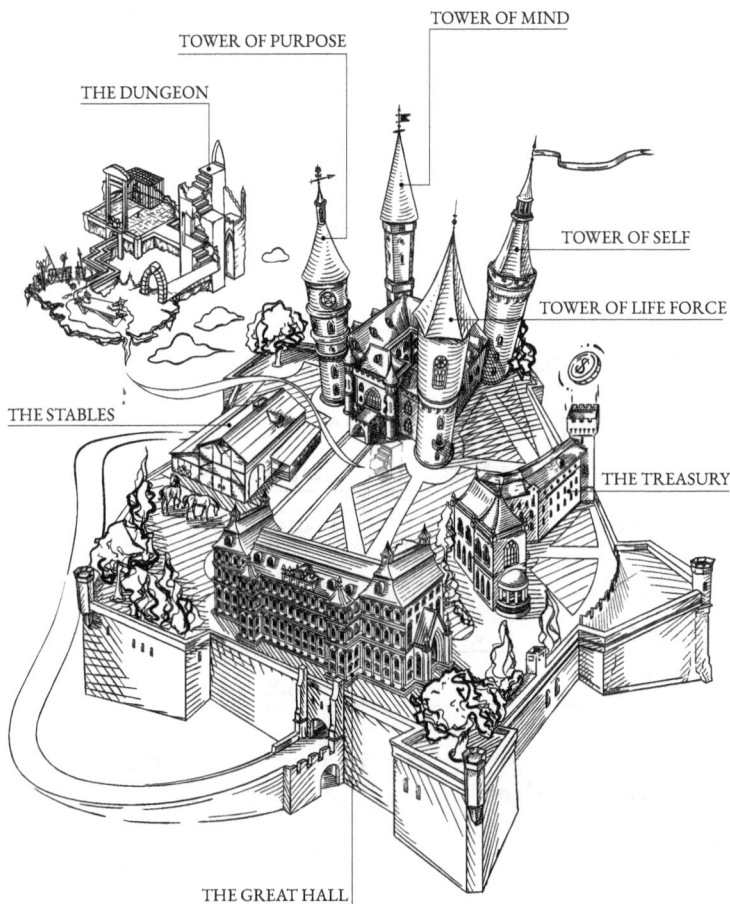

Congratulations on journeying literally to the end of this book. The Castle metaphor helps us visualise which areas of life we need to build up. In this chapter, we'll cover a 4-step process to put some dimensions to your Castle. *Figure 35* below gives the cross reference back to each of the eight parts of the Castle to make it easier to jump back to the section. This, as well as the other templates that can be used for each step, are also downloadable from the BAUU book site.[xxix]

Castle	Chapter Reference
1 – Tower of Purpose	**Chapter 1**
1.1 My Values	Life Purpose Formulation Step 1 Explore & uncover Core Values
1.2 My Life Purpose	Life Purpose Formulation Step 9 Life Purpose Statement
1.3 My Life Goals	Life Goals
1.4 My Legacy	Legacy
2 – Tower of Life Force	**Chapter 2**
2.1 Health	Health
2.2 Energy	Energy
2.3 Rest	Rest
2.4 Balance	Balance
2.5 Stress	Stress
3 – Tower of Mind	**Chapter 3**
3.1 Kaizen	Kaizen
3.2 Habits	Habits
3.3 How I Show Up	How I Show Up

[xxix] BAUU book resources can be found at RickYvanovich.com/BAUU/.

3.4 The Slight Edge	Living the Slight Edge
4 – Tower of Self	**Chapter 4**
4.1 Self-Confidence	Self-Confidence
4.2 Self-Efficacy	Self-efficacy
4.3 Self-Worth/Value	Self-Worth/Value
4.4 Self-Motivation	Self-Motivation
5 – The Dungeon	**Chapter 5**
5.1 Coach	Coaching and Mentoring Defined
5.2 Coachee	Coaching + Mentoring = Sports Coaching Dungeon Coaching Coaching Gurus
6 – The Great Hall	**Chapter 6**
6.1 Family	Community – Family
6.2 Friends	Community – Friends
6.3 Network	Community – Network
6.4 Community Service	Community – Community Service
6.5 Growing Connections	Community – Growing Connections
6.6 Culture	Culture
6.7 Leadership	Leadership
7 – The Stables	**Chapter 7**
7.1 Looking Forward to There	Looking Forward to There

7.2 Transforming (Here to There)	Transforming (Here to There)
7.3 Satisfaction	Satisfaction
7.4 Job Satisfaction	Job Satisfaction
8 – The Treasury	**Chapter 8**
8.1 Net Worth	Net Worth
8.2 Income	Income

Figure 35. Build a Castle – Cross-Reference

Step 1: What Success Looks Like

Define success on your own terms, achieve it by your own rules, and build a life you're proud to live.

Anne Sweeney

Grab your favourite weapons of choice, and using *Figure 36* below as a prompt, reflect on each of part of the Castle.

- Consider what success looks like to you for each and paint a vivid picture of that in your own words.
- Assign an importance 1 (low) to 10 (high) and insert it as "there" (like the mall map this is where you are heading).
- Allocate a timeline to each one e.g., six months, one year, five years, ten years, etc.

Castle	Timeline (Months/ Years)	There (1–10)	What Success Looks Like
1 – Tower of Purpose			
1.1 My Values			
1.2 My Life Purpose			
1.3 My Life Goals			
1.4 My Legacy			
2 – Tower of Life Force			
2.1 Health			
2.2 Energy			
2.3 Rest			
2.4 Balance			
2.5 Stress			
3 – Tower of Mind			
3.1 Kaizen			
3.2 Habits			
3.3 How I Show Up			
3.4 The Slight Edge			
4 – Tower of Self			
4.1 Self-Confidence			
4.2 Self-Efficacy			
4.3 Self-Worth/Value			
4.4 Self-Motivation			

5 – The Dungeon			
5.1 Coach			
5.2 Coachee			
6 – The Great Hall			
6.1 Family			
6.2 Friends			
6.3 Network			
6.4 Community Service			
6.5 Growing Connections			
6.6 Culture			
6.7 Leadership			
7 – The Stables			
7.1 Looking Forward to There			
7.2 Transforming (Here to There)			
7.3 Satisfaction			
7.4 Job Satisfaction			
8 – The Treasury			
8.1 Net Worth			
8.2 Income			

Figure 36. Build a Castle – Step 1: What Success Looks Like

Step 2: What's Stopping Me?

*The only thing standing between you and your goal is the bullshit
story you keep telling yourself as to why you can't achieve it.*

Jordan Belfort

Grab your favourite weapons of choice, and using *Figure 37*
below as a prompt, reflect on each of part of the Castle.

- Insert the "there" from Step 1.
- Like the mall map, to get to "there," we need to
  establish where we are now. Assign a 1 (low) to 10
  (high) of where you are now and insert that as "here."
- Calculate the difference between "here" and "there"
  and insert that as the Gap.
- Reflect on the gap and ask yourself, "What's stopping
  me from getting there?" Write down all the roadblocks,
  potholes, obstacles, and challenges that are in your way.

Castle	Here (1–10)	There (1–10)	Gap	What's Stopping Me?
1 – Tower of Purpose				
1.1 My Values				
1.2 My Life Purpose				
1.3 My Life Goals				
1.4 My Legacy				
2 – Tower of Life Force				

2.1 Health				
2.2 Energy				
2.3 Rest				
2.4 Balance				
2.5 Stress				
3 – Tower of Mind				
3.1 Kaizen				
3.2 Habits				
3.3 How I Show Up				
3.4 The Slight Edge				
4 – Tower of Self				
4.1 Self-Confidence				
4.2 Self-Efficacy				
4.3 Self-Worth/ Value				
4.4 Self-Motivation				
5 – The Dungeon				
5.1 Coach				
5.2 Coachee				

6 – The Great Hall				
6.1 Family				
6.2 Friends				
6.3 Network				
6.4 Community Service				
6.5 Growing Connections				
6.6 Culture				
6.7 Leadership				
7 – The Stables				
7.1 Looking forward to There				
7.2 Transforming (Here to There)				
7.3 Satisfaction				
7.4 Job Satisfaction				
8 – The Treasury				
8.1 Net Worth				
8.2 Income				

Figure 37. Build a Castle – Step 2: What's Stopping Me?

Step 3: #1 Action to Close the Gap

You don't have to be great to start, but
you do have to start to be great.

Zig Ziglar

Grab your favourite weapons of choice, and using *Figure 38* below as a prompt, reflect on what's stopping you in Step 2.

- Reflect on the size of the gaps and choose the priority order you choose to do them. Whilst doing this also consider the timeframe from Step 1. Write down the priority order.
- Think of the number one action you can take to overcome whatever is stopping you and close the gap. Write that down as the "#1 action to close the gap."
- Assign a specific date for you to do this number one action.

Castle	Priority	#1 Action to Close the Gap	Date to Do #1 Action
1 – Tower of Purpose			
1.1 My Values			
1.2 My Life Purpose			
1.3 My Life Goals			
1.4 My Legacy			
2 – Tower of Life Force			

2.1 Health			
2.2 Energy			
2.3 Rest			
2.4 Balance			
2.5 Stress			
3 – Tower of Mind			
3.1 Kaizen			
3.2 Habits			
3.3 How I Show Up			
3.4 The Slight Edge			
4 – Tower of Self			
4.1 Self-Confidence			
4.2 Self-Efficacy			
4.3 Self-Worth/Value			
4.4 Self-Motivation			
5 – The Dungeon			
5.1 Coach			
5.2 Coachee			
6 – The Great Hall			
6.1 Family			
6.2 Friends			
6.3 Network			
6.4 Community Service			

6.5 Growing Connections			
6.6 Culture			
6.7 Leadership			
7 – The Stables			
7.1 Looking Forward to There			
7.2 Transforming (Here to There)			
7.3 Satisfaction			
7.4 Job Satisfaction			
8 – The Treasury			
8.1 Net Worth			
8.2 Income			

Figure 38. Build a Castle – Step 3: #1 Action to Close the Gap

Step 4: Other Actions to Close the Gap

If you want things to get better, take action...
Don't just read and think about it. Do it.

Larry Winget

Grab your favourite weapons of choice, and using *Figure 39* below as a prompt, reflect on Steps 2 and 3 and what else is stopping you to close the gap.

- In Step 3, you wrote down the number one action you can take to overcome whatever is stopping you and close the gap. Now think of what other actions you can take to close the gap. Write them all down as "other actions to close the gap."

- Assign a specific date for you to do each other action and write it down as "date to do."

Castle	Gap	Other Actions to Close the Gap	Date to Do
1 – Tower of Purpose			
1.1 My Values			
1.2 My Life Purpose			
1.3 My Life Goals			
1.4 My Legacy			
2 – Tower of Life Force			
2.1 Health			
2.2 Energy			
2.3 Rest			
2.4 Balance			
2.5 Stress			
3 – Tower of Mind			
3.1 Kaizen			
3.2 Habits			
3.3 How I Show Up			
3.4 The Slight Edge			
4 – Tower of Self			
4.1 Self-Confidence			
4.2 Self-Efficacy			

4.3 Self-Worth/Value			
4.4 Self-Motivation			
5 – The Dungeon			
5.1 Coach			
5.2 Coachee			
6 – The Great Hall			
6.1 Family			
6.2 Friends			
6.3 Network			
6.4 Community Service			
6.5 Growing Connections			
6.6 Culture			
6.7 Leadership			
7 – The Stables			
7.1 Looking Forward to There			
7.2 Transforming (Here to There)			
7.3 Satisfaction			
7.4 Job Satisfaction			
8 – The Treasury			
8.1 Net Worth			
8.2 Income			

Figure 39. Build a Castle – Step 4: Other Actions to Close the Gap

Congratulations. You are the King/Queen of your Castle. You have a plan of what your Castle looks, and now it's time to continue your journey.

If it were easy to make lasting success happen, more people would be able to achieve and maintain it without effort. Success calls for leaders (that's you!) to grow, and you need to leave your comfort zone to do that. Growth requires taking risks and trying new things. It can feel intimidating to jump into unknown waters on your own, so grow your community and surround yourself with encouraging and supportive people who will help keep you accountable.

I hope you can now journey-on knowing how to do the following:

1. Formulate your life purpose.
2. Formulate your legacy.
3. Create life goals and put a plan of action into place.
4. Leverage tools, motivation, and strategies to execute your plan.
5. Build your own Castle.

You have the tools to coach and lead yourself and others on their own personal and professional journeys. As a result, you can create a sustainably successful Castle with a convivial and supportive community, culture, and a people-first leadership model that helps elevate Castle life, work, and business.

Your majesty, as your humble servant, allow me to continue to inspire and transform you for consistently higher achievement.

Long live King/Queen [insert your name], long shall you reign!

CHAPTER 8 KEY TAKEAWAYS

- Give dimensions to your Castle using the 4-step process.
- Step 1: What does success look like?
  - What's the timeline?
  - What's the importance?
- Step 2: What's stopping me from closing the gap?
  - Where am I now?
  - How big is the gap?
- Step 3: What's the #1 action I can take to close the gap?
  - What's the priority order?
  - When will I do it?
- Step 4? What other actions can I take to close the gap?
  - When will I do them?
- Before making any improvements, we always need to assess where we are, figure out where we want to go, and identify the daily actions that will help us bridge this gap.
- Never stop learning and growing. Always strive to better yourself and enrich the people around you.
- Build your Castle daily, help others build theirs, and keep on growing.
- Chapter 8 resources and downloads are available at RickYvanovich.com/BAUU/.
- Help from Rick can be requested at RickYvanovich. com/Contact/.

CHAPTER 8
REFLECTION PROMPTS

What's your **one** key takeaway from this chapter?

```
_____
_____
_____
```

And what else?

```
_____
_____
_____
```

What action will you take right away because of something you read in this chapter?

```
_____
_____
_____
```

And what else?

```
_____
_____
_____
```

ACKNOWLEDGEMENTS

Never, never, never, never give up.

Winston Churchill

To Sirian, Safena, and Katharina. Words are not enough, Thank You. I still love each one of you to the moon and back.

To the Leaders Press team past and present: Steven Pamplin, Grace O'Donnell, Megan Okonsky, Zella Mansson, Deborah Brannon, Marinel Balde, Anette Liwanag, Glenda Mae, Alinka Rutkowska, Lucas Mayer, and Anna Paige. Like all journeys, you've put up with me, some of you came and went, we laughed a lot, pulled our hair out and cried, had highs and lows, and just kept on going as the months flew way past the deadlines. We got here in the end and some of you even got multiple promotions— though it's not the end, is it—ready for LAUU?

To CCMC Cohort number 1. The book sprung to life during CCMC and so many of you contributed to the iterative process of creating and fine tuning my coaching models and tools, all of which are in this book. Thank you for being my cheerleaders and egging me on: Guy Rowse, Moorthy Murugaiah, Roby Tjiptadjaya, Angela Samson, Vellu Mahadevan, Floris Verhagen, and Lynn Ho. Huge extra thanks to the other two thirds of the CCMC Techies trio: Kian Leong Phang and Gregory Engalbert. You kicked me and my models to near death to make them better.

To ITD World and the team that delivered CCMC: Dr. Peter Chee, Serely Alcaraz, Dr. Marcia Reynolds, Dr. Marshall Goldsmith, Dr. Peter Hawkins, John Mattone, Mark C. Thompson, Dr. William J Rothwell, Peter Bregman, Aaron Ngui, and Nita. Marshall, you kicked my ass, and I'm better for that. Dr. Peter Chee, you are a huge inspiration for this book which is testament to what a wonderful coach and person you are and the absolute unquestionable power of CCMC. You and the other gurus are the giants whose shoulders I am now standing on.

To CBC, I met many talented people in the breakouts and that brought new perspectives. Thank you to fellow CBC and the Mindvalley team: Ajit Nawalkha, Coach Fran, and Coach Sid.

To CLO cohort number 1. I've met so many like-minded people and several of you have inspired me to get the book process finished. Thank you to CLO and Mindvalley team: Bianca, Ajit Nawalkha, Coach Sid, Yuri Minski, Ronan Diego De Oliveira, and Vishen Lakhiani.

To *The Conspiracy*: Michael Bungay Stanier, Ainsley Brittain, and my fellow conspirators, Kati, Ulli, Robyn, and James. Thank you for creating the space and supporting my slipperiness during this journey for my Worthy Goal.

To the Great People Inside team, yup you're all great! Thank you: Dr. Doru Dima, Cristi, Sasa, Betty, Lucian, and all those who must not be named.

To TRG International: Nguyen Nhu Quynh, I gave you the impossible task of freeing up my time and continually rescheduling so I could spend time on the book—you did it! Truong Quang Hoi for smiling though my just one more little change on the image I needed, and then another and another and another, and just one more. TRG Team leads and TRGers for putting up with my BAUU prioritisations and demands, and Academy team who know my Masterclasses are now a bigger priority!

To the many inspirational people, some of whom have never heard of me, but whose books I've likely read or whose courses I've attended: Jeff Olsen, Simon Sinek, Nir Ayal, BJ Fogg, Kristen Hadeed, Mark Green, Samantha Clark, and Jim Sirbasku.

To my coaches and mentors past and present. Maybe if you read this book, you'll see just how much you have helped to make me, me—and yup, I'm still open to you helping smooth out those rough edges! Thank you: Deiric McCann, Dr. Peter Chee, Coach Sid, Nicholas Kemp, Warren Eng, Gary Genard, Roger Martin, Ronan Diego De Oliveira, Yuri Minski, Ajit Nawalkha, Coach Fran, and Vishen Lakhiani.

To my friends, though I'm not sure if I've scared you all off during the last few years. Thank you.

To all the people who encouraged me to write this book as well as those who said to *not* write this book. You've all helped me to do it!

And finally, to all of you reading this book, I appreciate you investing your time in you and I hope it has helped guide you towards value and success.

Arigato.

ABOUT RICK YVANOVICH

Rick Yvanovich is a Master-qualified Business Coach skilled in helping people and companies consistently reach higher achievement by leveraging business experience with coaching interventions. He utilises systematic processes to envision goals and milestones and translate vision into actionable steps. He's a leader committed to employee empowerment, happiness, and development.

Rick's also an entrepreneur, techie, Brit, baby boomer, CFO, CEO, professional bean counter, and a *USA Today* and *Wall Street Journal* bestselling author. He has an eclectic forty-plus years' experience in supermarkets; accounting; breweries; newsagents; defence manufacturing; IT; talent; the food and beverage industry; property development; and BP in the UK, China, Singapore, Switzerland, and Vietnam. Rick first moved to BP China as Finance Manager, then relocated to BP Vietnam in 1990, likely making him the longest-lasting Brit in Vietnam. He's been directly involved in client engagements in thirty-nine countries.

He's a Board Member of BritCham Vietnam, Chairman of the Industry Advisory Committee RMIT University Vietnam, and Chairman of the South East Area Advisory Committee AICPA-CIMA. He's a founder, co-founder, CEO, CFO, investor, and advisor in multiple start-ups including TRG International and Great People Inside.

An active promoter of CIMA (Chartered Institute of Management Accountants), Rick's a regular speaker in Vietnam on multiple topics, including talent, accounting, ICT, digital transformation, cloud, project management, doing business in Vietnam, UK-Vietnam trade, and inward investment.

Rick's coaching journey includes CCMP (ITD World 2018), Leaders Create Leaders (2020), Genos Emotional Intelligence (2020), OKR Champion (2021), CCMC (ITD World 2021), ikigai coach (Ikigai tribe, 2021), and Certified Business Coach (Mindvalley, 2022).

For more information visit RickYvanovich.com.

About TRG International

Founded in 1994, TRG International is an exclusive Infor Gold Partner supplying Infor SunSystems, EPM, Syteline, LN, and Infor OS. We partner with hospitality, financial services, energy, real estate, manufacturing (and much more) customers in eighty countries to shine. TRG Talent solutions include Great People Inside and Team Tailor. We believe that with the right solutions working quietly in the background, our customers can be free to focus on their core business. The company has more than four hundred employees across ten countries. Rick is the founder and CEO. For more information about TRG International, visit TRGInternational.com.

About Great People Inside

Founded in 2016, Great People Inside (GPI) provides a fully customisable People Intelligence Platform, offering assessments and Talent Management solutions, specifically adapted to each organisation and job, based on a unique IMF-inspired global pricing model. GPI empowers the complete life cycle of every employee, securing optimum results for both employee and employer. GPI's assessments and reports provide an organisational and team diagnosis that offers a clear perspective on the dynamics, the development areas, and the team's common values, along with coaching and development suggestions and strategies that will help the leaders and their teams in their quest for reaching their maximum potential. GPI is available as a SaaS subscription from GPI and via partners in twenty-four countries. Rick is the co-founder and CFO. For more information about Great People Inside, visit GreatPeopleInside.com.

Life As UnUsual (LAUU)

As you explore Business As UnUsual, don't forget that business is just a portion of our life. And life has never been crazier. I think that's something each generation exclaims to compete with prior generations. That was, of course, until 2020. When the COVID-19 pandemic hit, the world was suddenly turned upside down. For some people, it quite literally happened overnight. In the blink of an eye, we stopped sending our kids to school, stopped leaving the house to go to work, and started panic-purchasing toilet paper. In 2020 and 2021, life truly had never been crazier. It has been an unusual time that has lingered far longer than most people would have expected or preferred.

Amid these unusual changes, something else has shifted in the collective. It's the desire for a greater purpose. People are stuck at home and feel disconnected from the things and people that used to make their day-to-day life feel more fulfilling. The result has been a mass exodus from the workforce, with people moving towards projects and positions that provide more meaning than a paycheck alone.

Somewhere among all the craziness and change, though, we have been able to accept that life, as we know it, will never be the same that it once was. Not completely. We will always have this new way of living. Online grocery shopping has replaced many trips to the supermarket and virtual yoga classes in our living rooms have replaced the trips to the gym. The pandemic has forever changed our entire lifestyle. The goal shouldn't be merely to survive, but to thrive.

How do we deal with Life as UnUsual? Fortunately, there's still more to discover in my next upcoming book, *Life As UnUsual*.

Work As UnUsual (WAUU)

Work in a traditional business or a less traditional organisation has changed for most people on the planet in some way since March 2020. This date jumps out for me because it was the first day we shut the office doors and sent people home indefinitely.

TRG has always had a hybrid work environment, but the forced global shutdowns were unprecedented. Working from home with our kids, pets, spouses, or even completely alone presents a unique set of challenges. So how do we keep employees motivated? How do we keep driving towards results whilst also ensuring employees are satisfied in their jobs?

Work no longer has water cooler chats and casual moments of relationship building. We no longer have the option to pitch in by tagging along for a coffee run or picking up the office lunch orders. In today's new work environment, leaders need to put their people first. Without people, there is no business. Instead of driving the bottom line and pushing for results, this new way of working requires coaching, motivation, and support to inspire people to drive results for themselves.

Work is changing. As shutdowns ease and restrictions lift, we continuously need to re-evaluate how to conduct business, how work works, and what we expect of the people who work for us.

How do we deal with Work as UnUsual? Fortunately, there's still more to learn in my third upcoming book, *Work as UnUsual*.

ENDNOTES

1   Edward Coke, *The Selected Writings and Speeches of Sir Edward Coke*, ed. Steve Sheppard, vol. 1 (Indianapolis: Liberty Fund, 2003).

2   Douglas Adams, *The Hitchhiker's Guide to the Galaxy*, 1st ed. (New York: Del Rey, 1995).

3   Doran, George T. "There's a S.M.A.R.T. way to write management's goals and objectives." Management Review 70.11 (Nov. 1981)

4   Chris Mcchesney, Sean Covey, and Jim Huling, *The 4 Disciplines of Execution: Achieving Your Wildly Important Goals* (New York: Free Press, 2012).

5   James C Collins and Jerry I Porras, *Built to Last: Successful Habits of Visionary Companies* (New York: Harper Collins, 1994).

6   Tom Peters, "From BHAG to CCAG," Tom Peters! (blog), n.d., https://tompeters.com/2007/11/from-bhag-to-ccag/.

7   Simon Sinek, *The Infinite Game* (Portfolio Penguin, 2018).

8   Andrew S Grove, *High Output Management* (New York: Random House, 1983).

9   John E Doerr, *Measure What Matters: How Google, Bono, and the Gates Foundation Rock the World with OKRs* (New York: Penguin, 2017).

10   Shawn Achor, *The Happiness Advantage: The Seven Principles that Fuel Success and Performance at Work* (London: Virgin, 2011).

11   Ian Hunt, "The Losada Ratio—How Does Your Team Fare?," www.linkedin.com, accessed September 6, 2021, https://www.linkedin.com/pulse/losada-ratio-how-does-your-team-fare-ian-hunt/.

12   Stephen G. Post, "Altruism, Happiness, and Health: It's Good to Be Good," International Journal of Behavioral Medicine 12, no. 2 (June 2005): 66–77, https://doi.org/10.1207/s15327558ijbm1202_4.

13   Georgia Tech, "As We Get Parched, Cognition Can Sputter, Dehydration Study Says | News Center," news.gatech.edu, July 16, 2018, https://news.gatech.edu/news/2018/07/16/we-get-parched-cognition-can-sputter-dehydration-study-says.

14   Saundra Dalton-Smith, "The Real Reason Why We Are Tired and What to Do about It," You Tube (TEDx, April 10, 2019), https://youtu.be/ZGNN4EPJzGk.

15   Saundra Dalton-Smith, *Sacred Rest: Recover Your Life, Renew Your Energy, Restore Your Sanity*, 1st ed. (Hachette Book Group, 2017).

16   Rick Hanson, "Confronting the Negativity Bias," Dr. Rick Hanson, October 26, 2010, https://www.rickhanson.net/how-your-brain-makes-you-easily-intimidated/.

17   Harvard Medical School, "Understanding the Stress Response," Harvard Health Publishing (Harvard Medical School, July 6, 2020), https://www.health.harvard.edu/staying-healthy/understanding-the-stress-response.

18   Julie Nguyen and Kristina Hallett, "Fight, Flight, Freeze, Fawn: Examining the 4 Trauma Responses," MBG Health (MindBodyGreen, September 11, 2021), https://www.mindbodygreen.com/articles/fight-flight-freeze-fawn-trauma-responses.

19   Sherry Gaba, "Understanding Fight, Flight, Freeze and the Fawn Response | Psychology Today United Kingdom," PsychologyToday.com, August 22, 2020, https://www.psychologytoday.com/gb/blog/addiction-and-recovery/202008/understanding-fight-flight-freeze-and-the-fawn-response.

20   Kelly McGonigal, *The Upside of Stress: Why Stress Is Good for You, and How to Get Good at It*, 2nd ed. (New York: Avery, 2015).

21   James Nestor, *Breath: The New Science of a Lost Art* (New York: Riverhead Books, 2020).

22   Kira M. Newman, "Feeling Anxious? The Way You Breathe Could Be Adding to It," Ideas.Ted.Com (TED Conferences, January 8, 2021), https://ideas.ted.com/feeling-anxious-the-way-you-breathe-could-be-adding-to-it/.

23   Herbert Benson and Miriam Z Klipper, The Relaxation Response (New York: Quill, 2000).

24   Massachusetts General Hospital, "Tips to Manage Stress with the Relaxation Response," Massachusetts General Hospital, October 15, 2019, https://www.massgeneral.org/children/inflammatory-bowel-disease/tips-to-manage-stress-with-the-relaxation-response.

25   Judson Brewer and TED, "Mind Going a Million Miles a Minute? Slow down with This Breathing Exercise," ideas.ted.com, May 26, 2020, https://ideas.ted.com/mind-going-a-million-miles-a-minute-slow-down-with-this-breathing-exercise/.

26   Jane McGonigal, *SuperBetter: A Revolutionary Approach to Getting Stronger, Happier, Braver, and More Resilient.* Powered by the Science of Games, 1st ed. (New York: Penguin Press, 2015).

27   "Declutter," in Cambridge Dictionary, n.d., https://dictionary.cambridge.org/dictionary/english/declutter.

28   Netflix, "Tidying up with Marie Kondo | Official Trailer [HD] | Netflix," YouTube, December 12, 2018, https://www.youtube.com/watch?v=WvyeapVBLWY.

29   Marie Kondo, *The Life-Changing Magic of Tidying Up: The Japanese Art of Decluttering and Organizing* (Ten Speed Press, 2014).

30   The Decision Lab, "Why Do We Make Worse Decisions at the End of the Day?," The Decision Lab, n.d., https://thedecisionlab.com/biases/decision-fatigue.

31   Barry Schwartz, *The Paradox of Choice: Why More Is Less*, 1st ed. (London: Harper Collins, 2004).

32   Sunny Fitzgerald, "Forest Bathing: What It Is and Where to Do It," National Geographic, October 19, 2019, https://www.nationalgeographic.com/travel/article/forest-bathing-nature-walk-health.

33   Simon Sinek, *The Infinite Game* (Portfolio Penguin, 2018).

34   Simon Sinek, *The Infinite Game* (Portfolio Penguin, 2018).

35   Napoleon Hill, *Think and Grow Rich* (Original Classic Edition) (New York: G&D Media, 2019).

[36]   Meik Wiking, *The Little Book of Hygge: The Danish Way to Live Well*, 1st ed. (London: Penguin Life, 2016).

[37]   Andriy Bas, "Hygge: 6 Steps to Danish Happiness," Medium, January 1, 2018, https://medium.com/@bass.andriy/hygge-6-steps-to-danish-happiness-896283b96855.

[38]   Niellah Arboine, "What Is 'Lagom'? Turns out It Could Have a Significant Impact on Your Levels of Happiness," Bustle, June 20, 2019, https://www.bustle.com/p/what-is-lagom-turns-out-it-could-have-a-significant-impact-on-your-levels-of-happiness-18016917.

[39]   Stephen R Covey, *The 7 Habits of Highly Effective People: Revised and Updated: Powerful Lessons in Personal Change*, 30th Anniversary edition (New York: Simon & Schuster, 2020).

[40]   Jeff Olson, *The Slight Edge*, 8th Anniversary (Plano, TX: Success, 2013).

[41]   Mel Robbins, "'The Space Where Your Dreams Live' – Mel Robbins | Knowing What to Do Is Not Enough. If You Have a Goal, a Dream, a Future 'You' in Mind, You Must Know HOW to Push Yourself in Moments When You're... | by Mel Robbins | Facebook," Facebook, April 7, 2016, https://www.facebook.com/melrobbins/videos/949539128475305/.

[42]   Katherine L Milkman, *How to Change: The Science of Getting from Where You Are to Where You Want to Be* (New York: Portfolio/Penguin, An Imprint of Penguin Random House Llc, 2021).

[43]   Dan Sperber, "The Function of Reason," The Edge, February 22, 2017, https://www.edge.org/conversation/dan_sperber-the-functlon-of-reason.

[44]   Wikipedia Contributors, "Motivation," in Wikipedia (Wikimedia Foundation, March 16, 2019), https://en.wikipedia.org/wiki/Motivation.

[45]   "Motivation," in Cambridge Dictionary (Cambridge University Press), accessed August 14, 2022, https://dictionary.cambridge.org/dictionary/english/motivation.

[46]   "Motivation," in Oxford Dictionary (Oxford University Press), accessed August 14, 2022, https://www.oxfordreference.com/view/10.1093/oi/authority.20110803100212318.

[47] "Motivation," in The Britannica Dictionary (Britannica Group), accessed August 14, 2022, https://www.britannica.com/dictionary/motivation.

[48] Jim Schleckser, "The Myth of Motivating People," Inc., September 18, 2018, https://www.inc.com/jim-schleckser/the-myth-of-motivating-people.html.

[49] MBS Works, "The Conspiracy," go.mbs.works, n.d., https://go.mbs.works/theconspiracysignup.

[50] Frederick Herzberg, Bernard Mausner, and Barbara Bloch Snyderman, The Motivation to Work (New Brunswick: Transaction Publishers, 1959).

[51] Rick Yvanovich, "Motivation Spotlight – What Have We Missed?," TRG International (blog), August 17, 2017, https://blog.trginternational.com/trg-news-media/bbgv-breakfast-seminar-motivation-spotlight.

[52] Abraham Maslow, "A Theory of Human Motivation," Psychological Review 50(4)(1943): 370–96, https://doi.org/10.1037/h0054346.

[53] Kim Scott, Radical Candor: Be a Kick-Ass Boss without Losing Your Humanity. (St. Martin's Press, 2019).

[54] Rick Yvanovich, "Motivation - How Does It Work for Sales?," TRG International (blog), July 20, 2016, https://blog.trginternational.com/motivation-for-sales.

[55] Richard M. Ryan and Edward L. Deci, "Intrinsic and Extrinsic Motivations: Classic Definitions and New Directions," Contemporary Educational Psychology 25, no. 1 (January 2000): 54–67, https://doi.org/10.1006/ceps.1999.1020.

[56] Charles Stangor and Jennifer Walinga, Introduction to Psychology – 1st Canadian Edition, Opentextbc.ca (BCcampus Open Education, 2014), https://opentextbc.ca/introductiontopsychology/.

[57] Kori D. Miller, "Operant Conditioning Theory: Examples for Successful Habit Formation," Positive Psychology (blog), March 20, 2020, https://positivepsychology.com/operant-conditioning-theory/.

58   Gary D Chapman, *The 5 Love Languages*, Reprint (Chicago: Northfield Publishing, 2015).

59   Gary D Chapman and Paul E White, *The 5 Languages of Appreciation in the Workplace: Empowering Organizations by Encouraging People* (Chicago: Northfield Publishing, 2019).

60   International Coaching Federation, "Experience Coaching," Experience Coaching, accessed June 13, 2022, https://experiencecoaching.com/.

61   European Mentoring and Coaching Centre (EMCC), "EMCC Definition of Mentoring," EMCC Global, accessed August 11, 2022, https://www.emccglobal.org/leadership-development/leadership-development-mentoring/.

62   Peter Chee and Marshall Goldsmith, 5 Levels of Mastery, Itdworld. com (ITD World Mega Guru Learning, 2019), https://itdworld.com/drpeterchee/books.php?book=6.

63   Marshall Goldsmith, "FeedForward," Business Week, January 22, 2007, https://marshallgoldsmith.com/articles/feed-forward/.

64   Marshall Goldsmith, "Try Feedforward instead of Feedback," Marshall Goldsmith, accessed August 13, 2022, https://marshallgoldsmith.com/articles/try-feedforward-instead-feedback/.

65   Jocko Willink and Leif Babin, *The Dichotomy of Leadership: Balancing the Challenges of Extreme Ownership to Lead and Win* (New York: St. Martin's Press, 2018).

66   Alinka Rutkowska et al, *Habits of Success: What Top Entrepreneurs Routinely Do in Business and in Life* (United States: Leaders Press, 2022).

67   Jack Canfield and Peter Chee, *Coaching for Breakthrough Success: Proven Techniques for Making the Impossible Dreams Possible* (New York: Mcgraw-Hill Education, 2013).

68   Marcia Reynolds, *Coach the Person, Not the Problem: A Guide to Using Reflective Inquiry* (Oakland, Ca: Berrett-Koehler Publishers, Inc, 2020).

69   Marcia Reynolds, *Coach the Person, Not the Problem: A Guide to Using Reflective Inquiry* (Oakland, Ca: Berrett-Koehler Publishers, Inc, 2020).

70   John Mattone and John Mattone Global Inc, "A Preview of John Mattone's Thinking," John Mattone Global, Inc., accessed August 10, 2022, https://johnmattone.com/about/preview-john-mattones-thinking/.

71   John Mattone and John Mattone Global Inc., "Intelligent Leadership – All You Need to Know," John Mattone Blog (blog), September 27, 2017, https://johnmattone.com/blog/intelligent_leadership/.

72   John Mattone and John Mattone GLobal Inc., "Why Success Depends on Bringing Abundant Value to Others," John Mattone Blog (blog), May 3, 2021, https://johnmattone.com/blog/why-success-depends-on-bringing-abundant-value-to-others/.

73   John Mattone and John Mattone Coaching Inc., "How Executive Coaching Helps You Define Your Leadership Legacy," John Mattone Blog (blog), January 4, 2018, https://johnmattone.com/blog/how-executive-coaching-helps-you-define-your-leadership-legacy/.

74   Peter Hawkins and Eve Turner, *Systemic Coaching: Delivering Value Beyond the Individual*, 1st ed. (London; New York: Routledge, Taylor & Francis Group, 2019).

75   Peter Hawkins and Eve Turner, *Systemic Coaching: Delivering Value Beyond the Individual*, 1st ed. (London; New York: Routledge, Taylor & Francis Group, 2019).

76   Bregman Partners, "Big Arrow Process," Bregman Partners, accessed August 13, 2022, https://bregmanpartners.com/big-arrow/.

77   HBR and Peter Bregman, "Execution Is a People Problem, Not a Strategy Problem," Harvard Business Review, January 17, 2019, https://hbr.org/2017/01/execution-is-a-people-problem-not-a-strategy-problem.

78   Theodora Blanchfield and Verywell Mind, "Why Is Dating so Hard?," Verywell Mind, February 25, 2022, https://www.verywellmind.com/why-is-dating-so-hard-5220113.

79   Business Executive Network, "[C] Vietnam - a Publication of the Business Executive Network," C Vietnam, accessed June 15, 2022, https://executives.asia/cvietnam/.

80   John C Maxwell, *The 21 Irrefutable Laws of Leadership*, 10th Anniversary (HarperCollins Leadership, 2007).

81   Vaish, A., Grossmann, T., & Woodward, A. (2008). "Not all emotions are created equal: The negativity bias in social-emotional development". Psychological Bulletin, 134(3), 383–403. https://doi.org/10.1037/0033-2909.134.3.383.

82   Amy Edmondson and Mark Mortensen, "What Psychological Safety Looks like in a Hybrid Workplace," Harvard Business Review, April 19, 2021, https://hbr.org/2021/04/what-psychological-safety-looks-like-in-a-hybrid-workplace.

83   Stephen R Covey, *The 7 Habits of Highly Effective People: Powerful Lessons in Personal Change.* (New York: Simon & Schuster, 2020).

84   Barbara L. Fredrickson and Marcial F. Losada, "Positive Affect and the Complex Dynamics of Human Flourishing.," American Psychologist 60, no. 7 (2005): 678–86, https://doi.org/10.1037/0003-066x.60.7.678.

85   Shawn Achor, *The Happiness Advantage: The Seven Principles That Fuel Success and Performance at Work*, 1st ed. (New York: Crown Business, 2010).

86   "What Leaders Must Learn about the First Follower Principle," Lighthouse Blog (blog), n.d., https://getlighthouse.com/blog/first-follower-principle-leader-learn/.

87   John C Maxwell, *The 5 Levels of Leadership: Proven Steps to Maximise Your Potential* (New York: Center Street, 2013).

88   Nadya Zhexembayeva, "HOW OFTEN DO WE NEED to REINVENT to SURVIVE?," Chief Reinvention Officer, October 1, 2018, https://chiefreinventionofficer.com/how-often-do-we-need-to-reinvent-to-survive/.

89   BBC, "BBC One - Planet Earth II," BBC, accessed October 12, 2021, https://www.bbc.co.uk/programmes/p02544td.

90   Marshall Goldsmith, *What Got You Here Won't Get You There: How Successful People Become Even More Successful* (Profile Books, 2008).

[91] Klaus Schwab, "The Fourth Industrial Revolution," Foreign Affairs (Foreign Affairs Magazine, December 12, 2015), https://www.foreignaffairs.com/articles/2015-12-12/fourth-industrial-revolution.

[92] Dweck, Carol S. *Mindset: The New Psychology of Success.* (London: Robinson, 2017).

[93] World Economic Forum, "Jobs of Tomorrow: Mapping Opportunity in the New Economy," World Economic Forum, January 22, 2020, https://www.weforum.org/reports/jobs-of-tomorrow-mapping-opportunity-in-the-new-economy.

[94] World Economic Forum, "The Future of Jobs Report 2020," World Economic Forum, October 20, 2020, https://www.weforum.org/reports/the-future-of-jobs-report-2020.

[95] Erica Dhawan, *Digital Body Language: How to Build Trust and Connection, No Matter the Distance* (London HarperCollins Publishers, 2021).

[96] World Economic Forum, "The Future of Jobs Report 2020," World Economic Forum, October 20, 2020, https://www.weforum.org/reports/the-future-of-jobs-report-2020.

[97] World Economic Forum, "The Future of Jobs Report 2020," World Economic Forum, October 20, 2020, https://www.weforum.org/reports/the-future-of-jobs-report-2020.

[98] World Economic Forum, "The Future of Jobs Report 2020," World Economic Forum, October 20, 2020, https://www.weforum.org/reports/the-future-of-jobs-report-2020.

[99] Carol S Dweck, *Mindset: The New Psychology of Success* (New York: Random House, 2006).

[100] Evy Poumpouras and Remie Geoffroi, *Becoming Bulletproof: Protect Yourself, Read People, Influence Situations, and Live Fearlessly* (New York, Ny: Atria Books, 2020).

[101] Courtney Ackerman, "What Is Instant Gratification? A Definition + 16 Examples and Quotes," PositivePsychology.com, June 19, 2018, https://bit.ly/3gG4pq2.

[102]   Neil Patel, "The Psychology of Instant Gratification and How It Will Revolutionize Your Marketing Approach," Entrepreneur, June 24, 2014, https://bit.ly/2WxUc7H.

[103]   Rick Yvanovich, 'Values | TRG International,' accessed September 3, 2021, https://www.trginternational.com/about-us/values/.

[104]   Mihaly Csikszentmihalyi, *Flow: The Psychology of Optimal Experience* (New York: Harper and Row, 1990).

[105]   Michael Bungay Stanier, *The Coaching Habit: Say Less, Ask More & Change the Way You Lead Forever* (Toronto, On, Canada: Box of Crayons Press, 2016).

[106]   T. R. G. International, "Certified Coaching & Mentoring Professional (ECCMP) 2021 Intake," blog.trginternational.com, accessed September 3, 2021, https://bit.ly/3kvzr5c.

[107]   T. R. G. International, "Certified Chief Master Coach (CCMC)," blog.trginternational.com, accessed September 3, 2021, https://bit.ly/38nuYMi.

[108]   Susan Fowler, *Master Your Motivation: Three Scientific Truths for Achieving Your Goals* (Oakland, CA: Berrett-Koehler Publishers, 2019).

[109]   Susan Fowler, *Why Motivating People Doesn't Work ... And What Does: The New Science of Leading, Energizing, and Engaging* (San Francisco, CA: Berrett-Koehler, 2017).

[110]   Masaaki Imai, *Kaizen: The Key to Japanese Competitive Success* (McGraw-Hill Education, 1986).

[111]   Mihaly Csikszentmihalyi, *Flow: The Psychology of Optimal Experience* (New York: Harper and Row, 1990).

[112]   Barry Schwartz, *Why We Work* (New York: Ted Books, Simon & Schuster, 2015).

[113]   Viktor Emil Frankl, *Man's Search for Meaning: An Introduction to Logotherapy* (Boston: Beacon Press, 1992).

[114]   Rick Yvanovich, "In a World of Volatility, Invest in Employee Engagement," August 31, 2018, https://blog.trginternational.com/enhance-the-employee-engagement-in-the-vuca-environment.

[115] Ken Honda, "Is It Time to Maro Up? Why the 'Maro Up' Philosophy May Lead to Success, Wealth & Happiness | Money," 30Seconds Mom, March 2021, https://30seconds.com/mom/tip/21424/Is-It-Time-to-Maro-Up-Why-the-Maro-Up-Philosophy-May-Lead-to-Success-Wealth-Happiness.

[116] *Maro Up: The Secret to Success Begins with Arigato: Wisdom from the "Warren Buffet of Japan"* eBook: Bray Attwood, Janet, Honda, Ken: https://www.amazon.co.uk/Maro-Up-Secret-Success-Arigato-ebook/dp/B018HDTZL6/.

[117] Serrat, Olivier. "The Five Whys Technique," ResearchGate, May 2007, https://www.researchgate.net/publication/318013490_The_Five_Whys_Technique.

www.ingramcontent.com/pod-product-compliance
Lightning Source LLC
Chambersburg PA
CBHW071540210326
41597CB00019B/3060